前　言

“意象”和“境界”是中国古典文论两个最常用的术语。它们没有定于一尊的释义和铨解，学术界一般认为“意象”是指艺术家心中的物象，是主观情思和外在物象相融合的心象；“境界”指由艺术作品，譬如一首诗，或一幅画，或一段音乐，或一座园林建筑所唤起当下世界整体的复合印象。

这两个概念运用于汉英翻译的学习和实践，将使我们的叙述显得简洁明了。

刘勰在《文心雕龙》中说，完善的文章可以达到“弥缝莫见其隙”。

汉英翻译作为再创作的艺术活动与此有相通之处：“意象”就是翻译过程中译者在想象中为汉语英语这两种语言之间建构的桥梁或路径；而“境界”则是他的思维意念活动产生的视觉图式，是他的作品获得理想的铢两悉称，神形兼备，天衣无缝的艺术效果。

意象并不是一个宏大叙事。就汉语而言，遣词、造句、语法、修辞、语体、语气、音韵、形体、篇章结构、语言文采、时代特征等等有关语言及其使用的各个方面的特色，都可以看成意象的表情；而格调、韵致、神思、本色、风骨、警策、机锋、含蓄、空灵、雕琢及艺术感染力等特质，构成了意象的神采。

境界则不同。王国维的《人间词话》开宗明义：“词以境界为最上，有境界，则自成高格。”在汉英翻译中，译者应以最大努力，将汉语审美价值因素尽可能地传达出去，实现音美、意美、形美，以期达到译文读者与源语读者获得最大限度相同的美的享受，实现读者反应相似。好的翻译让你无法分出翻译家与原作者，是为大境界。

汉英翻译并非一个简单的二项对应，而是一个多项系统，这是语言表达的多层次多维度决定的，我们正是通过汉语英语意象和境界的消长、藏露、虚实、隐显的彼此转换和重构，才能无限接近真实完美的对应。

意象之用，存乎一心，运用之妙，境界全出。

> 红颜自古多薄命。
>
> 〖译文 1〗A beautiful girl has often an unfortunate life.[1]
>
> 〖译文 2〗The beautiful woman suffered a harsh life.[1]
>
> 〖译文 3〗Though she is very beautiful, she is also very unlucky.[1]

以上译文均摘自汉英词典。

译文 1 句意为："一个美貌女孩往往有一个不幸人生。"

译文 2 句意为："那个美貌女人遭受过严酷人生。"

译文 3 句意为："虽然她非常美丽，却非常不幸。"

译文虽然意思都不错，但是只是对"红颜薄命"的字面解释，而且丢掉了原文的"自古多"。

本句的翻译需要我们如上面所说的在译者的思维路径中产生一幅小小的意象图景，将原文的"红颜薄命"转换为译文的"命薄红颜"。因此，我们建议将本句主谓宾的语序颠个倒儿：

> 〖译文 4〗Fortune scarcely favors the beauties.

原文出自古诗，长期以来经过反复引用，已成谚语。译文 4 句意为“命运之神极少光顾美女。”译文字面上没有出现“自古多”，但是意义上没有丢失，风格上更接近原文，境界也就出来了。译文如何选取主语，本书在第二章有详解，主语被确定之后如何统领全句，由第三章详解。

自从我画的马从案头走向社会，有人说它像徐悲鸿之马，有人说像刘勃舒之马。

〖译文 1〗 Since the horse I draw appeared in public from my study, it has been said to look like that of Xu Beihong or that of Liu Boshu. （上海交通大学英语专业 2004 年研究生入学试题参考答案）[2]

本句原文“从案头走向社会”是拟人说法，英语也可以采用拟人手法，但是谓语动词最好不用 go，或 come，或 enter，appear 之类。全句建议调整为：

〖译文 2〗 Since my drawing of horse found its way from my studio to gallery, it has been commented to be another Xu Beihong or another Liu Boshu.

作家的“书房”，study，与画家的“画室”，studio，汉语英语的用词都是加以区别的。

原文“我画的马”，从字面看是指作者的画作，这是汉语的形合表达。“徐悲鸿之马”是汉语意合表达方式，英语即更进一步，可以直接用 Xu Beihong 表示他的作品，也是意合。请看：

In real life, unlike in Shakespeare, the sweetness of the rose depends upon the name it bears.

在现实生活中，有别于在莎士比亚戏剧中，玫瑰花有多香，就全看它的名字有多好听了。

Give me Bach and Beethoven, not these modern crashing-tinkle composers.

给我一些巴赫与贝多芬作品，不要这些现代的喧嚣音乐作曲家的。

上面句中 Shakespeare 系指“莎士比亚戏剧”或“莎士比亚剧作品”。Bach and Beethoven 系指“巴赫和贝多芬音乐”或“巴赫和贝多芬作品”。

汉语英语的这种形合意合相互转换在本书的第五章有所介绍。

天生五材，民并用之，废一不可。(《左传》)

〖译文 1〗 Nature produces five kinds of materials and people depend on these materials to live. None of them can be dispensed with.[3]

原文的“五材”，晋代学者杜预注为“金、木、水、火、土”。如果是这样，那么“五材”中的“五”固然是 five，“材”就不再是 material，而是 element。“五材”可以理解为形而下的万民器用之材，理解为 material。但是“五材”也是中国古代一种宇宙本源论的形而上学，认为宇宙自然是由五种要素相生相克衍生变化所构成。于是 element 应该成为本句译文的首选。

“天”是中国文化中一个极为重要、极为特殊的概念。它是宇宙和人间的主宰，中国人心目中的造物主和神灵，既是苍穹星空，又是道德律令，被约定俗成地译为 Heaven，首字母大写。下面译文 2 是我们的修改建议：

〖译文 2〗None of the five elements created by Heaven and utilized by people could be dispensable.

原文虽然只有短短 12 个汉字，却包含三个句子，形成三个散点，三者合起来组成一个完整的句意。英译不能跟随原文亦步亦趋，做散点式直译，必须规整为一个严谨的句子。本句的翻译涉及如何提取原文的主要信息，以及译文的聚焦式表达技巧，请分别参阅第一章和第四章。

中国逐步成为世界矿产资源大国和矿业大国。

〖译文 1〗China has gradually become a major country in mineral resources and the mining industry. [4]

译文 1 对原文逐字直译造成了逻辑问题：中国从开天辟地三皇五帝至于今就是世界矿产资源大国，并非现在 gradually become（逐步成为）的。用心揣摩，细细体味，原来汉语句子说的是中国现在是一个矿产资源的开采、加工、供货大国。因此我们也就不难推出下面的修改建议：

〖译文 2〗China has gradually become a big supplier and big processor of mineral resources.

译文中 supplier 和 processor 分别表示“供货方”和“加工方”，两者押尾韵，组成一个意群，这在英语中被称为 parallelism，平行结构，旨在增添语言的音韵美、整饬美，实际上这也有利于读者的阅读理解，增添语言的可读性。关于英语的排偶和对称，本书第六章有专题讲解。

本书可供汉英翻译教学人员参考，包括大学、中学的学生和教师，还可供专业笔译人员、口译人员、同声翻译，以及英语自学者、翻译爱好者、学习汉语的外国留学生和从事中国经典英译的西方汉学家学习参考。通过阅读本书，你一定会获得全新的感受和体会，你的翻译水平将从汉语意象的此岸，达到英语境界的彼岸，你的译文将令你的同学同事、你的老师学生、你的读者，包括外国人，native speaker，刮目相看。

编著者

2015 年 10 月

目　录

第一章
归纳、演绎及其他

第一节　如何提取主要信息

汉语语句的一个鲜明特定，就是尽可能不突出重点，尽可能不出头、不表态，书不尽言，言不尽意，其意象讲究“不著一字，尽得风流”。不著一字，非无字也，而是无一字直奔主题，无一字揭橥底蕴，但全篇却蓄满着丰盈的意境，尽现它所描摹的情景与物事的意态风韵。体现在句法中，汉语句子的各个成分之间是一种主次关系，信息分布主呼次应、前呼后应、此呼彼应，信息呼应互相配合，不露痕迹，没有标识，有时甚至尽在不言中。

英语的句子成分是一种主从关系，只有一个主语和一个谓语执全句之牛耳，其他句子成分则如众星拱月，定位明确，不得僭越。英语的复合句有主句、从句之分，不管在主句中、从句中，还是在简单句中，主、谓、宾、表、补等句子成分各据其位，各司其职，句法的主从关系使句子中主要信息和次要信息对号入座，来不得半点错位。英语句子重点突出，表态明确，语法关系清晰。

汉语几乎无语法规则可循。中国古代传统的语文教学，从塾馆到黉宫，从句读到训诂，都是通过阅读理解，背诵记忆，来积累语感，培养语言能力。我们平时分析汉语句子成分，说这个是主语，那个是谓语，实际都是搬套印欧语系的语法术语，犹如用西医的神经系统来解析中医的人体经络，两者既不对应，又不互补。近代以来应运而生的各种《国语文法》《汉语文通》因无法摆脱西方语言学的束缚，无法指导语言学习，也只能风行一时，昙花一现。

英语有严密而完备的语法体系。从中世纪到近代，英国有“文法学校”（grammar school），相当于现代的中学（secondary school），人生识字后即开始学习语法。

英语经典作家们正是在这种体系的严谨规整下才能纵横捭阖，挥洒自如。

如果翻译是在汉语英语之间架起一座桥梁，那么我们要做的第一步就是将汉语句式的主次关系转换成英语句式的主从关系。

我们说汉语句式是“主次关系”，不是因为它主次分明，层次清晰，反是因为它主次不分明，层次不清晰。在汉英翻译中，对于汉语句子中的主要信息和次要信息以及它的层次，需要我们去分析、辨别和判断。汉语文本中的主次关系，比之英语文本的主从关系，隐藏得相对较深。主次—主从转换的难度不在转换本身，而在原文主次结构的辨别和提取。

> 我常常听人说，他想读一点书，苦于没有时间。我不太同意这种说法。
>
> 〖译文1〗Often I hear a person say that he intends to read some books but is short of time. However I disagree to this kind of wording. （北京大学英语专业2009年研究生入学试题参考答案）[5,6]

译文1没有传递汉语原文的意象，逐字直译，且词不达意，故没有译出英语的境界。

我们第一步要做的是提取主要信息：原文有两个逗号，两个句号，四个组成部分，共同表达了一个完整的意思。很明显，其中“我不太同意这种说法”是最主要的信息，其他句子成分只是它的铺垫或衬托。

第二步，其他句子成分中也要分清主次，其中“苦于没有时间”相对比较重要，我们姑且把它称为次要信息。那么“我常常听人说”和“他想读一点书”就是最次要信息。

第三步是将主要信息译作英语的主句，次要信息译作从句，最次要信息以介词短语形式译作状语。

有了这样三步按部就班的分析和辨别，剩下的工作十分简单，只需要对号入座：

> 〖译文2〗I don't quite accept such an excuse as someone told me frequently that they could not find time to do some reading.

以上只是就英语译文的大境界而言，在汉英词语转换方面，译文1还有不少值得商榷之处：

首先，“人”可以译作 person。我们知道 a person = a man or a woman，一个比较具体的“人”。当说话者不必、不愿或不便说出这个人是男人是女人时，就说 a person：

> I think she's a very caring person.
>
> 我看她是个善解人意的人。

Jane was the last person to see him.
简是最后一个去见他的人。

但是在本句的语境中，“人”应该是 someone，一个泛众的“人”：

As someone once said, all's fair in love and war.
有人说过，在恋爱和战争中什么事情都是合理的。
I don't want to clean the kitchen—get someone else to do it.
我才不打扫厨房呢，找别人去干吧。

其次，“读一点书”可以说是 read some books。但是这是指很具体的“读一些书”“读某些书”。本句却是泛泛而谈的“读一点书”：to do some reading。

然后，“不太同意”，表明作者的表态是留有余地，不强加于人的，毕竟人读不读书无关宏旨。disagree 则是郑重其事地宣布作者与别人的歧见。其中“太”的脱落加剧了语气的强势。因此“不太同意”拟译作 don't quite accept。

最后，“说法”与 wording 字面看来天衣无缝，实则貌合神离。wording 系指“措辞”。本文的“说法”系指“借口”，excuse；或者“托词”，pretext；作 don't quite accept 的宾语。

词语转换并不像表面看起来那么容易。一般词典、教科书、语法书可以找到 receive 和 accept 的辨异，rather 和 fair 的区别，对于上述这些词语之间的细微差别则语焉不详，要靠我们阅读积累。本书在具体例句上可以作一些详细的分析，但是这不是重点，也不成系统。因为本书仅仅把这作为切入口，它的重点是，系统地介绍汉语英语在信息分布和句式安排上的差别。

清晨，太阳从地平线上升起，天安门广场响起雄壮嘹亮的国歌，鲜艳的五星红旗冉冉升起，象征着伟大祖国如旭日东升、前程无限。

〖译文 1〗 In the morning, the sun rises above the horizon, and the majestic and resonant of the national anthem sounds on Tiananmen square, and the bright-colored five-star flag rises slowly, symbolizing the bright future for China.

〖译文 2〗 In the morning, accompanied by the majestic and resonant sound of the national anthem, the bright-colored five-star flag rises slowly with the sunrise on Tiananmen square, symbolizing the prosperous future for China. [7]

这是一个常见的句子，却又是主次不太清晰的典型的汉化文句。译文 1 语法无误，但是平均使用力量，将几组信息平铺直叙，所以行文略显平淡，只适合用于口语。

译文 2 将“清晨”“太阳从地平线上升起”用两个介词短语译出。“天安门广场响起雄壮嘹亮的国歌”用过去分词短语译出。“鲜艳的五星红旗冉冉升起”

则是句子的主语和谓语。“象征着伟大祖国如旭日东升、前程无限”用现在分词短语译出。从全句结构看，“鲜艳的五星红旗冉冉升起”给人视觉冲击力最强烈，也最能打动人心，是当仁不让的重要信息。相比之下，“清晨”“太阳从地平线上升起”，只能处于从属地位。但是，“天安门广场响起雄壮嘹亮的国歌”是第二重要信息，不该与次要信息“清晨”“太阳从地平线上升起”平起平坐，所以被放在第二重要地位。译文主次分明，可以说在深层次上忠实于原文，而且句式灵活多变，文采斐然。

夫以出乎众为心者，曷常出乎众哉？（《庄子》第11章）

〖译文1〗However, those who would like to outshine others are not necessarily those who really outshine others![8]

〖译文2〗Whoever really outshines others when he tries to do so deliberately?

原文在《大中华文库》被今译为：“那一心想出人头地的人，又何尝超出过大众呢？”这样，我们就看得很清楚了，它的重要信息是：“人又何尝超出过大众呢？”这个信息一定要译成英语主句，译文1也正是这样做的。剩下的句子成分“那一心想出人头地的”是次要信息，以英语从句侍候。译文2将主要信息提前，将次要信息置后并以状语从句译出，这就保留了原文的反诘句形式。

至山阴之明年，先生以亲老不远游，设帐于家。（［清］沈复《浮生六记》）

〖译文1〗During the next year at Shanyin my teacher decided he did not want to live so far from his parents because they were growing old, and he moved home.[9]

〖译文2〗Next year in Shanyin my teacher decided to give tuition at home, because he did not want to leave his senile parents.

本句原文句子不长，内容简单，但是译文1却有三处错误：

第一，在the next year之前加介词during是一种“硬伤”。

第二，以“he did not want to live so far from his parents because they were growing old”译出“先生以亲老不远游”有歧义。它可以理解成：

He did not want to live so far from his parents. The reason is that they were growing old.

他因为双亲年老而不想住得那么远。（他没有住得太远，可能还在我们村子里。）

又可以理解成：

He wanted to live so far from his parents not because they were growing old.

他想住得那么远不是因为父母年老。（请不要误会他，他离开父母那么远是应父母的要求，或者他有更要紧的事情去办。）

由此可见，译文“live so far from”云云是毫无依据、毫无必要的。

第三，译者还不理解“设帐”是指办学讲课授徒。《大中华文库》以这样的水平译介中国文化经典，不也谬乎。

言归正传，本句“设帐”应是主要信息，确定了这一点之后，句式就容易整理了。

美成深远之致不及欧、秦。唯言情体物，穷极工巧，故不失为第一流之作者。（王国维《人间词话》）

〖译文1〗Chou Pang-yen could not come up to Ouyang Hsiu and Ch'in Kuan in the achievement of depth and distance in his tz'u. But he was infinitely skillful in his expression of emotions and empathy for things. Thus he can still be ranked among the poets of the first class. [10]

〖译文2〗Chou Pang-yen could still be ranked among the first class poets for his infinite skill to express emotions and describe environments despite the fact that he was second to Ouyang Hsiu or Ch'in Kuan in far-reaching influence.

提示：“美成”，是宋代文学家周邦彦。“欧”，欧阳修。“秦”，秦观。

这一句我们就更清楚了：主要信息是“美成不失为第一流之作者”，英译主句。其余是次要信息，其中“言情体物，穷极工巧”是主要信息的直接原因，英译为原因状语。“深远之致不及欧、秦”，作让步状语。

我们提供的修改建议，保留了威氏拼音。

如果说上面的例句结构比较复杂，那么结构简单的汉语语句也不能等闲视之。

有利必有弊。

〖译文1〗Everything has its advantages as well as disadvantages. [1]

〖译文2〗Advantages are inevitably accompanied by disadvantages. [1]

〖译文3〗Where there are advantages there also disadvantages. [1]

〖译文4〗It's an ill wind that blows nobody good.

〖译文5〗Advantages will have disadvantages. ❶

---

❶ http://fanyi.baidu.com。

我们知道，这个句子“有利”是条件，次要信息。“有弊”是结果，主要信息。两者不能混淆。说得直白一点，本句报告了一个坏消息。

译文1混淆了，将“有利”译作主要信息，全句句意为“有弊必有利”，报告的是好消息。译文不准确。

译文2，Advantages“有利”作主语，取被动语态，突出宾语 disadvantages“有弊”的强烈影响和制约，消息不妙。译文准确。

译文3，“凡有利之处必有不利的一面。”there also disadvantages“有弊”是主句，译文准确。

译文4，“对大多数人不利的东西，总会对个别人有利。”英语确实有这种说法，并且已成为谚语。但是作为本句译文，不准确。

译文5意义不明确，故不准确。

汉语表达十分强调和倚重悟性，文句不刻意地突出重点。如果说有什么突出的话，汉语突出的是整体效果，其行文的表征是平均使用力量。

小骂大帮忙

〖译文1〗small scold big help❶

〖译文2〗less scold more help❶

〖译文3〗small curse but great help❶

〖译文4〗praise with faint damn

〖译文5〗compliment in the disguise of criticism

〖译文6〗a miner attack in words but a major help in deeds❶

从表面上看，这个汉语短语的两部分“小骂”和“大帮忙”好像一枚硬币的两面，不分彼此。这是汉语句子信息分布的特点。但是通过形容词“小”和“大”，通过语序的前和后，我们可以作这样的分析：“骂”是手段，“帮忙”是目的；“骂”是现象，“帮忙”是实质。结论：“骂”是次要信息，“帮忙”是主要信息。

译文1亦步亦趋一词一字地对应，意义不明确。网络上有的译文在中间加连接词，成为 small scold and big help，就比较容易理解，比较合理了。

译文2很容易造成歧义，可以理解为“骂得越少，帮忙越多”，这就不忠实于原文了。

译文3与译文1有相似之处。

译文4将“帮忙”译作中心语，这个“忙”可就“帮”得大了，将“骂”译作介词宾语，并且用 faint（微小的、模糊的）修饰，这个“骂”无非雷声大，

---

❶ 摘自网络。

雨点小，高高举起，轻轻放下。所以译文比较贴近原文。

译文5用名词词组译出，意为“伪装成批评的恭维”。

译文6意为“在言论上攻击小，在行动上帮助大”。在词典工具书及网络上都不难找到这种译法。中国传统权术文化和权斗艺术博大精深，译出此句译文也在情理之中。但是置身另一种文化背景的读者却只能从中读出人格的裂痕和逻辑的紊乱。

其他译法请参考下面例句：

Their censure of the government's policy turned out to be oblique praise.

〖译文1〗他们对政府这项政策的批评到头来是转弯抹角的赞扬。

〖译文2〗他们对政府这项政策原来是小骂大帮忙。

第二节 语序安排与信息分布

我们分析了汉语句子的主次关系，英译时在语序安排上要突出主要信息。我们这儿所说的“语序安排”，是指汉英对重要信息和次要信息在语序上的排列是不相同的。汉语的次要信息在前，主要信息靠后。英语刚好相反，主要信息不但占据主句，而且位置靠前。

父母呼，应勿缓。(《弟子规》)

〖译文1〗When your parents call you, answer them right away.

〖译文2〗When mother and father are calling, answer them right away.

〖译文3〗Don't delay to answer your parents' call.

父母命，行勿懒。(《弟子规》)

〖译文1〗When they command you to do something, do it quickly.

〖译文2〗When they give you instructions, obey them without hesitation.

〖译文3〗Don't hesitate to obey your parents' command.

父母教，须敬听。(《弟子规》)

〖译文1〗When your parents instruct you, listen respectfully.

〖译文2〗When your parents need to instruct you, respectfully do as you're told.

〖译文3〗Listen respectfully to your parents' instructions.

父母责，须顺承。(《弟子规》)

〖译文1〗When your parents reproach you, obey and accept their reproach, try hard to change and improve yourself, and start anew.

〖译文 2〗 Whenever your parents must scold you, acknowledge your errors and faults.

〖译文 3〗 Accept meekly your parents' reproach.

本例证四句话的译文 1 译文 2 均摘自网络。很明显，它们受到原文影响不小，将原文的开头以时间状语的形式也放在译文的开头，没有照顾到英语的表达习惯，结果拉长了句式，造成主句某些代词指代不明。“父母责，须顺承”的译文 1 甚至还作了一些解释和发挥，风格上与原文相去甚远。

盖柿须摘下煮一沸，始去其涩，余不知也。（［清］沈复《浮生六记》）

〖译文 1〗 After the persimmon is picked it has to be boiled for a while before it loses its bitterness, but I had not known this.[9]

〖译文 2〗 I had not known that after the persimmon is picked it has to be boiled for a while so that before it can lose its bitterness.

〖译文 3〗 I had not known that the persimmon has to be boiled to alleviate its bitterness after it is picked.

本句可以将“余不知也”的位置提到句前。

四龄失怙，母金氏，弟克昌，家徒壁立。（［清］沈复《浮生六记》）

〖译文 1〗 Yun's father died when she was four years old, leaving her mother, whose family name was Chin, and her younger brother, Ko-chang. At first they had virtually nothing, but as…[9]

〖译文 2〗 Yun's been living in grinding poverty with her mother, Chin, and her younger brother, Ko-chang, since her father died when she was four years old.

提示：“四龄失怙”，四岁死了父亲。

全句有三个部分，主要信息是最后部分“（芸）家徒壁立”，可以作为主句，放在最前面。其余部分表示家徒四壁的原因，是典型的因果句。其中，“四龄失怙”是根本原因，英译时应该放在后面。“母金氏，弟克昌”的中间位置不变。

那些口讲大众化而实是小众化的人，就要很当心……（毛泽东《反对党八股》）

〖译文 1〗 So whoever talks glibly about "transformation to a mass style" while in fact he is stuck fast in his own small circle had better watch out, …[11]

〖译文 2〗 So whoever is stuck fast in his own small circle while talking glibly about "transformation to a mass style" had better watch out, …

现代汉语由于受古汉语骈体文的影响，往往形式上追求词句的整齐对仗，实际内容并不完全对等。譬如本句原文的两部分“口讲大众化”“实是小众化”看似并列，但是翻译时还是需要分析：它们实际上时间有先后，语义有主次。换句话说，“口讲大众化”是表面现象，“实是小众化”才是本质，才是作者真正要反对的。译文1听起来似乎是作者在警告“口讲大众化”的人，在以言治罪，而后面的“实是小众化”则是入人以罪。请看，语序的倒错，引起的误解有多大！本句几乎无法按原文的语序翻译。

上海浦东新区地处中国海岸线中点和长江出海口的交汇处，紧靠繁华的上海市区，背倚物阜民丰的长江三角洲，面对太平洋及东南亚的发达国家和地区，有着得天独厚的地理优势。

〖译文1〗The Pudong New Area of Shanghai lies at the middle of China's coastline where the Yangtze River empties into the sea. As it is close to the prosperous downtown area of Shanghai, borders on the rich and populous Yangtze Delta, and faces the developed Pacific-Southeast Asia countries and regions, the New Area certainly enjoys a unique geographical advantage.[12]

〖译文2〗Pudong New Area, Shanghai, enjoys a unique geographical advantage as it lies at the middle of China's coastline and the estuary of Yangtze River, and it is close to the prosperous downtown of Shanghai, borders on rich and populous Yangtze Delta, and faces the developed Pacific-Southeast Asia countries and regions.

译文1由于没有提取主要信息“上海浦东新区有着得天独厚的地理优势”，只好断句处理，重复the New Area词组，致使主要信息管不住次要信息。如果突出主要信息，并作语序上的调整，就管住了。

近日，中国青年报社会调查中心开展了一项有8777人参与的调查，结果显示，34.7%的受访者在谈到自己的大学生活时，都觉得“后悔”。

〖译文1〗The social research center of China Youth Daily conducted a survey on college education recently and the results are alarming. More than a third (34.7 percent) of 8,777 students surveyed regretted their decision to attend university.[13]

〖译文2〗More than a third (34.7 percent) of 8,777 students regretted their decision to attend university, shows a survey on college education recently conducted by the social research center of *China Youth Daily*.

新闻报道开头的第一个段落被称为“导语”，其特点是“倒宝塔”结构，亦即将最重要的信息放在最前面，次重要的放在次前位置，以此类推。这种源于美国新闻界的格式由于迎合了受众的阅读心理，在全世界，包括中国得到普遍应用。即使在同一句子中，要尽可能使用直接引语，尽可能少作记者的观点表达；直接引语或数据尽可能靠前。我们随便翻翻东西方报纸便可感受到此种特点。只是汉语的新闻报道导语不可能完全照此处理，在语序上仍然要兼顾汉语的特点，本句原文便是这个情况。译成英语我们即可发挥英语的这个特点。

第三信号，是大学生中仍然普遍存在过高的期望值，缺乏对形势的清醒估计和脚踏实地的思想作风。同日的《中国青年报》还有一项调查数据显示，……

〖译文1〗Last but not least, many college students have high expectations but lack a correct assessment of the reality or a down-to-earth style of work. Another survey by China Youth Daily further proves this. [12]

〖译文2〗Last but not least, many college students have much more expectations than a correct assessment of the reality or a down-to-earth style of work, according to another survey by *China Youth Daily*.

本句的情况与上句略同。

第三节　时间的顺叙与倒叙

与主次句转换成主从句类似或相关的是，汉语的记叙文，在时间上总是顺序表达，亦即按照事件发生的先后顺序来记录和描述的。英语恰恰相反，如我们上面所说的，是按照事情发生的“后先”而不是“先后”来表达的。

从现在测得的重量中，减去空坩埚重量，从而计算油品试样重量。

〖译文1〗From the now measured weight subtract the weight of the empty crucible and calculate the weight of oil sample.

〖译文2〗Calculate the weight of oil sample by subtracting the weight of the empty crucible from the now measured weight.

汉语原文的叙事顺序是：现在测得重量（时间最先），减去空坩埚重量（中间），计算油品试样重量（最后）。

译文2的叙事顺序是：Calculate the weight of oil sample（时间最后），subtracting the weight of the empty crucible（中间）from the now measured weight（最先）。

英语汉语的叙事顺序和时间先后可以完全颠倒。

我们这里所说的“顺叙”“倒叙”是汉语英语一个非常明显的差异，如果我们不注意到这种差异，就根本无法从事语言的翻译。但是顺叙—倒叙的转换，绝非一成不变的刻板的公式，译文的转换仍然应该是灵活多变的。

He had met her early in the spring as he flying down the river after a big yellow moth, and had been so attracted by her slender waist that ha had stopped to talk to her.

他还是在早春遇到她的，那时他正沿着河流飞去，追一只黄色飞蛾，她的细腰很引起他的注意，他便站住同她谈起话来。（巴金译）

原文出自英国作家王尔德的《快乐王子》，文中的 he（他）是一只拟人的小燕子，her（她）是芦苇。译者以汉语流水句译出英语流水句，却是相当成功的译文。原来英语原文既不是记叙，也不是议论，而是一种描写文字，作者细节性地描写小燕子连贯性的动作，当然按照时间先后处理。作为小说家出身的译者灵感相通，自然心领神会，故其译笔几可与原创乱真。

（邓弼）一日，独饮娼楼，萧冯两书生过其下，急牵入共饮。（［明］宋濂《秦士录》）

〖译文 1〗One day when Deng was drinking alone in a brothel, scholars Xiao and Feng happened to pass it. He insisted on having them in to keep him company, …[14]

〖译文 2〗One day Deng insisted on having two scholars, Xiao and Feng, to keep him company, when they happened to pass by a brothel, where he was drinking alone…

本句汉语按时间先后讲了三件事：(1)“独饮娼楼”，(2)“萧冯两书生过其下”，(3)“急牵入共饮”。

译文 1 是很好的。但是我们可以按英语习惯的 (3) (2) (1) 次序表达，见译文 2。逆序表达不但是一个语言习惯问题，而且还有一个好处，就是这样容易将句子归并起来，把汉语散点式句子译成英语透视式句子。请参见第五章。

余谪居于黄，过岐亭，适见焉。（［宋］苏轼《方山子传》）

〖译文 1〗As I was relegated to the magistracy of Huang Prefecture, I happened to pass through Qiting and came across him.[14]

〖译文 2〗I came across him when I happened to pass through Qiting as a relegated magistrate of Huang Prefecture.

与上一句一样，这也是一个 (1) (2) (3) 和 (3) (2) (1) 次序问题。汉语原文“适见焉”放在最后，是最重要的信息。译文 2 按 (3) (2) (1) 次序表达，用I came across him译出“适见焉”，放在最前面，而且是全句唯一的主谓宾，所以这是另一种风格的译文。

有一次，在沈阳车站，有位外地来的中年妇女中途丢了车票，十分着急，他就自己掏钱给她买了一张车票，送她上了车。

〖译文1〗Once at Shenyang Railway Station he found a middle-aged woman in a quandary because she had lost her ticket. He bought one for her out of his own pocket and saw her aboard her train.[15]

〖译文2〗Once at Shenyang Railway Station he bought a ticket for a middle-aged countrywoman out of his own pocket and saw her aboard her train, because she had lost her ticket when he found her ill at ease in a quandary.

汉语这种语言非常适合按时间先后顺序叙事，如我们前面所看到的，倒叙显得没有条理。英语刚好相反，比较适合倒序，个别极端的例句顺序叙事反而别扭。

如果说前面的几个例句，英译顺叙还没有发生语义上的混乱与差错的话，本句的译文1就很成问题了。

本句原文是很好的汉语，“有位妇女丢了车票，他给她买了一张车票，送她上了车”，事情交代得有头有尾，清清楚楚。译文1没有转换，按此顺序译出，就显得不合逻辑了：“他在沈阳车站发现了她，因为她丢了车票。”英语读者不可能明白其中的因果关系。为了顺序翻译，译者不得不断句，将原文一句话分译成两句。

如果改为逆序翻译，说成“他给她买了一张车票，送她上了车”，是“因为她丢失了车票”，这些问题就迎刃而解了。

翟理思（1845—1935）于1867年来中国，历任英国驻中国各领事馆翻译、副领事、领事。

〖译文1〗Herbert A. Giles (1845-1935) came to China in 1867 and served as interpreter, vice-consul and consul in several consulates.[8]

〖译文2〗Herbert A. Giles (1845-1935) held positions of consul, vice-consul and interpreter in several British consulates after he came to China in 1867.

我们读外国学生的个人简历（Resume），就会发现他们写的工作经历总是从高到低，由近及远，比如从目前担任的副总经理，到以前的经理、副经理，直到业务员、实习生。学历总是从大学、中学到小学。而且工作经历在前，学历在后。这个习惯与我们中国人刚好相反。所以中国学生如果申请外资企业的岗位，递交英语文本个人简历时，你的经历最好逆序书写。

本句原文完全按汉语习惯表述：翟氏先来中国，后任翻译，接着任副领事，最后任领事。英译当然可以照此办理。译文 2 按照英语习惯仅供参考。

几个月前，一位年轻的企业家购买了一栋空房子，重新装修后以原价的两倍出售。

〖译文 1〗 A few months ago a young businessman bought a vacant house, redecorated it and sold it for twice the original price.

〖译文 2〗 A young businessman sold a vacant house for twice the original price, after he bought and redecorated it a few months ago.

上面两句译文无疑都是正确的。译文 1 突出这位商人的经营过程和手法，与此同时，揭示他待价而沽的目的和结果，但不突出。译文 2 突出这位商人牟取暴利的本性，突出他的本利翻番，后面附带地说穿他购进和装修房子只有区区几个月时间。顺序或逆序叙事应视语境而定。

时孙权曾致巨象，太祖欲知其斤重，访之群下，咸莫能出其理。（陈寿《三国志》）

〖译文 1〗 Once Sun Quan sent a big elephant as a gift to Cao Cao, who wanted to know its weight. Cao Cao asked all his men, but none of them could find a way to measure it.[16]

〖译文 2〗 Once Sun Quan sent a big elephant as a gift to Cao Cao. None of Cao Cao's subordinates could find a way to measure its weight, which Cao Cao wanted to know and sought advice from them.

译文 1 希望第一句捎带后面"太祖欲知其斤重"信息，但是英语的倒叙特性却拒绝捎带，使译文出了差错。译文 1 的句意是"孙权送了一头大象给欲知其重量的曹操。"好像曹操跑来打听大象的重量，孙权做个顺水人情，就把大象送给了他。这不符合事实。事实是曹操将大象牵回家去后才想起要了解它的重量。因此译文可以将"太祖欲知其斤重"并入后一句，并且放在稍后的位置，以示太祖垂询于前，群臣束手在后。

翻身农民没有听凭命运的摆布，他们组织了护地队，与反动派展开了殊死斗争，保卫了胜利果实。

〖译文 1〗 Meanwhile, the people, once liberated, would never truckle back to oppression or fatalism. They organized themselves into land-protection bands and started fighting against reactionaries, live or die. The fruits of revolution must never be robbed.[17]

〖译文 2〗 The liberated farmers had protected the fruits of revolution by organizing themselves into land-guards and starting life-and-death struggle against reactionaries, instead of being subject to fatalism.

本句我们可以提取句末的“保卫了胜利果实”作为主要信息，放在译文的开头；“组织……展开……”作为次要信息，放在中间；“听凭”放在句末。全句采用倒叙手法，形成右重句式，详见第三章。这样就使散点式汉语译成了透视式英语，详见第四章。

第四节 归纳型与演绎型

不少教科书对汉英叙事与议论的语序不同已经有所论及。我们也已经知道汉语叙事在前，议论在后；英语议论在前，叙事在后。但是仅仅知道这一点，还很难运用到翻译实践中去。

所谓叙事与议论的关系，实质上还是一个如何分辨和表达主要信息和次要信息的问题。

在此基础之上，我们还需要进一步了解：同是议论，汉语论证在前，结论在后；英语结论在前，论证在后。同是叙事，汉语交代客观情况在前，交代主观感受在后；英语交代主观感受在前，交代客观事实在后。概而言之，汉语属归纳型，英语属演绎型。所有这些不同还是来源于主次—主从关系的不同。

It would be superfluous in me to point out to your lordship that this is war.

倘若我向大人喻示此乃战争，未免饶舌。

英语作者先给自己戴上帽子：It would be superfluous in me，然后展开理由：to point out to your lordship that this is war。汉译无法这样做，只能调换过来，先交代情况“我向大人喻示”，后下结论“未免饶舌”。

本句如果按照英语原文的语序汉译，就是：“我未免饶舌，倘若我向大人喻示此乃战争。”这就是我们常说的“翻译腔”。要改变“翻译腔”，就一定要转换语序。

最近税收不断加码，他感到很不爽。

〖译文1〗Recently, the tax is increasing. He feels bitter against this.

〖译文2〗He feels bitter against the recent increase in tax.

译文1的毛病是按照汉语的语序英译，结果使句子一断为二。只要转换语序，句子就合而并一又通顺了。

我的工资要养活一个五口之家，真是太难了。

〖译文 1〗My salary was to feed a family of five. It was really a struggle trying.

〖译文 2〗It was really a struggle trying to feed a family of five on my salary.

严格地说，译文 1 有语病。try 意为“尝试”，try to 意为“竭力”。原文是后一种意思，但句末的 trying 脱落 to，故句子不通顺。解决的办法是将“真是太难了”（It was really a struggle）向前移至句首，try to 就连在一起了。

古人云：“死生亦大矣”，岂不痛哉？（［晋］王羲之《兰亭集序》）

〖译文 1〗An ancient said，“Life and death are matters of great magnitude.” How could they not be afflicted with sorrow？（耿亮译）[18]

〖译文 2〗As the ancient saying（by Confucius）has it—momentous is the matter of life and death：how awfully painful it is！（孙大雨译）[18]

〖译文 3〗How could the ancient sage not be afflicted with sorrow when he said “Life and death are matters of great magnitude”？

我们可以把本句看作叙事和表态的关系，调整原文语序译出。

借人典籍，皆须爱护，先有缺坏，就为补治，此亦士大夫百行之一也。（［南北朝］颜之推《颜氏家训》）

〖译文 1〗Take good care of borrowed books，and repair any damage previously done to them. This is one of the many kind deeds a scholar-gentleman will perform.[19]

〖译文 2〗It is one of the gentleman's kind deeds to take good care of borrowed books and mend breakage if any in them.

Repair 后面可以跟“房屋”“汽车”等，表示“修理”；Repair 后面跟 damage 意为“弥补损失”，而不是“修补破损”：repair the damage done，“补救造成的损失”。

damage 可以作“损坏”解，系指自然灾害或人为造成的破坏。书本使用日久的“破损”英语只能用 breakage 表示。

以上是题外话，言归正传。本句是判断句，汉语习惯先陈述现象，后下判断词，英语则相反。译文 1 没有转换，按汉语习惯表达，结果将判断句误译作祈使句，句意为：好好照顾借出的书吧，弥补它们先前遭受的损失吧，这是学者绅士将要表现的许多行为之一。

如君实责我以在位久，未能助上大有为，以膏泽斯民，则某知罪矣；如曰今日当一切不事事，守前所为而已，则非某之所敢知。（［宋］王安石《答

司马谏议书》)

〖译文 1〗 If you reproach me with my failure, despite my long service at court, to assist the Sovereign in achieving greater success in the reform so as to benefit the people, then I ought to acknowledge my guilt. But if you say that nothing should be done but adhere to the old ways, then I must beg to differ. [14]

〖译文 2〗 I would accept the blame if you reproach me with my failure, despite my long service at court, to assist the Sovereign in achieving greater success in the reform so as to benefit the people. But I would disagree with you if you argue that nothing should be done but adhere to the old ways.

原文标题中的“司马”，正文中的“君实”均指司马光。王安石和司马光都是北宋政治家。王力主变法革新，司马则是保守路线的领军人物。王在这封信中表达了坚持改革路线的决心。本句分成两部分，每一部分都是“铺垫—表态”的关系，亦即铺垫在前，表态在后，是典型的汉语表达方式。译文 1 因袭了这种表达方式，所以显得头重脚轻。为了解决这个问题，译者将“则某知罪矣”译作 then I ought to acknowledge my guilt，将“则非某之所敢知”译作 then I must beg to differ，都以 then 开头。其实这样做不妥。首先 then 只能用在“既然……那么……”的转折关系中。譬如：

You have accepted my criticism, then you should give up the conservative policies.

既然您接受了我的批评，那么就应该放弃保守路线。

原文不存在这种关系。其次 then 还能用在“首先……然后……”的时间先后关系中，原文也不存在这种关系。既然我们知道原文是“铺垫—表态”的关系，就一定要作“主次—主从”转换。另外“知罪”不能译作 acknowledge my guilt（承担罪责）。因为“知罪”是古人一种很特殊的客套话，并非他真的有什么罪行。要是王安石不小心冒犯了司马光的名讳，他在赔礼道歉的时候也会口称“死罪”。所以这儿的“知罪”意谓“接受您的批评”。

余生乾隆癸未冬十一月二十有二日，正值太平盛世，且在衣冠之家，居苏州沧浪亭畔，天之厚我可谓至矣。（［清］沈复《浮生六记》）

I was born in the winter of the 27th year of the Emperor Chien Lung, on the second and twentieth day of the eleventh month. Heaven blessed me, and life then could not have been more full. It was a time of great peace and plenty, and my family was an official one that lived next to the Pavilion of the Waves in Soochow. [9]

Born in the winter of 1763, on the 22nd day, the 11th month of lunar calendar, I was blessed so well to live in a time of peace and prosperity with my eminent family residing near On-Waves Pavilion in Soochow, Jiangsu Province, China.

原文是《浮生六记》开宗明义的第一句话。作者叙事不愠不火，在娓娓道来的平淡中显现其文字功底。

这是一个典型的中国人：他的出生日和出生地都是相对的时空点。作者作为知识分子，虽然能够准确地计算自己的出生日期，却是按照中国古代皇帝年号纪年，现代读者只是通过"康乾盛世"的说法，才对"乾隆癸未"有一个朦胧的把握。看惯了戏说乾隆的中国人对历史只有流传感，没有流动感。除了专业人员和江湖术士，一般人并不熟悉天干地支天文历法。虽然作者也知道自己出生的准确地点，但是读者却是通过"上有天堂下有苏杭"的说法，才对"苏州沧浪亭"有一个模糊的印象，除了进京赶考的士子和中央委派的官吏，一般老百姓通常不查阅"皇舆全览图"，对于全国行政区划也只有一点儿方向感，没有方位感。这是中国人思维方式的第一个特征：朦胧性、模糊性。

第二个特征是类比性、象征性。"太平盛世"也只是一种历史纵深和国际横向的大致比较，"衣冠之家"的象征意义，表示这是一个主流之家，体面之家，诗礼之家。

上面的文字还体现了中国式思维的第三个特征：归纳性。作者通过"乾隆癸未""太平盛世""衣冠之家""苏州沧浪亭畔"，归纳为"天之厚我可谓至矣"的结论。

我们认为，英译需要以人为本，以形传神。具体的翻译策略是：一，将原文的朦胧性、模糊性转变为译语的清晰性，精确性；二，直译或意译原文类比性、象征性的中国特色词汇；三，在句式上用英语的演绎性取代汉语的归纳性。

第五节 因果、转折与其他

在因果、转折、让步、递进等语句方面，汉语英语有相似之处。相异之处是汉语的句法关系有时不明显，英语必须明确地加以表达，而且还要分清主次。

金的价格昂贵，因此不能广泛用作导体。

〖译文1〗The cost of gold is high. That is why it is not extensively used as conductors.[20]

〖译文2〗The cost of gold is so high that it is not extensively used as conductors.

〖译文3〗The gold is of so high cost that it is not extensively used as conductors.

〖译文 4〗The gold is so precious that it is not extensively used as conductors.

〖译文 5〗The gold is too expensive to be extensively used as conductors.

〖译文 6〗Because the gold is expensive, it is not extensively used as conductors.

〖译文 7〗The gold is expensive, so it is not extensively used as conductors.

〖译文 8〗The gold is not extensively used as conductors, for its cost is high.

〖译文 9〗The gold is not extensively used as conductors for its high cost.

〖译文 10〗The gold's high costs prevent itself being extensively used as conductors.

〖译文 11〗The gold's high costs prevent its extensive uses as conductors.

本例虽然简单，却包含着因果关系，如果将原文句子看作前因后果，那么我们可以用 so…that…等句型译出，译法可以有许多种。

液体变成气体叫汽化。

〖译文 1〗The liquid becomes a gas. This is called evaporation. [20]

〖译文 2〗It is called evaporation when a liquid becomes gas.

〖译文 3〗The process is called evaporation in which a liquid becomes gas.

〖译文 4〗The process which makes a liquid become gas is called evaporation.

〖译文 5〗The process in which a liquid becomes gas is called evaporation.

与上句不同，本句原文是结论性陈述。译文 1 译成了个案，句意为“该液体变成了气体。这就叫汽化。”原文想说的是“任何液体变成气体，都叫汽化。”

汉语陈述原因在前，说明结果在后。译成英语一般结果在前，原因在后。为何存在这种区别和转换？究其原因，恐怕与汉语隐藏主体、掩蔽结果，英语突出主体、彰现结果有关。汉译英的过程，就是在汉语文句中分辨和提取出“结果”，并把它作为主要信息译入英语的主句，把“原因”作为次要信息译入英语从句或短语。

其他如转折句、递进句、让步句，译成英语一般都可以将结果提前。

糖醋排骨味道好极了，孩子们给吃得精光。

〖译文 1〗The taste of spareribs in sweet-and-sour sauce were very delicious and children ate it up completely.

〖译文 2〗The spareribs in sweet-and-sour sauce were so delicious that children licked every last bit of it.

译文1没有译出原文暗含的因果关系。译文2用 so that 短语，使因果关系在译文字面上得到彰显。

The younger son, Tungyu, was beheaded for the double crime of deceiving a family girl and abandoning her, and of attempting to kidnap a nun and defiling temple ground. (Lin Yu-tang: *Moment in Peking*)

次子东榆，一因诱拐良家女子，始乱终弃；二因企图绑架尼姑，玷污尼庵，两罪并论，斩首示众。(张振玉译)

原文出自林语堂先生的英文小说《京华烟云》。本例句的特点是：英语先判决，后宣布罪行，汉语先宣布罪行，后判决。

不责人小过，不发人阴私，不念人旧恶，三者可以养德，亦可以远害。(《菜根谭》)

〖译文1〗Do not reproach others for small faults; do not reveal their private matters; do not bear a grudge against them. To refrain from doing the above three things can help cultivate one's moral character and keep away from disaster.[21]

〖译文2〗It can help cultivate one's moral character and keep out of harm to do nothing of reproaching others for small faults, revealing their private matters, bearing a grudge against them.

〖译文3〗It can help cultivate one's moral character and keep out of harm not to reproach others for small faults, to reveal their private matters, to bear a grudge against them.

如果把本句原文中的“三者”去掉，我们就可以看清楚句子的结构了：“不……，不……，不……，可以……，可以……”，是判断句。作者用“三者”是很精当的，这是汉语行文的一大特色，我们后面还会详谈。译成英语可以把“可以……，可以……”提前。

在唐敖和他的朋友去过的三十三个国家中，一些国家作者自己只花了一两段来写。

〖译文1〗Of the thirty-three foreign countries which Tang Ao and his friends visited, however, the author himself devoted only a paragraph or two to some of them.[22]

〖译文2〗The author devoted only one paragraph or two to depict some of the thirty-three kingdoms which Tang Ao and his friends visited.

译文1采取直译法，很容易出现“of…some of them…”这样首尾不相顾的语病。将结果放在前面译出可纠正这个毛病。

李汝珍本想为这部小说写续篇，但没有写成。

〖译文 1〗 Li Ju-chen intended to write a sequel to the novel, but he never did. [22]

〖译文 2〗 Li Ju-chen never wrote a sequel to the novel as he once intended.

译文 1 的最后一词 did，译者希望它指代前面的不定式 to write，事实上它指代的却是谓语动词 intended。这就使句意成为：李汝珍本想为这部小说写续篇，但是他从没有想过。显然违背了形式逻辑矛盾律。解决的办法还是要将原文结果部分提到译文前面来。

宅边有五柳树，因以为号焉。（［晋］陶渊明《五柳先生传》）

〖译文 1〗 There were five willows around his house and he adopted the name "Five Willows" as his literary name. （厦门大学英语专业 2003 年研究生入学试题参考答案）[6,23]

〖译文 2〗 He adopted "Pentawillow" as his literary name after those five trees around his house.

译文 1 将原文简单句译成了两句，两次出现 five willows，不符原文风格。解决问题的办法是将原文两部分的后一部分“因以为号”作为主要信息，前一部分则是次要信息，并且用 Pentawillow 译出“五柳”。词缀 penta-意为“五”，源自希腊语，用在这儿意在塑造主人公读书人的形象。

货恶其弃于地也，不必藏于己；力恶其不出于身也，不必为己。（《礼记》）

〖译文 1〗 Goods seemed to dislike to lie on the ground, so there was no need to keep them in one's own house; the strength seemed to dislike not to come from the body, so there was no need to use it for one's own purpose. [24]

〖译文 2〗 Everybody dislike squandering the resources and goods, but nobody would like to take possession of them; everybody dislike sparing efforts for public affairs, but nobody would like to do so for himself.

原文描述的是孔子心目中的理想社会，在这个社会中人人为我，我为人人，世界大同，天下为公。译者对原文理解有误，逐字对译，译文哪得不误？从字面来看，“货”是指“财物”，可大致地译作 money，goods 或 property 等。“恶”是指“厌恶”“嫌恶”，可译作 dislike。问题在于：原文并不是说“财物厌恶躺在地面上”。而是说“人们厌恶财物被毁弃糟蹋”。“弃于地”只是一种形象化的说法罢了。重要的是，原文句子成分之间不是因果关系，而是转折关系。

虽有嘉肴，弗食，不知其旨也；虽有至道，弗学，不知其善也。(《礼记》)

〖译文1〗Although there is delicious dishes, if not taste, you will not know all are made from vegetables. Although there exists extremely beneficial theory, if you do not learn it, you will not know its benefits. (武汉大学英语专业2003年研究生入学试题参考答案/厦门大学英语专业2005年研究生入学试题参考答案)[6,25,26]

〖译文2〗Even when there is good food, you will not know its deliciousness if you don't taste it; even when there is good doctrine, you will not know its virtue if you don't learn it.[16,27]

〖译文3〗You can not tell the daintiness of a dish unless you taste it, nor you know the virtues of a doctrine unless you begin to learn it.

本句实际上是条件和结果的关系。它在字面上出现“虽有”，我们容易条件反射般地想起although，even之类英语词语。实际上“虽有”和“弗食”组成让步关系，两者共同组成条件，“不知其旨也”才是结果，或者结论，全句是因果关系。

是故，学然后知不足；教然后知困。(《礼记》)

〖译文1〗So, you will only know you are nescient through learning, and you will only understand the shortages of the current teaching method. (武汉大学英语专业2003年研究生入学试题参考答案/厦门大学英语专业2005年研究生入学试题参考答案)[6,25,26]

〖译文2〗Therefore, to learn makes us realize our deficiency, and to teach makes us know the difficulties.

〖译文3〗So, you are not aware of your nescience until you get learned, nor of your puzzlement until you engage yourself in teaching.

译文1似乎排版打印有误。除此之外，它的两部分句式不整齐，前面是only know + 从句，还跟一个介词短语。后面是only understand + 名词，不带介词短语，显得凌乱，影响表达和理解。更重要的是，译文1没有理解原文内在的逻辑关系，使英译显得逻辑混乱，不能令人信服。

第六节 论证与结论

顺着上文提到的思路向前看，于是我们顺理成章地看到了：汉语论证在前，结论在后；译成英语一般结论在前，论证在后。汉语说明手段在前，目的在后；英语则目的为主，手段为次。其根源仍然是，汉语的思维方式，使语句尽可能淡化行为的动机和目的，强化过程和手段。英语则把动机和目的放在最突出的位置，过程和手段只是陪衬。

It is fascinating and encouraging to observe the development of this immense process, a process in which man appears all the time to be engaged in the act of creating an extension of himself.

〖译文 1〗观察这种伟大过程的发展是令人感到神往和鼓舞的，在这个过程中，人似乎一直都在从事使人本身得以延伸出去的创造性劳动。[28]

〖译文 2〗人类似乎一直都处在孜孜不倦地追求延伸自己的过程之中，观察这个伟大过程的进展是令人欢欣鼓舞，心驰神往的。

译文 1 中出现一次“这种过程”，一次“这个过程”。但是该“过程”究竟是什么过程，似乎译者，或者原文作者一直没有交代，于是读者就发生了理解障碍。这是照搬原文，在译语中将主要信息、结论放在前面，将次要信息、过程放在后面造成的，所以是一种误译。如果充分利用汉语语序作用，将英语原文的不定式内容放在汉译的次要位置，即放在前面，结论放在主要位置，即放在后面，虽然也重复了“过程”，但是该“过程”是指“人类一直都处在孜孜不倦地追求延伸自己”，两个“过程”确凿无疑指向这同一“过程”，故不造成误解，见译文 2。

或传“建自隋文帝”，但都无碑志可证。

〖译文 1〗Or it was said that it was built in the Sui Dynasty. However, there are no records inscribed on any stone tablet to prove those true. [29]

〖译文 2〗It was said to be built in the Sui Dynasty. However, none of its many stone tablets support the statement.

〖译文 3〗None of its stone tablets bears any words or trace to support the argument that it was built in the Sui Dynasty.

先看原文，“或”不是“或者”，而是“有人”的意思，“或传”是“有一种传言”。再看译文 1，形式主语 it 可以用“塔”的代词 it 取代，使语句简练。no records inscribed 可以用 none 取代，也是为了使语句简练。全句译作译文 2。也可以将原文的后半句理解成主要信息，译成主句。原文的前半句理解成次要信息，译成从句。如译文 3：没有任何碑志可证实它“建自隋文帝”这种说法。

我讳穷久矣，而不免，命也；求通久矣，而不得，时也。（《庄子》第 17 章）

〖译文 1〗For a long time I've tried to get out of misfortunes, but I failed—it is destined by my fate. For a long time I've tried to gain success, but I failed—it is due to the adversity of times. [8]

〖译文 2〗It is destined by my fate that I failed long to get out of misfortunes, and it is due to the adversity of times that I failed long to gain success.

原文是孔子的话，属于陈述—判断句。意谓：

我困窘得很久了，仍不免交坏运，是命运啊；我追求好运很久了，仍得不到，是时机不利啊。

所以英语应该倒过来表达，译作：是命运，使我长久不免讳穷。是时机不利，使我长久不得成功。见译文2。

容闳一生追求光明，与时俱进，无愧为中国现代化的卓越先驱。

〖译文1〗Rong Hong pursued brightness and keep up with the pace of time all his life, worthy of the title of the outstanding pioneer of Chinese modernization. [30]

〖译文2〗Rong Hong may be rated as an outstanding pioneer of China's modernization for his lifetime of dignified pursuit and progressive thought.

译文1的worthy of the title of意为“对某某称号当之无愧”，例如：

He is worthy of the title of combat hero.

他是当之无愧的战斗英雄。

而“卓越先驱”只不过是作者或者我们大家，对容闳的肯定和赞扬罢了，并不是一个title。

另外，“光明”在汉语中象征着“真理”和“进步”。而brightness在英语中表示“聪慧”“敏锐”。虽然字面意思对等，象征意义不对等。

从结构上看，本句英译最好将结论部分“无愧为先驱”放在前面，而“追求光明”“与时俱进”作为理由，放在句末。当然它们也可以放在前面，甚至作主语：

Rong Hong's dignified pursuit and progressive thought made him a worthy among the outstanding pioneers of China's modernization.

这样原译文中的worthy一词就派上了用场。它在这儿的字面意思是“有价值的重量级人物”，亦即“杰出人物”，以译出原文的“无愧”“卓越”等内容。

子曰：“贤哉回也！一箪食，一瓢饮，在陋巷，人不堪其忧，回不改其乐。贤哉回也！”

〖译文1〗The master said, "Incomparable indeed was Hui! A handful of rice to eat, a gourdful of water to drink, living in a mean street—others would have found it unendurably depressing, but to Hui's cheerfulness it made no difference at all. Incomparable indeed was Hui!" [24]

〖译文 2〗The master said, "Hui was sagacious indeed! He remained cheerful when he living in a mean street with only a handful of rice to eat, a gourd of water to drink, that would mean a miserable life to others. Sagacious indeed was Hui!"

这似乎也是一个叙事—判断句，而且它分成两个判断层次，亦即用"人"与"回"做对比。我们可以用"回不改其乐"做主要信息，放在主句位置；"人不堪其忧"做次要信息，放在从句位置；"在陋巷"是次次要信息；"一箪食，一瓢饮"是最次要信息。

让我们再来看一看手段与目的的关系：

我们要大力推进外贸体制改革，走集团化的道路，组建以外贸为龙头的工贸、农贸、科贸相结合的企业集团，以增强企业的竞争力。

〖译文 1〗We must press forward with the reform in the management system of foreign trade. Conglomeration-forming allies with farming, manufacturing, or scientific research with foreign trade as the locomotive points the way ahead to strengthened competitiveness. ❶

〖译文 2〗We must make the enterprises more competitive by reforming the management system of foreign trade, conglomerating or forming export-oriented group corporations with farming, manufacturing, and scientific research as a whole.

译文 1 将"大力推进外贸体制改革"译成单独的一句，不符合原文的意思。而且译文的后一句也不通顺。原文的主要信息是"我们要增强企业的竞争力"。其他都是次要信息，是"增强企业竞争力"的途径和方法。"大力推进外贸体制改革"也是途径和方法之一，决不能译成单独的一句。有了这条思路，我们就有了译文的框架："我们要增强企业的竞争力，……通过大力推进改革，……通过走集团化的道路，……通过组建企业集团。"句子也就通顺了。

延安虽然还没有战争，但军队天天在前方打仗，后方也唤工作忙，文章太长，有谁来看？

〖译文 1〗Although there is as yet no fighting here in Yan'an, our troops at the front are daily engaged in battle, and the people in the rear are busy at work. If articles are too long, who will read them?[31,32]

〖译文 2〗Who will read too long articles when our troops at the front are dai-

❶ http://www.mofcom.gov.cn。

ly engaged in battle, and the people in the rear are busy at work though there is as yet no fighting here in Yan'an?

〖译文 3〗 Although there is as yet no fighting here in Yan'an, who will read very lengthy articles when our troops at the front are daily engaged in battle, and the people in the rear are busy at work?

译文 1 作为经典已进入《毛泽东选集》。但是我们换一种思路看，原文“有谁来看”形式上是疑问句，实际上是不需要回答的结论。

第二章 如何确定英译的主谓宾

第一节　主语的位置

由于汉语语句的主语弱化，甚至缺位，无固定的程式可循，所以在句意上点到为止，留有余地，有时候只需意会，不需言传。而英语语句的主语则居高临下，当轴处中，不可或缺，而且语法功能完备，强有力地支配着谓语动词和其他句子成分。原来，汉语总是竭力将主体，亦即反映在语句中的主题、话题，或者主语，尽可能地用其他句子成分包裹起来。包裹层可以是动态名词或抽象名词，可以是短语或句子。有时包裹层不止一层，可以有两层，甚至三层。于是主体退居幕后，似乎与语句中的主题、话题，或者主语，脱了钩，反倒成了修饰语。

这家餐馆的服务很周到。

〖译文1〗The service of this restaurant is very considerable.

〖译文2〗This restaurant provides very considerable service.

与第一章一样，本章也着眼于英汉的相异之处，以一个新的视角，把汉语句子看作“主题—述题”（topic-comment）句式，而把英语看作“主语—谓语”（subject-predicate）句式，探索两者的句法结构之间的差异和转换。所谓“主谓”是一个语法问题，所谓“主述”则属于语用学范畴，各种教科书均有所提及，但是如何用来指导翻译实践则语焉不详，暴露了它的局限性，因此我们有必要作进一步的解释与解析。

英语句子有主、谓、宾、补、表五大成分，通过它们的不同组合和搭配，英语又有五大基本句型，这是教科书告诉我们的。同时我们也知道，英语可以用名词、代词充当主语，除此之外，还可以用从句、不定式短语、分词短语、动名词短语、介词短语，甚至副词、数词等充当主语，形式灵活，丰富多彩。但是英语的主语并非与其他句子成分平起平坐，平分秋色，而是起着引领、统御其他句子成分的作用。

汉语主语的句法功能较弱，和谓语的关系比较松散，虽然不影响我们对句子的理解，如果译成英语，倘不加分析，也会带来一些问题。为此我们不再把汉语主语看作主语，而是“主题”，除了主题，其他句子成分就是“述题”。

他的工作效率非常高。

〖译文1〗His work efficiency is very high.

〖译文2〗His work has very high efficiency.

〖译文3〗He works efficiently.

〖译文4〗He is efficient in his work.

译文1和译文2语法无误，意思也对，更不影响交际，甚至在特定的上下文中有时还非得这么说不可。但它仍然有转换余地。按照句式转换的要求，就可以把原文“他”确认为主题，那么“工作效率非常高”就是述题，是用来描述和说明主题“他”的。然后再把“他”（he）确定为英语句子的主语，那么“工作效率非常高”就是它的谓语。英语表示“工作效率非常高”可以有多种说法，譬如“非常有效地工作”（译文3），“工作中很有效率”（译文4）等。

秘书的职责就是上情下达。

〖译文1〗The duty of a secretary is to relay information from an upper to a lower level.[33]

〖译文2〗A secretary is meant to relay information from an upper to a lower level.

如果把“秘书”划分为本句主题，那么“职责”可以根本不必译出，以突出“秘书”的作用。但是如果把译文2译回汉语，一定要增添“职责”一词，表达成本句的汉语原文。不能译成“秘书是用来上情下达的”。

中国的发展离不开世界，更离不开欧亚地区。

〖译文1〗The development of China is vitally closely-related to the world's and even more to Eurasia's.

〖译文2〗In her development, China is vitally closely-related to the world, especially to Eurasia.

〖译文3〗A developing China is vitally closely-related to the world, especially to Eurasia.

译文1是学生习作，将主语“中国”位置移后了，故句子译得很累。如果“中国”提前，就形成译文2。如果将“中国的发展”译作“发展的中国”，则形成译文3。

历史证明西藏的现代化离不开祖国的现代化，祖国的现代化也不能没有西藏的现代化。

〖译文1〗History has proved that Tibet's modernization cannot be separated from that of the motherland, and the motherland's modernization cannot be realized without that of Tibet.[34]

〖译文2〗History has proved that Tibet cannot be separated from the other part of China for modernization, and China cannot realize the modernization excluding Tibet.

本句说的是“西藏”和“祖国”的密切关系，但汉语却用“现代化”把主体裹得严严实实。

另外，“祖国”的英译确实是motherland，但是在本句具体语境中，最好还原为China。

比如贪污分子大多数还是个是非问题，还是可以改造的，他们与反革命不同。

〖译文1〗For instance, with most of the embezzlers, it is just a matter of right and wrong, for they are different from counter-revolutionaries and can be reformed.[31]

〖译文2〗For instance, most of the embezzlers just have no sense of right and wrong, therefore they should be reformed rather than be treated as counter-revolutionaries.

译文1是一个以it做主语的句子，it不知所指，故全句不知所云，显得逻辑混乱。原文主体稍稍被“比如”遮掩，译文如果仍以“贪污分子”作主语，整句就会贯通起来。

改革开放以来，上海的城市面貌和经济建设取得了令世人瞩目的跨越式发展。

〖译文1〗Since the reforming and opening policy was adopted, the appearance of Shanghai as a whole has greatly changed, its economy has been developing at galloping speed, and win the tremendous achievements that has surprised world.（《上海艺术博览会》j111/2344-1）

〖译文2〗Since adopting the reform and opening-up policy, Shanghai has scored tremendous achievements of world interest both in urban area renewal and in economic growth.

译文 1 采用“面貌”appearance 作主语，于是代词 its 的指代方向就不明确了，动词 win 的主语究竟是 appearance，还是 Shanghai，抑或 economy，就更含混了。如果用“上海”作主语，一切问题都可以迎刃而解了。另外，介词 since 的宾语 the reforming and opening policy was adopted 可以由从句改为短语 adopting the reform and opening-up policy，使短语的逻辑主语与主句主语一致。原文语句流畅，语气连贯，译文 1 却显得凌乱，如何纠正，请参考第四章、第五章相关内容。

说服的成功取决于受众对说服者言谈方式的认同。

〖译文 1〗 The success of persuasion depends on causing the audience to identify itself with the speak, both in what he says and how he says it. [35]

〖译文 2〗 The successful persuasion depends on the audience's identification with the speaker, both in what he says and how he says it.

“说服的成功”译成英语应该改为“成功地说服”。

唐代吕元膺任洛阳留守时，有位部下常陪他下棋。

〖译文 1〗 A subordinate of Lu Yuanying, a minister in Luoyang of the Tang Dynasty often came to play chess with him. [6]

〖译文 2〗 Lu Yuanying, the mayor of Luoyang in the Tang Dynasty, used to play chess with a subordinate of his.

〖译文 3〗 When Lu Yuanying was the mayor of Luoyang in the Tang Dynasty, a subordinate of his used to play chess with him.

译文 1 没有说清楚谁是洛阳留守，谁跑来和谁下棋。原文是个主体退至从句，客体成为主语的典型汉化句子。我们可以采用第二章节的方法，以吕元膺作主题，其他句子成分是述题，如译文 2。当然我们也可以按原文语序断句译出，如译文 3。

别人都不知道辞退他的原因，他自己也不知道为什么被辞退。临走时，吕元膺还赠送了钱物。

〖译文 1〗 No one else, not even the man himself knew why he was dismissed. Lu give that man some money when he left. [6]

〖译文 2〗 No one else knew, nor did the man himself, why he was dismissed. Lu give that man some money when he left.

译文 1 无误，译文 2 只是将谓语提前，使主谓关系更紧密，使宾语 why he

was dismissed 成为独立的意群。

第二节 主语的选择

“主述—主谓”转换与上一章所讲的“主次—主从转换”相互依存，关系密切。因为我们通过第一章确定了主要信息，本章要确定这些主要信息的句子结构安排。

“主述—主谓”转换为我们在汉译英中分析汉语句子，构思英语句子，提供了很好的方法。但是这并不意味着我们可以一成不变地机械地把汉语“主题—述题”结构移植为英语的“主语—谓语”结构。从上面几个例句中，我们可以看到：汉语句子的主语不等于主题，要寻找主题我们的目光不得不左移，亦即在这个主语的左面寻找主题。这样做的目的只有一个：就是要使原文句子中相当一部分内容译成英语后，出现在译文的右面，形成右重。

你的态度有问题。

〖译文 1〗Your attitude has problem.

〖译文 2〗You have an attitude problem.

原文是我们中国人非常习惯的说法，直译成英语则令人不习惯，甚至不理解。改变的方法就是选择“你”做主语。

中国可供出口的商品种类繁多。

〖译文 1〗Chinese commodities available for export are varied. [36]

〖译文 2〗China can provide great variety of exporting goods.

译文 1 和译文 2 说的是同一回事，多一种表达方式译者就多一份驾驭文字的能力。

本公司提供的数码照相机品种非常之多。

〖译文 1〗The strain of digital cameras this company provided is very much.

〖译文 2〗The digital cameras this company provided have so many varieties.

〖译文 3〗The digital cameras provided by this company have so many varieties.

〖译文 4〗This company provides very extensive line of digital cameras.

稍作比较，我们就可发现：译文 1 完全按汉语结构译出，听来似乎是中国商人的口吻。译文 2、译文 3 略带“翻译腔”。译文 4 才是欧美商人口吻。

本公司制作的监视照相机，既有传统的模拟 CCD 型号，又有以太网络照相机型号。

〖译文 1〗 Surveillance cameras that this Company manufactures have Ethernet network camera models as well as traditional analog CCD models.

〖译文 2〗 This Company manufactures surveillance cameras in Ethernet network camera models as well as traditional analog CCD models.

汉语原文又是一个“本公司”被产品遮蔽的句子，这符合汉语习惯。译文修改办法同上一句。

典型的转换速率按操作条件，将为每秒钟 5 至 10 次。

〖译文 1〗 The typical rate of conversion will be between 5 to 10 times per second, depending on the various operating conditions.

〖译文 2〗 The rate will typically be between 5 to 10 conversions per second, depending on the various operating conditions.

译文 1 是我们最常见的无可挑剔的那种译文。但是语言表达具有多样性，译文 2 将原文的形容词“典型”改由副词译出，另一个形容词“转换”改由名词译出，句子也是通顺的。

这些规则和准则的实施有望为考试增添理性、连贯和公正。

〖译文 1〗 The implementation of these rules and guidelines holds the promise of adding to the rationality, consistency and fairness of the tests. [37]

〖译文 2〗 These rules and guidelines will give the promise of adding more rationality, consistency and fairness to the tests.

〖译文 3〗 These rules and guidelines will be implemented to the tests with more rationality, consistency and fairness.

原文的“规则和准则”被“实施”有所遮掩。如果译文 1 删去 implementation，那么 rules and guidelines 就更突出了，见译文 2。另一个办法就是将“实施”译作谓语动词，这样既符合英语的表达习惯，而且简洁明了，又不漏掉原文的意义，见译文 3。

这次大会的目的是寻求平等、和平与发展。

〖译文 1〗 The aim of this conference is to seek equality, peace and development. [6]

〖译文 2〗 This conference aims to seek equality, peace and development.

译文 1 是正确的译文。但是，如果上下文的话题是“这次大会”的话，译义

2 更合理。

与以前的商业展销会有所不同，这次交流会的目的是为参展客商提供一个互动平台。

〖译文 1〗 Unlike previous commercial expos, the aim of this fair trade is to provide an interactive platform for those taking part.

〖译文 2〗 Unlike previous commercial expos, this trade fair aims to provide an interactive platform for those taking part.

译文 1 摘自某商业交流会资料。与上一句的情况有所不同，本句译文 1 算错。可能有人会提出 expo 和 fair 不能比较，此其一。其二是，就算拿 expo 和 fair 比较，译文 1 也没有做到，而是拿 aim 和 expo 比较。所以两个译文中，译文 2 是唯一正确的。

修筑万里长城的工程非常艰苦。

〖译文 1〗 The project of constructing the Great Wall was extremely hard and bitter. （武汉大学英语专业 2003 年研究生入学试题参考答案）[6,25]

〖译文 2〗 The Great Wall was constructed with appalling hardships.

译文 1 如果删去修饰语，句子化简为 project was hard and bitter（工程艰苦），我们马上可以看出搭配不当。因此要在“工程”的前面找主语。前面有“修筑”和“万里长城”，我们以“万里长城”作主语，以“修筑”作谓语，此时才发现“工程”可以根本丢下不译。

她的想法和做法与你可不一样。

〖译文 1〗 Her thought and action were different from you.

〖译文 2〗 She thought and acted differently from you.

译文 1 有语病，句子的最后一词应改为 yours 才对，yours = your thought and action。如果以“她”做主语，可以得到译文 2，句中的最后一词 you = you did，省略 did。

如果只知道 pH 值的近似值，我们就不能把它代入方程式中。

〖译文 1〗 If the approximate value of pH-value is known, we can not substitute it in the equation.

〖译文 2〗 If the pH-value is approximately known, we can not substitute it in the equation.

在英语民族看来，我们知道或不知道，或介于知道不知道之间的是 pH-value 本身。

译文 1 可删除一个 value。译文 2 直接用“pH 值”做状语从句的主语，这样动词 is 左面部分缩水了，右面比重增加了。

《孙膑兵法》总结了战国中期及其以前的战争经验，继承和发展了孙子的军事思想，包含着朴素的唯物论。

〖译文 1〗 Sunbin: *The Art of War* inherits and develops Sunzi's military thinking and sums up the war experiences during and prior to the Warring States Period (475—221BC). It contains many ideas resplendent with dialectics and naive materialism. [38]

〖译文 2〗 In his *The Art of War*, Sunbin inherited and developed Sunzi's military thinking and summed up the war experiences so far as the middle Warring States Period (475—221BC), and gave expression to some ideas of naive materialism.

在译文 1 中，我们首先看到的是 inherit 与前面的主语搭配不当。作为动词，inherit 的主语应该是人，或与人相关的机构等。而且“总结”“继承”“发展”“包含”译成英语后，其主语也应该是人。换言之，做这一切工作的是孙膑。另外，英语表示延续的时间，总是先说以前，再说以后，不能颠倒。“战国中期及其以前”应该译成 the early and middle Warring States Period，而不能译成 during and prior to…。如果我们认为原文的“以前”不仅仅指战国初期，而是包括更早的春秋时期，甚至夏商周三代，那么这个短语就应该译作 so far as the middle Warring States Period（晚至战国中期）。最后，原文的“包含”与前面的“总结”“继承”“发展”共用一个主语，译文就不必另起炉灶，当然“包含”不能照搬词典而直译成 contain。

但是自 1980 年代中期以来，尽管经济仍然保持快速增长，减贫却出现了放缓的趋势，并出现了一些新的贫困形态。

〖译文 1〗 However, the speed of poverty reduction has slowed down since mid-1980s in spite of rapid economic growth; in addition, some new forms of poverty have arisen. [39]

〖译文 2〗 However, the poverty-elimination has slowed down since mid-1980s in spite of rapid economic growth, in addition, some new forms of poverty arises.

译文 1 中 speed 可以删除。因为 slow down 就是“放缓速度”“减慢速度”的意思。slow down（或 slow up）= to reduce the speed or rate of production of（减慢事物产生的速度或速率）：

Business slows up at this time of year.
每年这个时候生意就冷清了。

Economic growth has slowed down.
经济发展的速度减慢了。

我们再来看看国内外报刊是如何表述“减贫”的。与原文最贴近的说法大约是 poverty relief，其他还有 to aid the poor（帮困），to get rid of poverty（脱贫），poverty-alleviation（扶贫）；西方媒体最常用的说法是 anti-poverty（反贫穷），to eliminate poverty（消除贫穷）。

与会者对这个问题的观点差别太大，以致发生了争吵，一时会场的气氛紧张起来。

〖译文 1〗 The opinions of the attendants were far from unanimous about this issue so that some of them began to quarrel with each other. The atmosphere at the meeting became tense at the moment.[32,40]

〖译文 2〗 The attendants were far from unanimous about this issue so that some of them began to quarrel with each other. The atmosphere at the meeting became tense at one time.

粗一看，原文的主语是“观点”。仔细分析，可以把“与会者”作为主题，“对这个问题的观点差别太大”是述题。主题“与会者”被名词“观点”稍稍遮蔽起来了。我们可以把译文 1 开头的三个词 the opinions of 删除。因为表语 unanimous 本身就意味着“观点一致”“无异议”，不必再用 opinion、mind 等词来说明和限定。用“与会者”（attendants）作英译主语的另一个好处是：so that 从句中的主语 some of them 就可以准确无误地指向 attendants，亦即“与会者”在争吵，而非“观点”在争吵。

历尽百年沧桑的中国未来实现复兴和崛起尽管不容置疑，但未来中国将以怎样的方式崛起？中国崛起将如何影响未来的国际秩序？

〖译文 1〗 It is beyond all doubt that China, after a long period of lagging behind, will rise up in the future. But how will it rise up? And how will its rise-up affect the future world?[41]

〖译文 2〗 China , after a long period of lagging behind, is determined to rise up. But how will it rise up and affect the future world?

先说后半句，“中国崛起将如何影响……”根据主语前移，可以译作“中国将如何影响……”。“崛起”承接上一句的“中国将以怎样的方式崛起”表达出来，并不丢失。再说前半句，介词短语 after a long period of lagging behind（经过长时期落后之后）译出“历尽百年沧桑”是可以的，但是经过长时期落后也好，历尽百年沧桑也罢，不是“复兴和崛起”的逻辑前提。落后必定挨打，然而落后未必导致“复兴和崛起”。所以“中国复兴和崛起不容置疑”应该换一种说法，说成“中国决心崛起”。

花蜜在变成蜂蜜的过程中所经受的几次变化是在蜜囊中开始的。

〖译文 1〗The changes nectar experiences in the transformation into honey begin in the honey crop.（南开大学英语专业 2006 年研究生入学试题参考答案）[42]

〖译文 2〗The nectar begins to be transformed into honey in the honey crop.

本句必须用“花蜜”作主语，“开始”作谓语，“所经受的几次变化”以被动语态的不定式作宾语，“过程”不译，句子才能通顺。

国将兴，听于民；将亡，听于神。

〖译文 1〗When a state is about to flourish, he receives his lessons from the people; and it is about to perish, he receives his lessons from spirits.

〖译文 2〗The state is about to flourish when the public opinions are prized. It is doomed to perish when fetishism prevails.

原文出自《左传》：“虢其亡乎，吾闻之：国将兴，听于民；将亡，听于神。”属无主语句，译文 1 设置的主语 he 无上下文依据。译文 2 选择以“国”为主语。

周恩来的品德、人格、风范、情怀为中华民族树立了一座精神丰碑。

〖译文 1〗Zhou Enlai's moral character, personality, style and noble sentiments constituted a paragon for the Chinese nation. [43]

〖译文 2〗Zhou Enlai becomes a paragon of moral character, personality, style and noble sentiments among the Chinese people.

译文 1 按原文结构译出，是不错的。但是如果我们换一种思路，首先划分主述，将原文理解成：“周恩来，他的品德、人格、风范、情怀为中华民族树立了一座精神丰碑。”然后，述题关键词“丰碑”用 paragon 译出，paragon 意为“杰出典范”“尽善尽美的人”“完人”，那么，周恩来本人，而非品德、人格等，是 paragon。接着，用品德、人格等修饰 paragon。最后，把原译文的 for the Chinese nation 改为 among the Chinese people，见译文 2。

有女阿宝，绝色也。日择良匹，大家儿争委禽妆，皆不当翁意。（［清］蒲松龄《聊斋志异·阿宝》）

〖译文 1〗He had a daughter Abao—an unrivaled beauty seeking for a good spouse—who was much sought after by wooers of lofty birth but none was elegible to her father. [27,44]

〖译文 2〗 His daughter Abao—an unrivaled beauty seeking for a good spouse— was much sought after by wooers of lofty birth but none was eligible to the father.

通观全句，主语应该选取“阿宝”才符合句意。这样做的另一个好处就是可以简化句子结构，详见第四章第六节。另外，译文 1 的 elegible 拼写有误。

第三节 在述题中提取主语

东西方人都有客体思维的现象。这是一种客观的、理性的、排除主体情感因素的思维方式，在语言表达上有时是客观情势所需要的。只是由于主观体验有“毋我”和“惟我”的不同，所以英汉语句采用的主语互有差异。

进行社会主义现代化建设必须尊重知识和人才。

〖译文 1〗 We must show our respect for knowledge and people of talent in the construction of socialist modernization. [45]

〖译文 2〗 People of talent and knowledge must be much respected in the construction of socialist modernization.

〖译文 3〗 Knowledge and talent deserve respect in the socialist construction and modernization.

原文以“进行社会主义现代化建设”为主语，也可以理解成无主语句。译文 1 回归主体，添补主语 we（我们）。原文作者是一位领袖级人物，语句带有号召性口吻，故译文主语也可以设为 you（你们）。由于原文作者不设主语，因此我们翻译可以采用“知识和人才”做主语，采用被动语态，如译文 2。另外，“人才”可以直接用 talent 译出；construction of modernization 可以改为 construction and modernization；全句采用主动语态，如译文 3。

在科技史上，曾经有人企图制造永动机，但都没有成功。

〖译文 1〗 In the history of science and technology, someone attempted to make the perpetual motion machine, but all of them had not succeeded.

〖译文 2〗 In the history of science and technology, all attempts to make the perpetual motion machine had proved unsuccessful.

本句“企图”用 attempt 译出，作谓语，当然不错，但是进一步推敲，我们可以发现“有人企图”和“没有人成功”的主语，都暗含在 attempt 之中了，所以我们可以径直采用 attempt 作主语。

尽管有许多人在猜这个微笑的谜，其实都是多此一举。

〖译文 1〗 Although many people are making guess about it, the try is indeed unnecessary.（上海对外贸易学院英语专业 2005 年研究生入学试题参考答案）[6,46]

〖译文 2〗 All attempt to guess it is indeed unnecessary.

〖译文 3〗 It is indeed unnecessary for all of the attempt to guess it.

这个译例颇耐人寻味。原文分成两个部分，表示让步关系。译文 1 完全按照这个模式译出，其实都是多此一举。经过分析，我们可以把“猜这个微笑的谜”作译文主语，“多此一举”作谓语。这样就把译文 1 的两个句子合成了一句。请参见第三章。

如果规章制度遭到破坏，就会引起混乱。

〖译文 1〗 If the rules and regulations are disrupted, they would cause chaos.

〖译文 2〗 Any violation of the rules and regulations would be chaos.

我们看到“如果”“一旦”“倘若”引领的汉语句子，首先会想到 if、once、in case 等词语，但是本句可以用“如果”后面的“破坏”（damage, disruption, violation 等）做主语，不用 if。这样译文在句式上更紧凑，在逻辑上更合理。

如果我们做进一步调查，就会发现市场行情已经变了。

〖译文 1〗 If we make a further survey we will find that the market quotations have changed.

〖译文 2〗 A further survey will find changed market quotations.

和上一句一样，这也是一个“如果”开头的条件句，我们可以换一种说法，用“进一步调查”作英译主语，如译文 2。虽然用抽象名词作主语，我们还是能够在这个抽象名词的背后找到执行动作的“人”。找到或确定主语后，要为主语安排合适的谓语动词和宾语。比如上面“市场行情已经变了”，就是整句的宾语，译作 a changed market situation 比之 that the market situation has changed 既简洁又地道。

倘若对这些现象有更多的了解，我们就会根本改变关于环境保护的观念。

〖译文 1〗 If we understand these phenomena more, we may completely change our conception of environmental protection.

〖译文 2〗 A better understanding of these phenomena may completely change our conception of environmental protection.

毫无疑问，本句可以用“倘若”后面的“对这些现象有更多的了解”做主语。

通过进一步调研，医学界权威们认为这种疾病并不容易传染。

〖译文1〗After further investigation medical authorities agree that the disease is not easy to infect.

〖译文2〗Further investigation leads the medical authorities to agree that the disease is not easy to infect.

本句用“进一步调研”作主语，“通过”不必译出，但是需要另外设置一个谓语动词。

你哪怕最简单地问问路，往往就会有人陪伴着你走。

〖译文1〗Even you simply request for directions often you could be accompanied by someone.

〖译文2〗The simplest requests for directions often result in guided tour.

本句当然可以用“你”作主语，然而也可以用“问路”作主语。有时原文句子成分中的“无”“没有”等否定词可以作译文的主语。

这家大型电子企业没有及时对新的市场需求作出反应，结果削弱了自身的竞争力。

〖译文1〗This electronic giant failed to respond promptly to new market demands, this has blunted their competitive edge.

〖译文2〗Failure to respond promptly to new market demands has blunted the electronic giant's competitive edge. [47]

译文1用“这家大型电子企业”作主语没有错。译文2用“没有”作主语，语句更贯通了。

谈来谈去，结果全无。

〖译文1〗Though they talked over and over again, there were no results.

〖译文2〗Nothing resulted from all of these talks.

〖译文3〗Nothing came out of all these talks.

本句可以用否定词“无”作主语，“结果”作谓语，“谈来谈去”作宾语，如译文2。“结果”也可以用come out of译出，如译文3。

工地上千万盏电灯光芒四射，连天上的星月也黯然无光。

〖译文1〗The work site was ablaze with thousands of lights so that even the moon and the stars appeared lusterless in comparison. [33]

〖译文 2〗 The brilliance of the thousands of lights on work site outshone even the moon and the stars.

译文 1 用"工地"做主语，译文 2 用"光芒四射"作主语，达到同样的效果。

为了您和大家的健康，吸烟请到吸烟区。

〖译文 1〗 For your and others' health, the passengers who smoke, please go to the smoking area. [13,48]

〖译文 2〗 For your and others' health, no smoking except the smoking area.

〖译文 3〗 For your and others' health, smoking is only allowed in the smoking area.

某汉英翻译实务指出：这条标语是想告诉大家候机室不准吸烟，如要吸烟请到吸烟区。标语的用意中国人一看就明白。但从它的汉式英译（译文 1）结构分析，英译文的意思便成了"为了健康欢迎候机乘客吸烟"，因为机场为吸烟者特意安排有吸烟的场所。这哪里还有禁止吸烟的提示，简直是在纵容人们去吸烟！

某汉英翻译策略认为：英译文（译文 1）含有歧义："为了健康，欢迎候机乘客吸烟"。因此也就未能实现广告的功能。

译文 2、译文 3 是我们的修改建议，根据本句的语境最好用"吸烟"作主语，可以译作否定式，如译文 2，也可以译作肯定式，如译文 3。

严格地说译文 2、译文 3 有语病，因为译文开头的介词短语的逻辑主语与主句主语不一致。但是这样的公共标示语，似乎英美国家也有。

与其他发展中国家贸易摩擦迅速增多已经成为中国近年来对外经济贸易遇到的一个突出问题。

〖译文 1〗 In recent years, China's trade frictions with other developing countries are increasing rapidly. [49]

〖译文 2〗 In recent years, the trade frictions between China and other developing countries are on the rapid increase.

〖译文 3〗 In recent years, China is confronted by the increasing knotted trade frictions with other developing countries.

译文 1 选择"贸易摩擦"作主语是很好的，但是不能用"中国"来修饰，而应该用"中国和其他国家"修饰。

另外，are increasing 如果改为 are on the increase，就显得更客观，更公正，而且后者含有"问题""困难"等负面因素"增多"的意思。

译文3提取“中国”作主语。在汉语的述题中寻找英译主语的过程是一个选择的过程，要经过反复推敲，审慎比较。

自古明王圣帝，犹须勤学，况凡庶乎。（［南北朝］颜之推《颜氏家训》）

〖译文1〗Wise kings and sage emperors down the ages were all diligent learners. If so, does the average man in the street have any excuse not to learn avidly?[19]

〖译文2〗Diligent learning is needed for wise kings and sages of all ages, let alone for the average man.

译文1根据原文语序，用“明王圣帝”做主语，是一种很自然的选择。但是我们也可以从后面寻找，选择“勤学”做主语。

城里充满一种奇异的平静。

〖译文1〗The city is filled with a strange quiet.

〖译文2〗A strange quiet pervaded the city.

译文1或译文2要根据上下文语境而定。不过译文2更能渲染某种气氛。

贫居闹市无人问，富住深山有远亲。

〖译文1〗If you are poor, though you dwell in the busy market place, no one will inquire about you; if you are rich, though you dwell in the heart of the mountains, distance relatives will come over to see you.[50]

〖译文2〗A poor man who lives in a downtown area is inquired about by nobody. A rich man who lives in a deep mountain and forest has distant relatives.[51]

〖译文3〗If a poor person lives in the busy city center, no one will visit him. Although the wealthy may live on a remote mountain, they have plenty of distant relatives.[51]

〖译文4〗No one would inquire about a poor man even if he dwell in the busy market place, all would come over to visit a rich man even if he retire into the barren mountains.

〖译文5〗One's poverty repels his friends, be he living in downtown. One's riches attract his relatives, be he in uptown.

译文1译作条件句是不错的，问题是if…though…可以合并为even if…，见译文4。

译文 2 听起来似乎在讲故事："一位穷人居于闹市无人询问，一位富人住在深山老林有远亲。"这就游离了原文揭露了世态炎凉、人心凉薄的深刻寓意。

译文 3 的句意是："如果一个穷人住在市中心，那么没有人会拜访他……"请问穷人该住哪儿？"……虽然富人住在遥远的一座山上，他们却有大量的远亲"，远亲的数量是上天分配的，无关乎住处和贫富，走动的次数才与贫富相关。可见句子逻辑不成立。当然，本句可以用原文句子开头的"贫""富"做主语，见译文 5。

第四节 谓语的选择

主语确定以后，谓语的选择应该符合英语的表达习惯。可以采用的方法有，以主语中心语做谓语：

投资回报率的计算应保持一致。

〖译文 1〗 The calculation of ROI (Return On Investment) should be consistent.

〖译文 2〗 ROI (Return On Investment) should be consistently calculated.

原文的主语中心语是"计算"，可以用作英译的谓语动词，突出句子的动态过程，符合英语表达习惯。

婚姻决定一个男人的成败。

〖译文 1〗 Marriage determines the success or failure of a man.

〖译文 2〗 Marriage makes or mars a man.

译文 1 选择"决定"作谓语。译文 2 采用两个谓语代替译文 1 的 determines the success or failure。这两个谓语动词 make or mar 押头韵，使用方法详见第六章。

中国照相洗印市场的结构与欧美市场略有不同。

〖译文 1〗 The structure of Chinese photofinishing market is slightly different from the U. S. and European markets.

〖译文 2〗 The Chinese photofinishing market is structured slightly different than the U. S. and European markets.

在我们的教科书中，"甲与乙不同"就是 A is different from B。套用这个句型，原文于是就被舒舒服服地译成如译文 1 的中式英语。译文 1 的 from 后面至少要加上 that of 才通。如果不加，译文 1 是将"中国市场结构"同"欧美市场"

比较，不合逻辑。加了之后，是“结构”同“结构”比较。其实，我们中国人关注着“结构”，西方商人却着眼于“市场”，故他们常常将 market 放在主语位置，用可以人为改变的 structure（结构）做谓语动词。而且美国英语认为 different 后面可以跟 from 也可以跟 than。

氢气的爆炸极限范围非常大。

〖译文 1〗The range of explosive limits of hydrogen is very wide.

〖译文 2〗Hydrogen has a very wide range of explosive limits.

本句一般按原文语序用“爆炸极限范围”作主语，也可以用“氢气”作主语，“爆炸极限范围”作宾语，另设一个谓语。译文 2 适合谈论氢气与其他化学元素的比较。

汽轮机的操作温度相对较高。

〖译文 1〗The operational temperature of the steam turbine is relatively high.

〖译文 2〗The steam turbine has a relatively high operational temperature.

〖译文 3〗The steam turbine operates at a relatively high temperature.

译文 1、译文 2 似乎是静态的说明，而译文 3 是一种动态的描述。本句的译文 1 有一个瑕疵，就是主语长，谓语短，头重脚轻。译文 2、译文 3 则不存在这个问题。译文 3 的翻译技巧在于从主语中心语“操作温度”中挑选“操作”作全句的谓语动词。

现代经济泡沫的复杂性，不仅体现在金融资产的独立运行规律上，而且体现在系统的内在脆弱性上。

〖译文 1〗The complexity of modern economic bubbles displays itself not only in the independent running of financial assets, but also in the inherent fragility of financial system. [52]

〖译文 2〗The modern economic bubbles displays its complexity not only by the independent running of financial assets, but also the inherent fragility of financial system.

原文的主题可以从“复杂性”前移到“泡沫”甚至“经济”，而“复杂性”则充当宾语。

家贫，常为官佣书以供养。（《后汉书·班超列传》）

〖译文 1〗The want of his family required that Ban Chao frequently copy books in the employment of local authorities to support himself and his mother. [16]

〖译文 2〗His poor family was supported by his casual employment as a transcriber for local authorities.

〖译文 3〗His poor family was supported by his casual employment as an official transcriber.

说明：原文句意为：班超家贫，常为官方打工，靠抄抄写写养家糊口。译文 1 用 want 和 require 作为主谓搭配，比较勉强。译文 2、译文 3 选择 family 和 support 搭配，使译文意思更明了。

她不太遵守时间，肯定又是迟到了。

〖译文 1〗She doesn't quite observe time and is sure to be late again.

〖译文 2〗She's not very punctual and is sure to be late again.

〖译文 3〗She's a poor timekeeper and is sure to be late again.

英语中并无 observe time 的搭配，"遵守时间"只能用 be punctual 表示。

第五节　宾语的选择

以上的例句涉及如何选择主语谓语，下面涉及如何选择宾语。

学习绝不能半途而废。

〖译文 1〗One must not give up halfway in one's study. [21]

〖译文 2〗One must not give up his study halfway.

〖译文 3〗Study must not be given up halfway.

这儿可以用"学习"作宾语，"学习"也可以作主语。

她母亲希望她早日康复。

〖译文 1〗Her mother wished that she recovered soon.

〖译文 2〗Her mother wished her a quick recovery.

谓语动词 wish 可以跟双宾语，这就使"她早日康复"不必用宾语从句译出。

那时我确实期望宴会上有极其美味的佳肴。

〖译文 1〗I did expect that there were delicious foods in the feast.

〖译文 2〗I did expect a most delicious feast.

汉语用句子"宴会上有极其美味的佳肴"充当宾语，英语可以用名词词组译出。

有人预测这家公司的倒闭指日可待。

〖译文1〗Someone has predicted that this company's bankruptcy is impending.

〖译文2〗Someone has predicted this company's impending bankruptcy.

“这家公司的倒闭指日可待”是一个句子，它可以用英语名词词组译出。

厉行节约就能解决资源短缺吗？

〖译文1〗Can economy solve the resource shortage?

〖译文2〗Is economy a solution to resource shortage?

这里既可以采用“解决”solve作谓语，也可以用它的名词形式solution作表语。

他结识了不少企业家。

〖译文1〗He has got to know many entrepreneurs.

〖译文2〗He has a numerous acquaintance among entrepreneurs.

译文1将原文“企业家”充当谓语动词的宾语，译文2用它充当介词宾语，可供比较。

单单商店的客流量还不能完全衡量成败。

〖译文1〗The number of customers alone can not measure success or failure completely.

〖译文2〗The number of customers alone are not a complete measure of success.

译文1语法无误，意思也到了，但是略嫌就事论事，只管一时一事。如果用measure的名词形式作表语译出，句子便地道了。这是汉译英的一个技巧：汉语的谓语，有时可以译成英语的表语。例如：

在我们过于网络化的文化里，什么流言蜚语、家长里短都出现在博客和微博里。

In our over-networked culture, every rumor and mundanity is blogged and microblogged.

汉语述题“出现在博客和微博里”译成了英语被动语态。

公冶长，可妻也，虽在缧绁之中，非其罪也。(《论语》第五章)

〖译文1〗Kung-ye ch'ang might be wived; although he was put in bonds, he had not been guilty of any crime. ❶

---

❶ http：//blog. netat. net。

〖译文 2〗The master said of Gongye Chang, "I may marry my daughter to this man. Although he has been put in prison, he was not guilty of any crime." He married his daughter to him. [53]

〖译文 3〗Gongye Chang would be a qualified husband. Though suffered imprisonment, he is innocent. —The Analects V

原文是孔子对他的学生公冶长的评价。"可妻也"是指可以把闺女嫁给他为妻。这儿的"妻"用 wife 译出显得生涩，如果逆向思维，用 husband 反而顺畅，译为"他可以是一位称职的丈夫"。后半句也可译得更紧凑些，以便与原文的风格有所照应。

物权法中的平等保护不但来源于民法中的平等原则，同时也是私法自治理念在物权法中的体现，其经济基础则根植于市场经济的土壤。

〖译文 1〗The equal protection of jus rerem not only stems from the principle of equality of civil law, but also reflects on the idea of autonomy of private law, the economical foundation of which lies in the market economy. [54]

〖译文 2〗The equal protection of jus rerem not only stems from the principle of equality of civil law, but also reflects on the idea of autonomy of private law, which based on the market economy.

〖译文 3〗The equal protection of jus rerem is based on the market economy, whether it stems from the principle of equality of civil law, or reflects on the idea of autonomy of private law.

译文 1 后半句意为："其经济基础是市场经济"，重复了同源词 economical 和 economy。可以改为"以市场经济为基础"。也可以把"基础"作为主要信息，放在前面译出，仍以"基础"充当谓语动词。

一些语言学者担心，这些字母词的使用会污染汉语的纯度，会导致沟通上的混乱。

〖译文 1〗Some language scholars fear such usage will contaminate the purity of Chinese and cause confusion in communication. ❶

〖译文 2〗Some language scholars fear such usage will contaminate Chinese and confuse communication.

所谓"字母词"是指国内媒体上经常出现的 MP3，DVD，DJ 这样的英文缩略语。原文"污染汉语的纯度"被译作 contaminate the purity of Chinese，其中 the

❶ http://www.chinadaily.com.cn。

purity of 是冗词。

请看例句：

The water supply has become contaminated by factory waste.

水源被工厂废料污染了。

如果 contaminate 后面跟 purity，等于说“使……纯度不纯”，不符合逻辑。所以原文宾语“汉语”被名词“纯度”包裹起来了。另外，“导致混乱”：cause confusion in。这是一个动词 + 名词 + 介词的结构，可以用一个动词 confuse 代替，这样可以使译文在句子结构上达到 contaminate Chinese 与 confuse communication 的排偶。

早在6,000年前，就有一个原始部落在此定居。现在的无锡始建于公元前二世纪。

〖译文1〗As early as 6,000 years ago, there had been a primitive tribe settled here. Today's Wuxi began to be built in the second century B. C. [6,55]

〖译文2〗Established as early as 6,000 years ago by a primitive tribe, the present city was first built in the second century B. C. [6,55]

〖译文3〗It was settled by a primitive tribe as early as 6,000 years ago, and began to be built in the second century B. C.

本句译文用“无锡”作主语，大概不会有争议。问题是用什么作谓语。既然是“定居”，那么用 settle 作谓语可能会使译文句子更明朗、更简洁、更符合事实一些。

老子对世界的认识是深刻的，但是他认识世界的方法却是隐者的方法。

〖译文1〗Although Laozi has a profound understanding of the universe, his epistemological approach is one that a recluse usually holds. [56]

〖译文2〗Although Laozi has profound insights into the universe, his epistemology is of a recluse.

描述客体转换为描述主体。我们详细讨论了汉语主体被遮蔽现象，主体在主语中成了修饰词。在翻译中我们固然应该以主体作英译的主语，但是其他句子成分也需要配合跟进。

我这一辈子给自己树立了一系列目标，然后努力去达到，一次一个，我必须了解自己能力有限。若开始就知道某个目标根本达不到却硬要去实现，那不会有任何好处，那只会带来失败的苦果。

〖译文1〗I have built a series of goals all my life. Then I tried to reach them, one at a time. I had to know my limitations. It was no good to try to realize something, which I knew at the start, was totally out of reach. If I did, that would only bring me the bitterness of failure. [57]

〖译文 2〗 All my life I have set ahead of me a series of goals and then tried to reach them, one at a time. I had to know my limitations. It was no good to try for something, which I knew at the start, was wildly out of reach because that only invited the bitterness of failure. [57]

〖译文 3〗 So far I have set ahead of me a series of goals and then tried to reach them, one by one. I had to recognize my limitations. It was no good to try for something wildly out of reach, if it was clear to me from the start. That only led to a miserable failure.

"我这一辈子" All my life 似应改为 So far，以适应英语逻辑严密的要求。

"开始" at the start 可以改为 from the start，两者是有区别的：I knew at the start 我开始是知道的（后来才犯迷糊）。I knew from the start 我开始是知道的（现在也还明白）。

"失败的苦果"，改为"痛苦的失败"。

第六节　其他句子成分被遮蔽

实际上汉语的其他句子成分，包括宾语也存在着主体被遮蔽、被包裹、被掩盖的现象。改变这种现象的办法，就像上面"失败的苦果"改成"痛苦的失败"，通过换位，在译文中突出该句子成分。也可以直接把修饰语、范围语之类省略了，这就是人们常说的"减译法"。

构建市场经济的步子必须加快。

〖译文 1〗 The pace of market economy construction should be accelerated. [58]

〖译文 2〗 The construction of market economy should be accelerated.

〖译文 3〗 The market economy should be constructed with more quickening pace.

accelerate，quicken 等词本身就含有"加快速度""加快步子"的意思，所以原文中的"速度""步子"字样不必用对应的用 speed，pace 译出。某汉英词典有例句：

我们要加快我厂技术创新的步子。

We must quicken the pace of technical innovation in our factory. [17]

句中 pace of 虽然在右面，还是应该删去。再如《大中华文库》总序的最后一段说：

各国人民的优秀文化正日益迅速地为中国文化所吸取。

China is accelerating its pace of absorption of the best parts of the cultures of other countries.

主体也被遮蔽了，应删除 its pace of。

解决问题的最好办法是调查研究。

〖译文 1〗 The best way to solve the problem is to conduct investigation. [59]

〖译文 2〗 The best way to a solution is investigation.

〖译文 3〗 The best solution is investigation.

原文“解决问题”和“调查研究”可以如译文 1 译成动宾结构。有时候 Solution 就是“解决问题”，investigation 就是“调查研究”，见译文 2。甚至“最好办法”有时也可不必译成偏正结构，如译文 3。

在分配问题上，我们必须兼顾国家利益、集体利益和个人利益。

〖译文 1〗 On the question of distribution, we must take the interests of the state, the collective and the individual into account. [31]

〖译文 2〗 As for distribution, we must take the interests of the state, the collective and the individual into account.

distribution 既是“分配”，也是“分配问题”。没有 question 句子更清晰。

一个人的生命究竟有多大意义，这有什么标准可以衡量吗？

〖译文 1〗 What is the significance of life? Is there any criterion for its measurement? [60]

〖译文 2〗 Could there be any standard to valuate the meaning of one's life? (2000 年全国高校英语专业八级考试汉译英试题参考译文) [61,62]

〖译文 3〗 What is the significance of life? Is there any measurement for it?

〖译文 4〗 What is the significance of life? Can it be measured?

〖译文 5〗 Is there any measurement for the significance of life?

〖译文 6〗 Can the significance of life be measured?

〖译文 7〗 Can the value of life be measured?

译文 1 逐词译出“标准”和“衡量”，其实 criterion 和 measurement 可以合并，见译文3。译文4删除了原文“有什么标准”字样，剩下“这可以衡量吗?”译文5则将两句合并成一句。译文6更进一步，将译文5的measurement改作谓语动词。译文7在译文6的基础上将原文重新组织成：“生命的意义，可以衡量吗?”

您能否简单介绍一下上海市政府在这方面的工作特点?

〖译文1〗Could you please give us a brief introduction to the work features of Shanghai Municipal Government in this aspect?[63]

〖译文2〗Could you please brief us on the work features of Shanghai Municipal Government in this aspect?

本句最好用brief译出。brief作形容词是“简单的”；作名词是“摘要”“概要”；作动词是“简单介绍”，及物动词，可以带宾语，与on或about搭配。例如brief the press（向新闻界通报情况）。而give a brief introduction则是指为开个头而做一番介绍，后面自己还要详谈，或让别人讨论。

玉不琢，不成器。

〖译文1〗If a jade is not polished, it cannot become a thing of use. ❶

〖译文2〗If a jade is not cut and polished, it can not be made into anything. [1,64]

〖译文3〗Jade can not be made into anything without being cut and polished. [51,64]

〖译文4〗One cannot become useful without education[1,51,64]

〖译文5〗The finest diamond must be cut. [1,64]

〖译文6〗An uncut gem does not sparkle.

原文出自《三字经》，以物喻人，鞭辟入里，短小精悍，一字一珠。原文将“人的成才”比作“玉的成器”，亦即成为统治者的工具。这在汉语文化中是顺理成章的事。统治者在下一盘很大的棋，你被当作一枚棋子，他就是“器重”着你。否则的话，你只能在网络上发发牢骚，爆爆粗口，这就叫“不成器”。

译文1将这个意象译作a thing of use，将使西方读者无法理解：人，或者玉，怎么变成了器用之物？难道人，或者玉，本身不是价值和目的吗？难道这个世界上还有什么其他价值和目的吗？

译文2和译文3，我们可从语言表达看，玉jade，原本就是something，很稀罕的东西，怎么还要被折腾成一文不名的anything呢？

译文4听起来好像在谈教育的重要性，与玉不玉的无涉。

---

❶ 摘自www. EnglishCN. com和某外语学习博客。

译文5听起来好像一伙盗贼在坐地分赃，其中分得最少的那一位提出一个新的分配方案。

在英语文化中，“人的成才”可以比做“玉的发光”。“发光”的英译，可用sparkle一词，它也作“才智焕发”“才华横溢”解。译文6取自英谚，巧合的是，它以六个英语单词译出了六个汉字，文字的对应也可谓铢两悉称。

翻译技能以你的语言技能为基础。语言技能的获得是不能通过理论学习和纯粹的理论研讨完成的。

〖译文1〗The translation skill is based on the foundation of your language skills. The acquisition of language skills can not be achieved through the study of theories or pure theoretical discussions. ❶

〖译文2〗The translation skill is based on your linguistic capacity, which can not be acquired through the study or discussion on pure theory.

译文2按照本章节的要求对译文1做了全面修改，另外，对词语意群、排偶、句子结构的整合方法，请阅读下面几个章节。

正是本着对中国人民和世界的负责精神，我们才有计划、有组织地对我国的经济和政治结构进行调整。

〖译文1〗Just for the spirit of being responsible for Chinese people and the whole world, we designedly and organizedly adjust the economic and political structure of our country. [65]

〖译文2〗Just for the spirit of being responsible for Chinese people and the whole world, we in a designed and organized way adjust the economic and political structure of our country. [65]

〖译文3〗Just for the responsibility for Chinese people and the whole world, we adjust the economic and political structure of our country in a designed and organized way.

〖译文4〗Just for a sense of responsibility towards the Chinese people and the whole world, we adjust the economic and political structure of our country in a designed and organized way.

原文的“精神”遮蔽了“负责”，实际上responsibility这个词本来具有“责任感”“责任心”“负责能力”“负责精神”的意思。但是“责任感”可以用a sense of responsibility译出，其语势有所减弱。

---

❶ 摘自网络。

第三章 英语文句的脉络

第一节　天人合一与天人二分

在中国文化“天人合一”的观念中，虽然“天”和“人”相依相存，相融相合，但是两者的地位和名分却不容丝毫倒错或混淆。反映在语言表达的次序上“天”在前，“人”在后；在语句结构上“天”为主，“人”为宾；在句法功能上，“天”为静态，“人”为动态。推而广之，就是客体在前，主体在后；客体反客为主，主体反主为宾；客体静态，主体动态。再推而广之，环境在前，景物在后；环境为主，景物为宾；环境静态，景物动态。总之，以乾阳主坤阴，以不变应万变。

于是，表现在语句上就是把“天”放在动词的左面，而整个句子的左面，是展开的、铺陈的、静态的；动词后面的“人”是收敛的、短促的、动态的。我们把这称为“左重”。

英语刚好相反，语句的主语谓语处于最前面，亦即最左面，句子的右面则可以从句套从句，短语叠短语，洋洋洒洒，一泻千里。这就是所谓的“右重”。

这里关键是看一个句子谓语动词两边的侧重点在左边还是右边。汉语是“左重”，即使一个简短的汉语句子，很可能它的开头部分，亦即左边部分是展开的、复杂的，甚至叠床架屋，雕章镂句。其结尾部分，亦即右边部分却是短促的、简单的。反观英语，句子的主语谓语部分占据开头的位置，不事枝蔓和铺陈，让句右，亦即结尾部分来充分描述、议论、说明主体。这就是右重。有的书上把这个现象称为“尾重”“右分支”，是一个意思。

That man is the richest whose pleasure are the cheapest.（Henry David Thoreau）

不要花多少钱便可获得快乐的人才是最富的人。[66]

原文译文摘自公开出版物，都未加修改，都是活生生的、具有典型意义的句子。如果我们数一数，就可以看到：原文英语动词 is 的左面有 2 个词，右面 7 个词。译文汉语的动词“才是”的左面有 14 个词，右面 4 个词。这样，我们就看得很清楚了：原文的句左（即句头）和句右（即句尾）用词 2∶7，译成汉语成了 14∶4，等于 7∶2。这虽然是巧合，但是用来说明英汉句子结构不同的侧重点及其转换则大致无误。

换一句话说，汉语句子的谓语动词有尽可能靠后的倾向，即倾向于把动词及其宾语放在句末。而英语的谓语动词则尽可能靠前，句后真要表示什么动作，一定要用非谓语动词，而把谓语动词倾向于放在句前。

Should we succumb to a protectionism that history tells us that in the end protects no one?

〖译文 1〗我们该屈服于一种历史表明最终谁也保护不了的保护主义吗?[67]

英语原文取自英国前首相布朗（Gordon Brown）的讲话，右重的特点很明显。句子的主语是 we，谓语是 should succumb to，宾语是 a protectionism，这个宾语带一个冗长的后置的定语从句，这就是所谓的右重。

译文 1 取直译方法，将“一种历史表明最终谁也保护不了的”作修饰语放在中心语“保护主义”前面，因为定语后置不符合汉语的表达习惯，译文 1 当然只好译成了右重句式，亦即欧式汉语。

我们模仿一位中国领导人说同样的话，大约会是这样的：

〖译文 2〗历史表明保护主义最终谁也保护不了，难道我们还应该屈从它吗?

将两句译文一比较，我们就可以看出译文 1 的动词“屈服于”非常靠前，靠近主语。译文 2“屈服于”非常靠后，靠近宾语。所以译文 2 是符合汉语“左重”——左分支特点的。

他的《庄子》是《道家经典》的一部分，收入《东方圣书》第 39 卷和第 40 卷，是最有权威性的一个英文全译本。

〖译文 1〗His *The Writings of Kwang-tsze*, part of *The Tests of Taoism* in Volume XXXIX and Volume XL of *The Sacred Books of the East*, is an authentic English rendering of the Book.

〖译文 2〗*The Writings of Kwang-tsze* by him is an authentic English rendering, which is included in *The Tests of Taoism*, in Volumes 39 and 40 of *The Sacred Books of the East*.

译文 1 令读者有点眼花缭乱。问题在于动宾结构置于句末，形成左重，虽然加了 of the Book 也无济于事。译文 2 将 is an…提前，全句稍加整理，即成右重。

夫圣贤之书，教人诚孝，慎言检迹，立身扬名，亦已备矣。（［南北朝］颜之推《颜氏家训》）

〖译文 1〗 In their books, ancient sages preach loyalty and filial piety, advocate careful speech and prudent behavior, and urge people to attain integrity and celebrity. [19]

〖译文 2〗 In their books, ancient sages comprehend all their teachings on the loyalty, the filial piety, the prudence on speech and behavior, and the attainment of integrity and celebrity.

译文 1 的特点是以三个谓语动词组成三套动宾结构。译文 2 的特点将"诚孝，慎言检迹，立身扬名"这些宾语共用一个谓语动词，这样可以缩紧句左，使句右呈展开状。译文 2 将"亦已备矣"作为主要信息，提到前面去，以进一步缩紧句左，展开句右。

如果排气管装在陆路车辆上，则总是配以消音器。

〖译文 1〗 If an exhaust pipe is fixed (or attached) to a road vehicle, it will always be fitted with a silencer. [17]

〖译文 2〗 An exhaust pipe will always be fitted with a silencer, if it is attached to a road vehicle.

英语习惯将名词放在主句，从句采用代词作主语。英译可以按此惯例调整，使译文更具右重特点。

理论必须密切联系实际，这是我们应当牢记的一条原则。

〖译文 1〗 That theory must go hand in hand with practice is a principle we should always keep in mind. [68]

〖译文 2〗 We should always keep the principle in mind that theory must go hand in hand with practice.

英语可以将名词概念放在前面，解释发挥放在后面，形成右重特点。

随着中国综合国力的增强，中国政府高度重视文化建设，传统文化保护工作得到前所未有的重视。

〖译文 1〗With China's comprehensive national strength increasingly growing and the Chinese government giving more and more importance to the cultivation of culture, the cause of protecting our traditional culture has attracted unprecedented attention.[69]

〖译文 2〗With the increase of China's comprehensive national strength and the importance attached to the development of culture by Chinese government, the protection of Chinese traditional culture has attracted unprecedented attention.

〖译文 3〗With the increase of China's comprehensive national strength, Chinese government gives more and more importance to the development of culture, therefore the protection of Chinese traditional culture has attracted unprecedented attention.

译文 1 读起来不舒服，是因为介词和它的宾语距离太远。如果将宾语提前，使之直接跟在介词后面，情况可能有所好转，见译文 2。译文 3 以“中国政府”作主语。

第二节　主体与环境的关系

汉语句式倾向于突出环境，弱化主体。在天人关系中，以“天”为主，以“人”为次；“天”在前面，“人”在后面。这样，就在一定程度上加剧了句式的左重。在西方人的观念中，“天”“人”虽不对立，但也不合一。“天”“人”可谓井水不犯河水，表现在语言上甚至“人”优先于“天”。

本省现代美术馆欢迎您。

〖译文 1〗This Provincial Museum of Modern Art welcome you.

〖译文 2〗You are welcome to this Provincial Museum of Modern Art.

〖译文 3〗Welcome to this Provincial Museum of Modern Art.

上面例句的汉语原文符合“天”在前“人”在后，展开在前收敛在后的特点，是地道的汉语。译文 1 照此办理，是我们常见的那种中式英语。译文 2 符合英语的表达习惯，也符合西方人的文化心理习惯。译文 3 虽然丢掉“人”，却不失右重，所以是合格的。

本句表达的是“本省现代美术馆”——环境、天与“您”——主体、人的关系。汉语“欢迎您”落在句末，体现左分支的特点。英语必须表达为译文 2 的右分支。译文 3 是省略句。

中国西部的自然资源很丰富。

〖译文1〗The west of China's natural resources are rich.

〖译文2〗The western China is rich in resources.

〖译文3〗The west of China abounds in natural resources.

原文说的是主体“中国西部”与客体“自然资源”的关系。译文1译作了：中国西部的资源很“富有”。实际上是中国西部，不是资源“富有”。美国作家亨利·大卫·梭罗（Henry David Thoreau）说：

I was rich, if not in money, in sunny hours and summer days.

如果说我一文不名，但我拥有无数个艳阳天和夏日。

他说：“我”很富有，富在阳光和夏日，不在金钱。所以我们可以说：西部富有，富在资源，如译文2。这样说，逻辑通过了，右重的语言习惯也通过了。

“很丰富”也可以译作 to abound in，如译文3。

中国的潮汐能潜力很大。

China's tidal power potential is enormous.

China has enormous tidal power potential.

本句类似上句，故不再分析。

对不起，这样不停地打断使我无法工作。

〖译文1〗I'm sorry—these continual interruptions make me unable to work.

〖译文2〗I'm sorry—I can't work with these continual interruptions.

译文1用“这样不停地打断”作主语，造成了左重，虽然句子是通顺的。译文2用“我”作主语，“这样不停地打断”作介词宾语，形成右重，句子更通顺。

宣传工作的另一个重点是企业。

〖译文1〗Another emphasis of publicity work is enterprises.[63]

〖译文2〗Next, the publicity must lay stress on the enterprises.

原文所谓“宣传工作”是指宣传知识产权保护。原文作者是上海市政府有关方面的领导干部，而企业大概是侵权和被侵权的“事故多发区”，所以他才这么说。原文将“是企业”这个动宾结构放在句末，汉语左重的特点非常鲜明。

译文1也用 emphasis（重点）作主语，is enterprises 也放在句末，全句呈现左重。可以改由“宣传工作”作主语，“重点”作谓语，形成右重。

我国经济社会发展的基本面和长期向好的趋势没有改变。

〖译文1〗Neither the fundamentals of China's economic and social development nor its positive long-term trend has changed. [70]

〖译文2〗Nothing has changed for the fundamentals and the long-term positive trend of China's economic and social development.

〖译文3〗All remains unchanged for the fundamentals and the long-term positive trend of China's economic and social development.

译文1是不错的。但是，我们发现原文的谓语动词“改变”落在句末，译文1对应地将has changed也放于句末。如果我们用原文的“没有”作主语可以改变这种状况，使has changed大为提前，见译文2。

我们还可以另外添加一个主语All，这样谓语动词也提前了，见译文3。

公园里几乎同时开放的几千朵美丽的红玫瑰吸引了许多游人。

〖译文1〗Several thousands of beautiful red roses that blossomed almost at the same time in the park attracted many visitors. [17]

〖译文2〗Several thousands of beautiful red roses blossomed almost at the same time in the park attracting many visitors.

原文略微有一点人为设计的痕迹，比较自然的表达大约是：“公园里几千朵美丽的红玫瑰几乎同时开放，吸引了许多游人。”当然，译文1是不错的。译文2仅供参考。

李汝珍，1763年生于中国河北省的大兴，可能死于1830年。当时通过科举考试是入仕的一个先决条件，而做官又是读书人谋生的唯一的方式，李汝珍却不愿学习八股文（一种固定的作文形式，为科举考试的一项）写作，因为他反对这种形式。这样，他只通过了乡试，和他小说中的主人公唐敖一样，只是个秀才，文人中最低的一级。（［明］李汝珍《镜花缘》）

〖译文1〗Li Ju-chen was born in 1763 in Tahsing, Hopei province in China and probably died in 1830. At a time when passing the Imperial Civil Service Examinations was the prerequisite for an official career, and an official career was the only way of living open to scholars, Li would not learn how to write *pa ku wen*, a fixed style of composition which was one of the requirements of the Examinations, because he objected to this form. Thus, he failed to pass any but the county level of the Imperial Examinations, and like Tang Ao, the hero of his novel, was only a *hsiu-tsai*, or scholar of the lowest rank. [22]

〖译文2〗Li Ju-chen was born in 1763 in Tahsing, Hopei province, China, and probably died in 1830. Li failed to pass beyond the county level of the Imperial

Examinations and was only *a hsiu-tsai*, or scholar of the lowest rank, like Tang Ao, the hero of his novel. Because he was reluctant to be absorbed in *pa ku wen*, a stereotyped style of composition, which was the prerequisite of the Imperial Examinations that offered the only way for scholars to earn their livelihood and officialdom.

汉语原文除了介绍李汝珍的生卒年份、出生地点之外，将“天”——环境，亦即科举制度放在前面；李的态度和行为居中；“人”，亦即李本人，在体制系统中的位置则放在最后面，这完全符合汉语的叙事顺序和思维习惯。

译文1照此办理，可能不符合英语表达习惯，故难以组织语句。译文2则将叙事顺序调换了，可能情况有所好转。

第三节　祈使句的右重特点

我们上面说过，英语谓语动词靠前，体现右重特点，如果走向极端，移到句子的开头，便成了英语的祈使句。祈使句是英语右重规则的特例，也就是省略了主语you的陈述句。

需要更多信息可联系我们的售后服务部。

〖译文1〗If you need more information please contact our after-sale-service department.

〖译文2〗Contact our after-sale-service department for more information.

译文1语法无误，但是可以把动词contact提到句首，简省状语从句。

把它用烤箱的中等温度烘烤。

〖译文1〗Use a moderately hot oven and bake it.

〖译文2〗Bake it in a moderately hot oven.

译文1也是语法无误，但是句子成了左重。修改的办法是把汉语句中最后的“烘烤”提到句首。

在完成分光仪校准后，切记须用250μm切片取代100μm切片。

〖译文1〗After finishing the spectrometer calibration remember to replace the 100μm slit with the 250μm slit.

〖译文2〗Remember to replace the 100μm slit with the 250μm slit after finishing the spectrometer calibration.

与上面的句子不一样，本句最好把动词Remember放在句首。

松开两个位于显微镜安装支架上的螺丝，从仪器的前面，取出显微镜。

〖译文 1〗Loose the two screws on the microscope mounting bracket and remove the microscope from the front of the instrument.

〖译文 2〗Remove the microscope from the front of the instrument by loosing the two screws on the microscope mounting bracket.

原文是科技文本，是说明书中常见的祈使句。译文 1 按照原文的语序，译出原文的两个短句，当然是很好的，意思也明白易懂。译文 2 将原文最后的“取出显微镜”以 Remove the microscope 译出，放在句首，显得更地道。

老吾老以及人之老，幼吾幼以及人之幼。

〖译文 1〗Respect and love the elders of one's blood relations should be extended to the elders of other families, and love and concern for the young of one's blood relations should be extended to the young of other families. ❶

〖译文 2〗Respect your own elders and do unto those of other's, cherish your own youngsters and do also the same.

译文 1 的前一句似乎有语法问题，后一句似乎有逻辑问题。译文 2 改为原型动词开头的祈使句。

第四节 倒装句的作用

某英语语法教材指出：倒装（inversion）是一种语法手段，用以表示一定句子结构的需要和强调某一句子成分的需要。英语的最基本的结构是主、谓结构，倒装就是将这种比较固定的词序加以颠倒。[71]

学习这一结论，我们的体会是：从本质上讲，倒装就是将原来正常的左重的词序加以调整或颠倒，以符合英语右重的表达习惯。

拥有梦想，并愿意付出努力实现梦想的人是幸福的。

〖译文 1〗Those who have dreams and are willing to pay price to make them come true are happy.

〖译文 2〗Happy are those who have dreams and are willing to pay price to make them come true.

这个句子的正常语序应该是译文 1，从修辞角度看，译文 2 倒装结构似乎更文从字顺，读起来更舒服。

---

❶ http://ahongqi. blok. sohu. com。

工地上传来了马达声。

〖译文 1〗 The rumbling of the machines comes from the construction.

〖译文 2〗 From the construction site comes the rumbling of the machines.[27]

译文 1 正常语序，是记叙性文本，译文 2 倒装，是描述性文本。

南京，她自从新中国建立以来发生的巨大而深刻的变化更加令人欢欣鼓舞。

〖译文 1〗 The tremendous changes that have taken place in Nanjing since new China was founded are even more inspiring. （西安外国语学院英语专业 2003 年研究生入学试题参考答案/韩素英青年翻译奖竞赛题参考译文）[6,57,62,72,73]

〖译文 2〗 Even more inspiring are the tremendous changes that have taken place in Nanjing since P. R. China was founded in 1949.

译文 1 的从句谓语与主句谓语位置比较靠近，当然没有问题。然而译文 2 将两者放在句子的一头一尾，遥遥相望，似有呼应，加上中间的动词，使全句很有节奏感。

标样的冲程长度及其最大频率详细说明如下。

〖译文 1〗 A detailed description for the stroke lengths and their maximum frequency of the standard specimens is given below.

〖译文 2〗 Given below is a detailed description for the stroke lengths and their maximum frequency of the standard specimens.

译文 1 作为科技英语是准确的，但是可以在文采上再美化一点，那就是将语序调整成倒装。

中国京剧艺术形成至今的一百七十余年里，诞生了众多伟大的艺术家。通过他们的代代相传，创作积累了数千个承载着精彩表演艺术的优秀剧目。

〖译文 1〗 During the past 170-old years since Peking Opera came into being, many great artists have emerged. They have passed down a repertoire consisting of outstanding titles they have created through the years.[69]

〖译文 2〗 For 170 years or more since Peking Opera came into being, have emerged many generations of great artists who have passed down a repertoire consisting of outstanding dramas they created and performed.

译文 2 在译文 1 的基础上将语序倒装，目的是使全句更严谨，更规整。如何使散点式语句合并成完整的句子，第四章将详细讲解。

工人阶级、劳动人民和革命知识分子，将在斗争中取得经验，受到锻炼，这是很有益处的。

〖译文1〗The working class, the other sections of the working people and the revolutionary intellectuals will gain experience and temper themselves in the course of struggle, and this is a great advantage.[31]

〖译文2〗Would the working class, the other sections of the working people and the revolutionary intellectuals gain experience and temper themselves in the course of struggle, this is of great advantage.

〖译文3〗It is of great advantage for the working class, the other sections of the working people and the revolutionary intellectuals to gain experience and temper themselves in the course of struggle.

本句原文的两部分不是并列关系。所以译文1读起来给人一种行文不严密，逻辑不牢靠的感觉。我们分析后认为前一部分是条件，后一部分是结论。所以我们建议修改成倒装句，以稍稍体现这种关系。译文2将助动词提前了，也稍稍化解了主语的臃肿。

我们也可以按第一章节结论在前条件在后的原则，译作译文3。

国家航海博物馆于2010年7月在上海浦东新区开馆。该航海博物馆是中国最大的综合性航海博物馆，也是世界最大的专业航海博物馆。

〖译文1〗The National Maritime Museum was opened in Pudong district of Shanghai in July 2010. The museum is the largest comprehensive maritime museum in China and is also the world's largest professional maritime museum.[74]

〖译文2〗Opened in Pudong district, Shanghai, in July 2010 was the National Maritime Museum, which is not only China's largest comprehensive but also the world's largest professional one.

本句采用倒装句可以使全句更规整，详见第四章，而且句中的 maritime museum 不必一次次重复。

教科书上所讲授的 there is, there are 句型，究其本源，应该也算是一种倒装。

大多数人对学生的要求持同情的态度。

〖译文1〗The most people sympathize the demands of students.

〖译文2〗The most people offer sympathy for the demands of students.

〖译文3〗There is considerable public sympathy for the students demands.[75]

译文1和译文2有一种说不清道不明的翻译腔，原来中国人所谓的“大多数人”，只具有道义力量，并不具备数理统计依据，不能直译为 most people。译文3

则显得无懈可击，而且采用 there is 句型，语气从容不迫，恰如其分，符合当年的实际情况。

登其艇，即躬身笑迎，搴帏入仓。旁列椅杌，中设大炕，一门通艄后。如呼“有客”，即闻履声杂沓而出。（［清］沈复《浮生六记》）

〖译文 1〗She bowed and welcomed us to the boat with a smile, and pulled aside the curtain so that we could enter the cabin. Chairs and stools were arranged along each side and in the middle was a large couch. A door led to the stern of the boat. The woman shouted that guests had arrived, and we immediately heard the sound of shoes pattering out.[9]

〖译文 2〗When we were on board, she bowed and smiled to meet us, and pulled aside the curtain for us. In the cabin arranged along each side were chairs and stools and in the middle was a large couch. A door led to the stern of the boat. The woman shouted "welcome", and we immediately heard the footsteps shuffling and pattering out.

这段文字描述作者和朋友们造访烟花船，老鸨迎接的情形。译文 2 按照原文的语序，采用一系列谓语或非谓语动词，描写老鸨一连串的动作。中间“旁列椅杌，中设大炕”如果正常语序英译应该是 chairs and stools were arranged along each side and a large couch was arranged in the middle。现在采用倒装，一可以将动词 arranged 提前，形成句式右重，二可以避免 arranged 的重复，同时保持句式整齐，三可以使描述更生动。

学生问：下面英语句子中，为什么她偷自己的东西？昨天之事是否应该用过去时？这里为什么用过去完成时？

Yesterday she had stolen the television set which her mother had sent her as a birthday present from Japan.

她的电视机昨天被人偷去，那电视机是她的母亲以前由日本送给她作生日礼物的。（许孟雄译）

许教授答：假定这样写 Yesterday she had her television set which her mother had sent her as a birthday present from Japan stolen. 这句按寻常章法是对的，但因这句子的宾语长得很，而把 stolen 远远地丢到后面去，使听者或读者迷途，因而不得不把 stolen 提到前面来。我想在口语中大约会截成两句来说，例如：Yesterday she had her television set stolen. It was sent to her as birthday present by her mother from Japan.

近十多年来，中国教育在过去的基础上，又取得了令人瞩目的成就，已形成了学前教育—基础教育—职业教育—高等教育—成人教育—老年教育这样一个教育体系。[76]

〖译文1〗Remarkable progress has been made in the past decade. and a complete educational system, covering the entire process from preschool to elementary, vocational, university and adult education has taken shape. [27]

〖译文2〗Remarkable progress has been made in the past decade. and a complete educational system has taken shape, covering the entire process from preschool to elementary, vocational, university and adult education.

如果译文1将最后三个词组成的谓语提到前面，没有一点问题，句子就更通顺了，见译文2。

第五节 引导词it的作用

引导词it充当形式主语或形式宾语,在本质上是为了适应英语右重句式的需要。

我们上面已经讲过英语的长句式，它的主要信息往往放在句子的前面。次要信息放在后面。主要信息往往只包含主语谓语，显得简约短促；次要信息则包含宾语、表语、补语等，这些常常需要用从句、不定式短语、分词短语、动名词短语、引用语、同位语等来表达，故显得铺陈枝蔓。

但是，如果出于某种表达需要，句子的主语或宾语采用冗长的从句、不定式短语、分词短语、动名词短语等来充当，句子就会显得头重脚轻，比例失调。这时就需要用it作引词，充当句子的形式主语或宾语，将那个冗长的从句、不定式短语、分词短语、动名词短语放在后面表述，以符合英语右重行文习惯。

这就是it用作引导词最本质的意义。

凡事不求人就好。

〖译文1〗Not to be dependent on others is nice.

〖译文2〗It's nice not to be dependent on others.

译文1显得头重脚轻，译文2将过长的成分（不定式短语）移到后面去，句子就显得顺畅了，于是就需要it派用场了。

不管黑猫白猫，捉住老鼠就是好猫。

It is a good cat that catches mice, be it black or white.

这个句子按正常语序表达，应该是：

That catches mice is a good cat, be it black or white.

用了it之后，动词is稍稍提前了，而动宾结构is a good cat整体前移了，句子读起来就舒服多了。事实上，西方媒体引用时，也是采用带 it 的那个句子。

秦之间言曰："秦之所恶，独畏马服君赵奢之子赵括为将耳。"（《史记》）

〖译文 1〗Then the spy sent by Qin spread a rumor, saying: "Qin has only one thing to worry about. They are afraid that Zhao Kuo, son of Zhao She, might come out to command the army."[27]

〖译文 2〗It was rumored by the Qin's spy that "Qin has only one thing to worry about. They are afraid that Zhao Kuo, son of Zhao She, might come out to command the army."

译文 1 以"秦之间"为主语，译文 2 以流言的内容为主语，用 it 引导。

为了了解人们当今所处的环境，并使自己能适应这种环境，就要求具有一定的科学素养。

〖译文 1〗To understand one's environment today and to be able to adapt oneself to it demand some appreciation of the scientific attitude.[20]

〖译文 2〗The understanding of one's environment today and the ability to adapt oneself to it demand some appreciation of the scientific attitude.

〖译文 3〗It demands some appreciation of the scientific attitude to understand one's environment today and to be able to adapt oneself to it.

译文 1 用不定式短语，译文 2 用名词短语作主语，都是可以的，符合语言表达和思维习惯。译文 3 仍用不定式作主语，但是用代词 it 前导，形成明显的右重。

是是非非谓之知，非是是非谓之愚。（《荀子》第 2 章）

〖译文 1〗To recognize as right what is right and as wrong what is wrong is called wisdom. To recognize as wrong what is right and as right what is wrong is called "stupidity".[77]

〖译文 2〗It is called wisdom to recognize as right what is right and as wrong what is wrong. It is called "stupidity" to recognize as wrong what is right and as right what is wrong.

〖译文 3〗It is called wisdom to recognize what is right as right and what is wrong as wrong. It is called "stupidity" to recognize what is right as wrong and what is wrong as right.

原文"是是非非"是动宾结构，第一个"是"意为"肯定"，动词；第二个

“是”意为“正确的东西”，名词；第一个“非”意为“否定”，动词；第二个“非”意为“错误的东西”，名词。上半句的句意是：肯定正确的东西，否定错误的东西，这就叫智慧。下半句的句意是：肯定错误的东西，否定正确的东西，这就叫愚昧。

这种动宾结构，译文 1 采用英语动词不定式译出，充当句子主语，是不错的。

我们考虑，原文谓语“谓之知”处于句末，译文 is called wisdom 是否可以提前，放在句首，见译文 2。另外，宾语从句也存在一个右重问题，是否可以调整，取左重句式，见译文 3。

夫水行不避蛟龙者，渔父之勇也；陆行不避兕虎者，猎夫之勇也。（《庄子》第 17 章）

〖译文 1〗To travel by the water in defiance of the flood dragons shows the valour of the fishermen; to travel on the land in defiance of the rhinos and tigers shows the valour of the hunters. [8]

〖译文 2〗It is the valor of the fishermen to travel by the water in defiance of the flood dragons; it is the valor of the hunters to travel on the land in defiance of the rhinos and tigers.

〖译文 3〗Fishermen show their valor when they compete with crocodiles and sharks in the waters, hunters show their valor when they compete with rhinos and tigers in the jungles.

同上句一样，译文 1 的不定式主语较长，可以用 it 充当形式主语。也可以根据“结论在前，论证在后”的原则，先译出“渔父之勇”，后译出“水行不避蛟龙”；先译出“猎夫之勇”，后译出“陆行不避兕虎”。这样就从根本上取消了不定式主语，如译文 3。

夫帝王之德，以天地为宗，以道德为主，以无为为常。（《庄子》第 13 章）

〖译文 1〗The virtue of the emperors and kings takes the heaven and the earth as its root, the morals as its stem and non-action as its norm. [8]

〖译文 2〗It is the virtue of the emperors and kings to take root between the heaven and the earth, to rule the state by the morals, and to do nothing against nature as norm.

原文句意为：“帝王的德行以天地为根本，以道德为主宰，以无为为原则。”“无为”是道家主张的统治原则，意思是：to govern least。本句可以采用 it 形式主语。

下面两个例句可以用 it 作形式主语和形式宾语，使英语句子形成右重。

故生于深宫之中，长于妇人之手，是后主为人君所短处，亦即为词人所长处。(王国维《人间词话》)

〖译文 1〗Therefore, having been born deep within the palace and raised among women accounts Li Yu's failure as a ruler of men but success as a tz'u writer.[10]

〖译文 2〗Therefore, it is Li Yu's advantage as a lyricist as well as his disadvantage as a sovereign to be born in the imperial palace and raised by royal maids.

提示："后主"系指五代文学家李煜。这里可以用 it 引导不定式短语，it 作主语。

看到同寝室里的人都上图书馆去学习，到深夜闭馆才回，而自己却去看电影，他们就会有一种内疚感。

〖译文 1〗If their roommates are studying in the library until it closes at midnight while they go to a movie, they will feel guilty.[75]

〖译文 2〗They would feel it guilty to go to a movie while their roommates are studying in the library until it closes at midnight.

这是又一个用 it 引导不定式短语的实例，但是 it 作形式宾语。

英语在不违背右重原则的前提下也可以直接用不定式、动名词等做主语，不用 it 代替。比如，在谚语，俗语或名言中，而且句式短小精悍：

Seeing is believing.
眼见为实。

To err is human, to forgive is divine.
犯错误是人性，原谅错误是神性。

英国作家赫兹里特（William Hazlitt）说：

To die is only to be as we were born; …
被译作：死亡就像我们的出生。[78]

西方报刊曾经把"谁致富谁光荣。"译作：

To get rich is glorious.

并以讹传讹地把原文说成是邓小平的话。这个句子当然可以译成：

It is glorious to get rich.

但是原译非常简洁，仅用五个单词，也就没有必要用 it 形式主语了。而且用不定式作主语风格更庄重。

学我者生，像我者死。

〖译文 1〗Those who learn from me will succeed, while those who imitate me will fail. (上海交通大学英语专业 2004 年研究生入学试题参考答案)[2,6]

〖译文 2〗To study me will succeed, to imitate me fail.

〖译文 3〗To study me means success, to imitate me failure.

原文是国画大师齐白石先生的名言。既是名言我们可以考虑用不定式作主语。

第六节 最高级用比较级表示

某些包含“最”的汉语句子，不一定适宜用 most, best 或者后缀-est 形式来表示，而必须采用否定式 + 比较级翻译。这样，英语句子就有可能形成明显的右重句式：

汉语使用的人最多，但英语使用的范围最广。

〖译文 1〗People who use Chinese are the most while English covers the widest scope.[79]

〖译文 2〗The Chinese is spoken by the most people while the English is covered on the widest scope.

〖译文 3〗No language is spoken by more people than Chinese, while no goes around wider area than English.

〖译文 4〗None of the other languages is spoken by more people than Chinese, while none goes around wider area than English.

译文 1 可能套用了教科书 Yangtze river is the longest river in China 句型，成为中式英语。而且，它头重脚轻的弊端非常明显。译文 2 也是如此，尽管它将主语前移，以 Chinese, English 做主语也无济于事。译文 3 和译文 4 更换主语，采用否定式 + 比较级译出，才更符合原文意思。

在所有的词汇中，摩登是最适合形容上海的。

〖译文 1〗Fingering through a list of endless adjectives in the enormous vocabulary bank, MODERN, the word stemmed from the late Latin modernus, would be most likely chosen to characterize Shanghai, the Chinese metropolitan who has been inextricably associated to Western World since the early thirtieth of last century. [80]

〖译文 2〗 None of the other adjectives is more precise than MODERN to define Shanghai.

〖译文 3〗 Of all the adjectives, MODERN may be the precisest one to define Shanghai.

〖译文 4〗 The word MODERN best defines Shanghai.

与上句不同，本句的“最”是一种绝对最高级，而不是相对最高级，因此既可以用否定式+比较级译出，如译文 2。也可以用最高级译出，如译文 3。还可以用 best 修饰谓语动词译出，如译文 4。

（金刚宝座塔）其中以北京正觉寺金刚宝座塔建的年代最早，雕刻也最精美。

〖译文 1〗 Of these pagodas mentioned above, Beijing Jingang Throne Pagoda in the Temple of the Great Awakening is the earliest in its building and finest in carvings. [29]

〖译文 2〗 None of these pagodas mentioned above was built earlier and carved finer than Beijing Jin'gang Throne Pagoda in the Temple of the Great Awakening.

译文 1 首先框定范围，说明在此范围内该宝塔建造最早，这是可以的。问题是译文谓语动词选择错误，造成中式英语。如何选择谓语，我们在第二章已有过讨论。

困难之大，莫甚于此。

〖译文 1〗 This is the most difficult thing.

〖译文 2〗 Nothing could be more difficult.

〖译文 3〗 There is nothing more difficult than this.

〖译文 4〗 One can imagine nothing more difficult.

虽然原文字面上没有出现“最”，但是意思含有“最”，又最不能用最高级译出，仍可采用否定式+比较级。

人生就是大胆的历险，否则毫无意义。

〖译文 1〗 Life is a daring adventure, otherwise it is meaningless.

〖译文 2〗Life is either a daring adventure or nothing. (Helen Keller)

译文 2 用否定词 nothing 取代了译文 1 后面的句子 it is meaningless，使全句趋于右重。

当一个女人突然意识到自己是一个女人，并且为自己的性别感到自豪时，是她最美的时候。

〖译文 1〗When it is occurred to a woman that she is a woman and is proud of the sex it is the time when she looks the most beautiful.

〖译文 2〗A women is never more beautiful when the full sense of being a female dawned on her and makes her very proud of the sex.

本句将主句提前，同时用 never 加比较级表达“最美”，使全句形成右重。

第四章 散点式汉语，透视式英语

第一节 营造“第四堵墙”

我们可以把汉语和英语分别比作中国画和西洋画。中国画是一种散点式构图，以风景画为例，画面上层峦叠翠，移步换景，横看成岭，侧看成峰，不尚纤毫毕现，但求写意传神，纳天地于丹青，得自然之风骨。汉语也是如此，句式长长短短，句法松散，行文自由，如果不从整体上把握，那你就真的不识庐山真面目了。西洋画则是一种透视构图，视觉反映景物在三维空间以精确的实际距离再现在画面上。与此相似，英语句式划一，句法严密，语法层次分明，语意主次分明，各种信息、意念和形象都规整在语句的景物框架之中。

汉语句法无拘无束，灵动飘逸，句子的各个部分相对独立。英语观察事物的视角，其表现方式为透视式，以我为主，一主多客，构架稳定，逻辑严谨，牵一发而动全身。

英美文坛有一段时间兴起短句式，以海明威为代表的现代作家，采用电报式的短句，表现并适应现代社会快节奏的生活方式。但是时过境迁，流风不再。现在，在英语的报刊媒体上、学术专著上、政府文告上、经贸文件上，尤其在议论文和说明文中，传统的长句式仍然是主流。

我们借用美术理论“散点”和“透视”这两个术语，分别描述汉英这两种语言的句式特点。据此，汉译英就要求将原文散点式句法转换成译文透视式。英译汉则反道而行，将透视式转换成散点式。

汉语句子可以有许多个主述题，主题可以随意转换，述题可以即兴发挥，甚至包含几个小的主述句，句子成分之间的关系不言自明。古代文言文和古典通俗小说概莫能外。只是到了近代新文化运动兴起，白话文中才出现诸如“因为……所以……”“不但……而且……”“虽然……但是……”“只有……才能……”这样的欧化连接词。

我们学习、理解和应用汉英翻译的“散点—透视”转换，也应该与前面三章的内容结合起来。

英语的长句式与英语的右重句法不无关系。

我们在第一章中提到过：英语句子语意中的结论或结果往往放在前面，论证或原因放在后面。这就要求把英语的单词、词组、意群、从句都规整在一个严谨的语法框架内，使铺陈和展开出现在句子后面，这就是所谓“右重”（right weight）。

在传统镜框舞台上，写实的室内景只有三面墙。沿台口一面不存在的墙，被称为“第四堵墙”。有些戏剧家和导演要求演员想象第四堵墙的存在，以便与观众保持距离。英语写作者也是如此，他关在四堵墙围住的空间内，从容不迫地组织文句，于是他的句子就像一部机器一样庞大精准。一个英语长句子我们读起来即使要换两三次气，仍觉得浑身舒坦，回味无穷。不难设想，英语句子如果三词一逗，五词一句，不仅它的美感丧失殆尽，会加重读者的心理负担，甚至对读者的理解都会造成极大的障碍。

汉语的“散点式”结构又容易使人联想起以京剧为代表的中国经典戏剧。京剧舞台上，演员四周根本没有哪怕一堵墙，他心中想要说的话，哪怕片言只字，都可以随时随地与观众交流；他手中的马鞭，就表示一匹高头骏马，他叩门的动作，就表示他正面对一扇关闭着的门。他甚至可以跳出角色，以旁观者的身份嘲笑自己扮演的角色。那么观众能理解吗？如果我们与他达成默契，不但能理解，而且能够从中获得极大的审美愉悦。

下面推荐一篇值得精读的英语短文及其汉译。

Let us consider, too, how differently young and old are affected by the words of some classic author, such as Homer or Horace. Passages, which to a boy are but rhetorical common-places, neither better nor worse than a hundred others which any clever writer might supply, which he gets by heart and thinks very fine, and imitates, as he thinks, successfully, in his own flowing versification, at length come home to him, when long years have passed, and he has had experience of life, and pierce him, as if he had never known them, with their sad earnestness and vivid exactness. Then he comes to understand how it is that lines, the birth of some chance morning or evening at an Ionian festival, or among the Sabine hills, have lasted generation after generation, for thousands of years, with a power over the mind, and a charm, which the current literature of his own day, with all its obvious advantages, is utterly unable to rival. Perhaps this is the reason of the mediaeval opinion about Virgil, as of a prophet or magician; his single words and phrases, his pathetic half lines, giving utterance, as the voice of Nature herself, to that pain and weariness, yet hope of better things, which is the experience of her children in every time.

〖译文1〗让我们也考虑一下，像荷马或贺拉斯这样的古典作家的言语对年轻人和老年人产生怎样迥然不同的影响。一些在年轻人看来修辞上不过很普通的章节，和任何聪明的作家所能写的上百篇别的东西相比较既不好也不差，他将它们背下来，认为写得不错，并且以为在他自己流畅的诗文里模仿得很成功，最后，很多年过去了，他有了阅历，这些文字的真谛他才理解，并以其悲伤的真诚和生动的准确深深打动了他，似乎他从来就不知道这些文字。然后，他渐渐懂得，这些某个早晨或晚上在古希腊爱奥尼亚人的节日或在萨宾山上偶得的诗行，以其震撼心灵的力量和他那个时期的文学（尽管它有明显的优点）完全与之无法媲美的魅力，是如何一代接一代地传颂了几千年。也许，因此才有了中世纪对维吉尔的评价：他犹如一个预言家或魔术师；他的单个的词和单个的短语，以及他那带有感伤情调的半行的诗句，就像大自然自己的声音一样，表达着那种痛苦和厌倦，然而，也表达着追求更加美好事物的希望，而这也正是一切时代一切大自然之子的经验。[81]

英语原文只有四句话，即构成一篇严谨完整的议论文，是一种典型的透视句式。译文1也译成四句话，忠实地再现了原文的思想和风格。我们读来确实有一股欧式气息，就像一位外国专家用中国话和我们讲话。译文2则模仿一位中国文人和我们讲话，说的也是这四句话，内容不变，但是他的语句是散点式的。

〖译文2〗让我们也考虑一下，像荷马或贺拉斯这样的古典作家的言语对年轻人和老年人产生怎样迥然不同的影响。某些篇章，在一位少年看来只不过是些普普通通的辞藻，把它们混同于其他优秀作家数以百计的作品，也无法分辨出个高下优劣。他将它们背下来，另眼相看，并且满有把握地在自己滔滔的诗文加以模仿。直到最后，很多年过去了，他有了阅历，这些文字才真正归属于他，他就像头一次知道它们。这些悲伤而真诚，生动而准确的文字深深打动了他。然后，他渐渐懂得，那些某个早晨或晚上在古希腊爱奥尼亚人的节日或在萨宾山沿途偶得的诗行，是如何一代接一代地传颂了几千年。它们震撼心灵的能量和魅力是他那个时代的文学完全无法与之媲美的——尽管后者也有明显的优点。或许唯因如此，才有了中世纪对维吉尔的评价：他犹如一个预言家或魔术师；他的片言只字，以及他那伤感的半行诗句，就像大自然自己的声音一样，表达着那种痛苦和厌倦，然而，也表达着追求更加美好事物的希望；而这也正是一切时代一切大自然之子的体验。

英译汉是如此，汉译英又如何？

汉译英往往有这样的情况：有一些汉语长句子可以，应该，甚至必须断开才能译成英语，这个问题我们在前面有所涉及，后面还会探讨，但是对于我们来说这不是一个难点。我们应该学会的是相反，即把完整的汉语句子用完整的英语句子来准确表达。而且汉译英也面对着这样的要求：我们如何将汉语原文中语意的散点收集起来，加以咀嚼、消化，然后加以合成、整编。具体的做法是：在汉语句子成分之间找出因果、转折、假设、让步、条件、偏正、递进等关系，然后将这种关系整合到英语复合句中。

如果我们习惯、擅长于撰写英语长句式，不仅仅用简单的散点式的短句来表达，就能尽可能摆脱了中式英语，达到表达上得心应手，纵横捭阖的自由境界。

我们需要营造第四堵墙。

在这种场合陌生人相识，如果是亚洲人，他们往往开口之前先毕恭毕敬地用双手把自己的名片呈递给对方，这好像是不可缺少的礼节。

〖译文 1〗On such occasions, strangers may get to know each other. If they are Asians, they will, very respectfully and with both hands, present their calling cards to their interlocutors before any conversation starts. This seems to be the required courtesy on their part. （全国高校英语专业八级考试试题参考答案）[48,82]

〖译文 2〗It seems to be the required courtesy for Asians to present their calling cards to their interlocutors with both hands respectfully before any conversation may start on such occasions as strangers get to be acquainted with each other.

译文 1 无误。但是译文可以采用前面三章的“提取主要信息”“顺叙—倒叙转换”“左重—右重转换”“it 作形式主语”等手段，使全文透视化。透视以后，句子的风格将为之改观，面貌为之一新，境界就出来了。译文 2 提供了修改建议。当然，这仅仅是建议，因为修改的方法可以有多种。

1997 年，在南海发展银行同样面临支付困难的情况下，又把 28 家面临危机的城市信用社接管下来，这更是雪上加霜。

〖译文 1〗In 1997, as the Hainan Development Bank got bogged down in the difficulty of payment, it had to take over 28 tottering credit unions, and this sealed its fate. It was like rubbing salt on an open wound.[48]

〖译文 2〗In 1997, Hainan Development Bank went from bad to worse when it got bogged down in the difficulty of payment, and had to take over 28 tottering credit unions.

〖译文 3〗In 1997, matters went from bad to worse with Hainan Development Bank, which had to take over 28 tottering credit unions as it got bogged down in the difficulty of payment.

〖译文 4〗 In 1997, it was the last straw for Hainan Development Bank to take over 28 tottering credit unions as it got bogged down in the difficulty of payment.

译文 1 无误。但是我们从翻译的角度看，“雪上加霜”是最重要信息，可以作为主句，另两个信息作为从句译出，译文就更忠实原文。这就是我们上面所说的“透视化”和后面章节所说的“并句”。海南发展银行曾经宣告破产，所以译文 1 使用 sealed its fate、rubbing salt on an open wound 这样的词语是不错的，缺点是断句了。

第二节 中式英语与欧式汉语

通过分析“翻译腔”，亦即欧式汉语，我们也可以从中受到有益启发。

There are occasional items of news in the papers that pull us up and tempt us to examine our attitude in regard to some questions as if for the first time.

〖译文 1〗 报上偶然有使我们阅读时猛然停住并且审视我们对某些问题的态度的新闻，好像初次遇到一样。[83]

〖译文 2〗 报纸上时不时有些新闻，会打住我们的阅读，促使我们反思对某些问题的看法，真有相见恨晚之感。

《上海翻译》对译文 1 的评论是：在英汉翻译中如果一味地添加英语的形合标记，造成恶性西化，就会破坏汉语固有的美感，使读者产生视觉疲劳，增加心理负担。译文倒真是亦步亦趋与原文形式上忠实对应，但让中国读者读起来，恐怕谁都会觉得有点儿气短，不停下来想想，一时也难明白说的是什么意思，更没有什么美感可言。这并不在输入“新的表现手法”，引进美学素质，而是“格里格达，吉里吉八，拖拖拉拉一长串，要折断人家的嗓子，其害处相当于误译。”

可惜，这个评论虽然措辞激烈，却没有给出解决方案和修改译文。

我们的评论是：原文是一个典型的英语长句子，带有后置的定语从句。这与汉语差别很大。汉语大多是散点短句，定语大多前置，一般都不长，而且也长不了。所以译文 1 中“有使我们阅读时猛然停住并且审视我们对某些问题的态度的新闻”，“新闻”的定语嫌长。“有”的宾语又是一个动宾结构，这个动宾结构的宾语则是一个很长的主谓结构，既叠床架屋又尾大不掉。“有”字结构用来修饰“新闻”，使偏正结构头重脚轻，整句好像患了鼓胀病。解决办法是将原文句意断开，先译出中心语“新闻”，然后将修饰语一一道来，方能泄滞，使文句显得从容不迫。

这就是我们所说的在英译汉中将透视式原文转换成散点式译文的一种方法。我们强调一点：汉译英需要营造第四堵墙，让演员独自发挥。英译汉需要强拆第四堵墙，让演员与观众直接交流。译文 2 是修改方法，也是我们克服欧式汉语的一种尝试。细心的读者也许会发现：译文 2 在字面上反而与英语原文的语序一一对应。

上面的例句是英译汉。汉译英，我们从一个简单的句子开始。

传说黄河里有个河神，人们尊称他为河伯。

〖译文 1〗It was said that there was a God of the river in the Yellow River. People respectably call him Hebo. [84]

〖译文 2〗It was said that there was a God in the Yellow River by the respectable name of Hebo.

〖译文 3〗It was said that there was a God in the Yellow River, whom people respectfully called Hebo.

原文是一个完整的句子，它分成两个散点，各自可以单独成句，表达两个非常简单的句意；放在一起却表达另一个稍稍复杂而又完整的句意。译文 1 断句，也译成两个散点。其实英译一定要将原文的定语放在中心语前面，理解成“传说黄河里有个被人们尊称为河伯的河神”即可，修改办法是将“尊称”用介词短语译出，见译文 2。

当然附带地说一说人民群众对河伯，亦即黄河的敬畏也未尝不可，译文 3 用宾语从句表达这层意思。

另外，respectably 只能用来修饰受尊敬者，而尊敬别人必须用 respectfully，译文 1 是误译。

从地下开采到的石油不能直接使用，首先必须进行提炼。

〖译文 1〗The petroleum which comes out of the ground cannot really be used for anything. It must first be refined. [20]

〖译文 2〗The petroleum which comes out of the ground cannot really be used for anything before it is refined.

〖译文 3〗The petroleum which comes out of the ground cannot really be used for anything unless it is first refined.

〖译文 4〗The petroleum which comes out of the ground must first be refined before it can really be used for anything.

译文 1 的前后两个句子可以简单地用连接词连接起来，见译文 2 和译文 3。我们分析原文：它将主要信息“首先必须进行提炼”放在最后，符合汉语的习惯。译成英语就可以将它放在前面，这样句子也串起来了，见译文4。

周处年少时，凶强侠气，为乡里所患。（［南北朝］刘义庆《世说新语》）

〖译文1〗When he was a young man, Zhou Chu (240—299) was tough and fond of fighting. Residents of Yi Xing, his hometown, both feared and hated him.[85]

〖译文2〗As a young man, Zhou Chu (240—299) was tough and fond of fighting. Residents of Yi Xing, his hometown, both feared and hated him.[85]

〖译文3〗Zhou Chu (A. D. 240—299) was feared and hated by the residents of his hometown, Yi Xing, when he was a young bellicose swordsman.

〖译文4〗Zhou Chu (240—299) was a young bellicose swordsman, who was feared and hated by the folks of his hometown, Yi Xing.

原文出自《世说新语》中的“周处自新”，改编成京剧叫作《除三害》。

原文有三个散点，很明显，第一个散点表示时间状语，后两个散点组成因果关系。译文1用散点译出，所以乍听起来好像在说两个人：当“他”年轻时，“周处”已经是一个好勇斗狠的人。为了避免这种误解，英语有一条语法规则，就是状语从句的主语谓语若与主句主语谓语一致，可以省略。例如译文2，前面的he was被省略了，状语从句被修改成介词短语As a young man了。

全句如何进一步修改呢？首先，在“年少时”中，我们一看见“时”容易有when或as的条件反射，但是本句只需要用young修饰名词，再配合过去式动词就可以译出“年少时”。然后将“为乡里所患”作为主要信息，放在译文开头，便可得到译文3。也可以反过来，将“凶强侠气”作为主要信息，便得到译文4。

花蜜是一种香甜的、多水分的流体，总是含有一种特殊的香味，这种香味跟从它采集蜜汁的花的香味有关。

〖译文1〗Nectar is a sweet, washy fluid. It has a special scent, which has much to do with the flavor of the flower from which the honeydew is gotten.（南开大学英语专业2006年研究生入学试题参考答案）[6,42]

〖译文2〗As a sweet, washy fluid, nectar has a special scent, which has much to do with the flavor of the flower from which the honeydew is gotten.

原文属科技文体，似无必要断句而译作口语化句子。译文2用介词短语代替译文1句首散点句子，使全句语气贯通，修改原理见上面“周处”句。

四门塔外形简朴，结构坚实，经历一千三百余年，至今依然完好。

〖译文1〗The Four Door Pagoda has a simple appearance and a solid structure. Having undergone over 1,300 years, it still remains intact.[29]

〖译文2〗Having weathered over 1,300 years, the Four-Door Pagoda still remains intact with its simple appearance and solid structure.

本句“外形简朴”“结构坚实”可以用介词短语，不用简单句译出，那么全文就合并成一句了。

在经济高度发展的社会，仅一小部分人从事农业，农业生产率较高，而大部分劳动力则从事于其他商品生产及服务性行业。

〖译文1〗In a society with highly developed economy, only a small proportion of population is engaged in agriculture. Its agricultural productivity is relatively high, and most of the working population is engaged in production of other goods and services.[43]

〖译文2〗In a society with highly developed economy, only a small proportion of population is engaged in agriculture with high productivity, so that most of the working force can be engaged in processing or service industries.

原文经分析后可以发现是一句因果句，句中“而”不是“而且”，是“从而”“因而”的意思。全句可以不断句，不分译成两句。“农业生产率较高”可以不照字面译成单独的一句句子，句中的 Its, agricultural, relatively 都是冗词，整个句子可以用介词短语 with high productivity 代替。另外，“劳动力”宜译成 working force，这绝不是说译成 working population 就错了，而是为了避免与主句中的 population 重复。

湖中有四岛。并且有湖心亭坐落在一个小岛上。它建于1552年，是西湖最大的亭子。在这个岛上有一些水池，又形成一个小湖，这就像是“岛中有湖，湖中有岛”了。

〖译文1〗There are four islands in the lake. And the Heart of Lake Pavilion situates on an islet. It was built in 1552 and it is the largest pavilion on the West Lake. There are some pools on this island, which form a miniature lake, so it seems an “islet in a lake within an island in a lake” .[86]

〖译文2〗There are four islands in the lake, one of which has the Midlake Pavilion, the largest pavilion on the West Lake, built in 1552. Part of this island is under water, forming a miniature lake, as saying goes “islet in lake, lake in islet” .

〖译文3〗One of the four islands in the lake has the largest of pavilions on the West Lake, which was built in 1552 by the name of Midlake Pavilion. There are some pools on this island, which form a miniature lake, as saying goes "islet in lake, lake in islet".

原文有四句，译文1也对应地译成四句，但是读起来没有原文舒服。比如译文1的第三句，主语it是代词，它可以指代前面的the Heart，Lake Pavilion和an islet，读者在这儿存疑，要往下读才会明白。我们可以将全句转换成透视式，还可以将"湖心亭"译作Midlake Pavilion，使句子读起来更流畅。

中国有些伟大的贤哲对于艺术的价值观似乎跟罗马教皇格里高里所坚持的看法相似。他们把艺术看成一种工具，用以提醒人们回忆过去黄金盛世的美德典范。

〖译文1〗Some of the great teachers of China appear to have had a similar view of the value of art to that held by Pope Gregory the great. They thought of art as a means of reminding people of the great examples of virtue in the golden ages of the past. ❶

〖译文2〗Some of the great Chinese thinkers appeared to share the same view on the value of art with Pope Gregory the Great, who believed the art should be means to remind people of the great examples of virtue in the golden age.

译文1是不错的，但是译文2将后一句散点句子改译成从句，办法是把"他们"改译成"他"（罗马教皇），因为两者"看法相似"，而且译文中的the golden age是西方神话中古代政治、经济、文化发展的全盛时期。这样，既归并了句子，又避免了英译中的逻辑矛盾。

1957年，他向著名内画艺术家叶晓峰和叶小三学艺，在师承的基础上，兼收各家之长，将传统的勾竹、木笔和勾毛笔结合并用，形成自己的风格。

〖译文1〗In 1957, Wang studied under the famous artists Ye Xiaofeng and Ye Xiaosan. He further developed the art by absorbing the good points of different schools and using the traditional tools, bamboo and wood slips, as well as writing brushes. Finally he created a style of his own. [13]

〖译文2〗In 1957, Wang created a style of his own after studied under the famous artists Ye Xiaofeng and Ye Xiaosan, and further developed the art by absorbing ideas from different schools and using traditional tools, bamboo and wood slips, as well as writing brushes.

这位艺术家拜师学艺，兼收并蓄，终于功德圆满，自成一家。汉语的陈述是

❶ http://www.52en.com。

正序的，所以容易取散点句式。英语要透视，就必须倒叙。

我们没有见过孔子，也没有见过老子和庄子。但是我们却可以毫不费力地就把孔子、老子和庄子区分开来，而我们区分他们的依据就是他们的思想。

〖译文1〗None of us has seen Confucius, or Lao-tzu, or Zhang-tzu（369—286 B. C. ）. However, we can easily distinguish these philosophers. The distinction is based on their different thinking.[87]

〖译文2〗We can easily distinguish Confucius from Laozi, or Zhuangzi（369—286 B. C. ）, depending on their different thinking, although none of us has seen these philosophers.

〖译文3〗We can depend on the different thinking of Confucius, Laozi, or Zhuangzi（369—286 B. C. ）to distinguish their writings although none of us has seen these philosophers.

译文1是不错的，可能在具体的上下文中该译文是唯一正确的。我们提供译文2、译文3还是为了显示语言表达的多样性丰富性。

《现代汉语词典》在整个编写和修订过程中，得到了全国一些科研机构、大中学校、工矿企业、部队有关机关以及很多专家、群众的大力协助。我们在这里敬向有关单位和有关同志表示衷心的感谢。

〖译文1〗Throughout the process of compilation and revision of *the Contemporary Chinese Dictionary*, we have received strong support from research institutes, universities, middle schools, industrial enterprises and relevant army units from across the country, and from many experts as well as ordinary people. To all of them we would like to express our sincere thanks.[88]

〖译文2〗We would like to express our sincere thanks to readers for all of the support we have received from the research institutes, universities, schools, industrial enterprises and relevant army units from across the country, and from many experts as well as ordinary persons throughout the process of compilation and revision of *the Contemporary Chinese Dictionary*.

译文可以把感谢说在前面。原文是出版物的前言，对于这种官样文章，译文句式适当拖长一些，读起来反而舒服。

此后，武汉先后与一些世界名城如美国的匹兹堡市、德国的杜伊斯堡市、英国的曼彻斯特市、罗马尼亚的加拉茨市和乌克兰的基辅等建立了友好关系，从而揭开了武汉与外国城市建立友好关系的新的一页。

〖译文1〗Since then Wuhan has established friendly relations with several famous cities of the world, such as Pittsburgh in the United States, Duisburg in Germany, Manchester in Britain, Galatz in Romania, and Kiev in Ukraine. Thus a new page is opened in the history of Wuhan on the establishment of sister city relations with cities in the other countries.[40,89]

〖译文2〗Thus a new page is opened in the history of Wuhan on the international exchanges as Wuhan has established friendly relations with several famous cities in other countries, such as Pittsburgh in the United States, Duisburg in Germany, Manchester in Britain, Galatz in Romania, and Kiev in Ukraine.

译文1如果删除最后一个定冠词the，该译文总得来说是不错的。这个句子我们也可以按照逆序翻译，先说“揭开了新的一页”，再说“与世界名城建立了友好关系”，如译文2。

中国的耕地面积只占世界耕地面积百分之七，她凭着这么少的耕地却养活占世界人口四分之一的人。真是一个了不起的成就！

〖译文1〗The area of China's arable lands is only 7% of that of the world. With so few lands, China supports 1/4 of the global population. What a marvelous achievement it is!（华东理工大学英语专业研究生入学试题参考答案）[6,90]

〖译文2〗What a marvelous achievement it is for China to support 1/4 of the global population with so few arable lands, which cover only 7% of that of the world!

这是一个典型的感叹句，只要我们简单地套用感叹句句型即可译出地道的英语。

上智不教而成，下愚虽教无益，中庸之人，不教不知也。（［南北朝］颜之推《颜氏家训》）

〖译文1〗For the wisest, education is superfluous; for the very stupid, it is futile. But for the average man, education is essential for him to acquire knowledge and reason.[19]

〖译文2〗Education is superfluous for the wisest, futile for the very stupid, but essential for average men to acquire knowledge and reason.

原文出现三个“教”，所以是最重要的信息，原译文译作education，并放在主语位置是不错的。但是没有进一步提取主要信息，仍不符合英语表达习惯。如果进一步提取主要信息，英语可表达为：“教”是多余的……是徒劳无益的……是至关重要的……关键是将“多余，徒劳无益，至关重要”放在重要位置，即谓语部分。“上智，下愚，中庸之人”放在次要位置，即介词宾语部分。

子祀、子舆、子犁、子来相与语曰：“孰能以无为首，以生为脊，以死为尻，孰知死生存亡之一体者，吾与之友矣。”四人相视而笑，莫逆于心，遂相与为友。（《庄子》第六章）

〖译文1〗Four men—Zisi, Ziyu, Zili, Zilai—were having a discussion when one of them said, “Who can take nothingness as his head, life as his back and death as his rumps? Who believes that life and death, survival and perishament are one and the same? That man shall be my friend.” The four of them looked at one another and smiled. They were of the same mind, and so they became friends at once.[8]

〖译文2〗“Whoever could take nothingness as his head, life as his backbone and death as his rumps, whoever believe that life and death, survival and perishment are one and the same should be my friend.” said one of the four men, Zisi, Ziyu, Zili and Zilai, who were having a discussion. They looked and smiled at one another, for they were of the same mind, and so they became friends ever since.

〖译文3〗“He should be my friend who could take nothingness as his head, life his backbone and death his rumps, and believe that life and death, survival and perishment are one and the same.” said one of the four men, Zisi, Ziyu, Zili and Zilai, who were having a discussion. Being of the same mind, they looked and smiled at one another, and became friends ever since.

原文的“孰”当然可以理解成“谁”，但是也可以理解成“哪个”或“哪些人”。“孰”译作 Who，全句只能取散点式。译作 Whoever 或 He…who，即成透视式。从原文上下文来看，后面的理解是正确的。

我们在第一章主次—主从转换中谈到过，英语句子通过倒叙突出主要信息，突出现在。本章所说的散点—透视转换也需要通过倒序整合，亦即倒叙是转换的一种语法手段。

第三节 断句容易并句难

有时候，一个一气呵成的汉语句子，译者无法用复合句译出，就只能断句。相对而言，断句译法比较容易。

蜀中有杜处士，好书画，所宝以数百。有戴嵩牛一轴，尤所爱，锦囊玉轴，常以自随。（苏轼《东坡志林》）

〖译文1〗There was a hermit scholar in Sichuan whose name was Du. Being fond of the art of calligraphy and painting, he had hundreds of masterpieces in his collection. Out of them all he cherished most was a painting of bulls by Dai Song, and so he had it mounted on a jade scroll roller and wrapped in a silken bag to be carried with him all the time. [16]

〖译文2〗Mr. Du, a hermit scholar in Sichuan, was fond of the art of calligraphy and painting. Among the hundreds of masterpieces in his collection, he cherished most was a painting of bulls by Dai Song, and so he had it mounted on a jade scroll roller and wrapped in a silken bag to be carried with him all the time.

汉语原文属记叙文，由七个部分组成。译文1做断句处理，应该说是正确的。译文2也断句，但是断开处不一致，算是聊备一格。关于断句，我们仅举此一例。

本书先前介绍了如何将片段的零碎的汉语句意，组织成英语的主从复合句。下面要介绍另一种并句的方法：独立分句用副词或介词短语译出。

上级的布置，我们能当耳边风，不严格执行吗？（孙犁《风云初记》）

〖译文1〗Should we let instructions from above go in one ear and out the other? Or should we carry them out seriously? [51]

〖译文2〗Shouldn't we carry instructions from the above seriously, rather than let them go in one ear and out the other?

译者将"耳边风"译作go in one ear and out the other是不错的。但是译文没有聚焦，分成两个散点，成为二选一的问题，使整个句子语势有所削弱。

办法是有的。按照第一章要求，我们可以将"上级的布置不严格执行吗"作为主要信息，放在前面，"当耳边风"作为次要信息，放在后面，用连接副词连接起来就可以了。

成都民物丰盛，邑宇逼侧，旧制禁民夜作，以防火灾。（范晔《后汉书·廉范传》）

〖译文1〗In the Han Dynasty, people were well-to-do and products abundant in the city of Chengdu. Only the houses were adjoined too closely. At first, people were forbidden to work at night in order to protect the houses from fire. [16]

〖译文2〗Although people of Chengdu were well-to-do by help of rich natural resources, their residential districts were crowded with all kinds of houses, so the old rules and regulations forbade people from working under torch or candle at night to avoid fire risk.

原文叙事一气呵成。译文1却断成三句。译文2试图吸收译文1的内容，使之规整在一个句子之内。

我们还可以通过表态在前，陈述在后；结论在前，论证在后；叙述结果在前，过程在后，使英语句子透视化。但是有时候这种表态轻描淡写，一笔带过，语势较弱，那么译文不必译成主从复合句，也可以降格为简单句。

当我骑车到那儿的时候，已经大汗淋漓。

〖译文 1〗 I was already perspiring on my bike when I got there. [57]

〖译文 2〗 I was already perspiring when I got there on my bike. [57]

〖译文 3〗 I got there on my bike sweatily.

译文 1 和译文 2 将“大汗淋漓”作为主要信息译出当然不错，而且使用大词 perspire（排汗），可用于正式文体。我们不妨换一种思路，译文 3 将“我到那儿”作为主要信息译作主句，“大汗淋漓”只用副词译出，可用于日常口语。

她竟拒绝了他的盛情邀请，令他惊诧莫名。

〖译文 1〗 He was surprised that she refused to accept his kind invitation.

〖译文 2〗 To his surprise, she refused to accept his kind invitation.

译文 1 本身是一个很好的透视式句子，译文 2 将译文 1 的主句内容改由介词短语表达。所以本句的翻译要视上下文而定，如果原文谈来谈去的是“他”，最好采用译文 1，如果谈“她”，应该采用译文 2。

老一辈教育家对青年教师这样关心，真叫我感动。

〖译文 1〗 The educators of the old generation have shown so much concern about young teachers. This has moved me greatly. [17]

〖译文 2〗 I am so moved that the senior educators have shown so much concern about young teachers.

同上一例一样，“真叫我感动”可以用单独的句子译出，也可以用主句译出。

公司总部坐落在天津经济开发区，交通便利，进出口方便。

〖译文 1〗 The headquarter of this co. is located in Tianjin Economic Technological Development Area and its transportation is convenient and easy for import and export. [68]

〖译文 2〗 The headquarter of this company is located in Tianjin Economic Development Area with convenient transport facilities for import and export business.

原文是三个散点，译文译成两个句子。其实这两个句子还可以进一步合并成一个，后一句可用介词短语取代。

译文中 convenient = easy，也可合并。

“交通方便”最好不用主谓结构，而用偏正结构 convenient transport facilities 译出。这样语气连贯，逻辑合理。

“公司”不用在名称中最好不采用缩略语。

“进出口”最好补足“业务”（business）。

这座城市因其夜总会而闻名，的确不无道理。

〖译文 1〗 It is reasonable that the city is famous for its nightclub.

〖译文 2〗 The city is justly famous for its nightclub.

我们同意译文 1，因为它本质上是一种透视结构。我们也同意译文 2，它只用 justly 一词译出“的确不无道理”的确不无道理。justly 在这儿可以理解成“名副其实的”“恰如其分的”。

对改革开放，一开始就有不同意见，这是正常的。

〖译文 1〗 Opinions were divided over the reform and opening policy at the very beginning. This is normal.

〖译文 2〗 In the beginning opinions were divided about the reform and opening policy. This is normal.

〖译文 3〗 In the beginning opinions about the reform and opening policy were divided. This is normal.[12]

〖译文 4〗 Opinions were naturally divided over the reform and opening policy at the very beginning.

译文 1、译文 2 和译文 3 三句都是正确的表达，译文 4 提供新的思路，仅供参考。

说也奇怪，许多关于“鬼屋”的秘密现在都不复存在了。

〖译文 1〗 It is curious that much of the secrecy that surrounded the spirit house has now disappeared.

〖译文 2〗 Much of the secrecy that surrounded the spirit house has now curiously disappeared.

〖译文 3〗 Curiously enough, much of the secrecy that surrounded the spirit house has now disappeared.

译文 1 语法无误，属于主从句层次。译文 2 将“说也奇怪”用副词译出，全句变成简单句，减少了层次。译文 3 强化了“说也奇怪”的语势，但没有增加层次。

可是，等他进了市区一看，只见街头一片混乱。

〖译文 1〗 However, when he went deep into the city, he only saw a chaotic scene in the street.

〖译文 2〗 However, he went downtown only to see chaos in the street.

译文 1 是某出版社要求笔者担任复审而提交的稿件原文，笔者信手做了如译文 2 的修改。敝帚自珍，我们认为修改后意思没有丢失，虽是简单句，但仍是透视式。

我们说断句容易并句难，就是因为有时候汉语句子太长，用英语长句子译出有困难，这就需要断句。断句容易分布信息，组织句子。

第四节 汉语的多代词，多散点

汉语句子取散点式，如果一个散点有一个主语，那么几个散点就有几个主语，这就是“多主语”。英语取透视式长句子，一般只有一个主语，这就是“单主语”。汉语句子虽然呈多主语，但是如果这些主语系指同一事物，那么我们还是把它看作是“单主语”。

换言之，汉语倾向于多用代词，截断句子，舒缓语气。我们还是看实际例证：

When the best-selling author Cornel West, now a Harvard professor, and the critic Stanley Crouch appeared on the Charlie Rose show to discuss the connection between race and cities during the Los Angles riots, they contributed to a tradition of urban social philosophy which originated with Lewis Munford. When Henry Louis Gates Jr. , also of Harvard, denounced black anti-Semitism on the New York Times op-ed page, he no doubt reached a wider audience than Norman Podhoretz ever did with similar pieces on black-Jewish relation. When Stephen Carter, of Yale, appeared on the Today show to talk about the intricacies of competing affirmative-action policies in the wake of Justice Clarence Thomas's nomination, he took his place alongside Lionel Trilling and Alfred Kazin in explaining the travails of a successful minority figure in a WASP-dominated culture.

〖译文 1〗 当畅销书作家现任哈佛大学教授科尔内尔·威斯利和评论家斯坦利·克劳奇在洛杉矶骚乱期间在“查理玫瑰展”节目中露面，讨论种族和城市的联系时，他们宣扬了路易斯·芒福德创立的城市社会哲学。当小亨利·路易斯·盖茨（他也是哈佛大学的）在《纽约时报》专栏版上谴责黑人反犹情绪时，他的读者群无疑比诺曼·彼多雷茨论述黑人犹太人关系的类似文章要广泛得多。当耶鲁大学的斯蒂芬·卡特在“今天”节目里露面，讨论克拉伦斯·托马斯大法官被提名后各种反种族歧视政策的错综复杂关系时，他是在和莱昂内尔·特里林以及艾尔弗雷德·卡津一起，解释一个少数民族人物在以美国新教徒为主体的文化中通往成功的艰辛历程。[91]

〖译文 2〗畅销书作家考内尔·威斯利是现任哈佛大学教授。他和评论家斯坦利·克劳奇曾经在“查理玫瑰展”节目中露面，讨论过洛杉矶骚乱中种族和城市的关系，并对路易斯·芒福德创立的城市社会哲学作了引申。小亨利·路易斯·盖茨也是哈佛的。他在《纽约时报》专栏版撰文谴责黑人反犹情绪，在读者群中的影响无疑比诺曼·彼多雷茨论述黑人犹太人关系的类似文章要广泛得多。斯蒂芬·卡特则是耶鲁大学的。他在“今天”节目里露面时，讨论了克拉伦斯·托马斯大法官被提名后各种反种族歧视政策的错综复杂关系。他与莱昂内尔·特里林以及艾尔弗雷德·卡津殊途同归，解释了一个少数民族人物在白人新教徒一统天下的文化中通往成功的艰辛历程。

译文 1 摘自《英汉语比较与翻译》[91]，该书对译文的批评是：三个以“当……时……”连接的从句，分别夹着 60 字、33 字、52 字，这样夹缠的句子只能勉强自治，无法上口，也很费解。

可惜的是该书作者没有进一步分析，也没有给出修改译文，因此没有解决问题。但是好在给出了原文，于是我们对照原文，加以分析，就可以看出汉译的问题：一是对原文理解有误；二是原文的人名太多，这些人物在西方大都有一定的知名度，而中国读者不熟悉，故客观上增添了阅读理解难度；三是汉语表达有问题，汉译没有按“透视—散点”转换要求将原文透视式句子断开，转换成汉语散点短句，而是用长句译长句；四是按原文自然语序逐词对译，使译文正如被批评的那样“夹缠”不清。

原来汉语句子可以是一个“主题（主语）+谓语”引领数个“代词+谓语”，后者环绕前者呈扇面状展开。英语句子一般只有一个主语，这个主语引领谓语和其他句子成分，呈环状链接，后者前者环环相扣。因此英语句子在译为汉语后可以而且必须分拆开来，多设置几个“代词+谓语”结构。比如 the best-selling author Cornel West，译文 2 译作“畅销书作家科尔内尔·威斯利”“他”。Henry Louis Gates Jr. 译作“小亨利·路易斯·盖茨”“他”。Stephen Carter 译作“斯蒂芬·卡特”“他”。这样，英语原文三句句子的三个主语，译成了汉语的七句句子的七个主语。这就成功地将英语的透视句式转换成了汉语散点句式。译文 2 是我们的尝试。

同样，如果将译文 2 译回至英语，文中的那些个“他”“他”“他”及其引导的独立句子，都没有必要，也不应该译作英语独立句子。

鉴此，汉语散点句式中的多个主语，如果系指同一主体，可以归并成英语的一个主语。

拱北宾馆位于拱北海关毗邻，构思源自秦代阿房宫，衬以现代建筑形式，是具有最完美设施之酒店。

〖译文1〗Gongbei Hotel is situated near the Gongbei Customs. The hotel is modeled on the architecture of Epang Palace in the Qin Dynasty with modern architectural forms added. It is a perfectly equipped hotel. [40]

〖译文2〗Gongbei Hotel is situated near the Gongbei Customhouse, equipped with most perfect apparatuses and constructed after the style of Epang Palace of the Qin Dynasty mixing some modern architectural elements.

〖译文3〗Being situated near Gongbei customhouse, Gongbei Hotel is perfectly equipped, and constructed by mixing style of Epang Palace of the Qin Dynasty with some modern architectural elements.

译文1译成了散点式，包含了三个主语，即Gongbei Hotel, the Hotel, it, 组成了三个句子。实际上全句只有一个对象，说的是一回事。从表面上看，原文有三个部分，第一部分讲宾馆的位置，第二部分讲宾馆的建筑，第三部分讲宾馆的设施。我们可以采用任一部分作主要信息，以主句译出，其余两个部分以其他句子成分译出。

（包公祠）在主殿中，陈列着高3米、重2.5吨的青铜色的包公雕像。它戴着头冠，系着腰带，正襟端坐：一手扶椅，一手握拳，仿佛要拍案而起，这姿势向我们显示了他的浩然正气。

〖译文1〗In the Main Hall, a bronze statue of Lord Bao, which is 3 meters in height and 2.5 tons in weight, is displayed. With his hat and waistband on, Baozheng sits upright. One of his hands places on the chair and the other clenches. It looks like he stands immediately. The pose shows us his rectitude. [86]

〖译文2〗In the Main Hall, displayed is a bronze statue of Lord Bao, which is 3 meters in height and 2.5 tons in weight. Lord Bao is officially dressed with hat and waistband on, and sits upright with one of his hands on the armchair and the other clenching, meanwhile he looks like to stand immediately. The pose suggests his rectitude.

译文1的第一句语法无误，但是主语有一个尾大不掉的定语从句，根据第三章要求，可以倒装，改为右重句。第二句逻辑有误，包公雕像“戴着头冠，系着腰带”，恐怕还“穿着官袍”。而且“包公”译作Baozheng，与前面的Lord Bao

不统一，为了减少阅读负担和理解障碍，最好统一起来。第三句译文本身是个散点，句内又包含两个散点，可以考虑归并。第四句主语 It 指代不明。第五句的双宾语使谓语动词 show 的语义不明。明白了译文 1 的问题所在，我们就可以有针对性地加以解决。见译文 2。

不少老年人有气血虚弱的现象，气虚者必定血弱，血弱者必兼气虚，因此气血往往合治。

〖译文 1〗Phenomenon of Qi and blood deficiency is a common phenomenon in old persons. The case With Qi-deficiency or blood-deficiency will certainly have both blood and Qi-deficiency at the same time so Qi and blood deficiency are often treated together. [92]

〖译文 2〗Deficiency of Qi and blood is common among the aged. Deficiency of Qi inevitably leads to deficiency of blood and vise versa. That is why Qi and blood are frequently treated at the same time. [92]

〖译文 3〗*Chi* and blood are frequently treated at the same time because deficiency of *Chi* inevitably leads to deficiency of blood, and vise versa, and both is common among the aged.

法缘先生评论译文 1 时说："译文在词语的选用和拼写、句子的布局和照应以及语义的解读和再现等方面，均有瑕疵。如 phenomenon 在一简单句中出现两次，且拼写有误，介词 with 在句中大写。这些小误，略加注意即可避免。译者需要万分注意的，是对原文的理解和对译文的布局。本句译者似已领会原文之意，惜译文结构涣散，致使语意难以再现。"先生之言甚是。译事虽重在释意，然无形意亦难立。译文 2 是先生对此例的改译。

译文 1、译文 2 以及上述评论摘自同一本书。法缘先生和作者之言甚是，但是我们还发现：本句原文的三个部分可以倒过来翻译，亦即（1）"不少老年人有气血虚弱的现象"，（2）"气虚者必定血弱，血弱者必兼气虚"，（3）"气血往往合治"，可以按（3）（2）（1）顺序翻译，我们在第一章中已经谈过这个技巧。这里要说的是如何将原文的各个散点合并成一个透视式句子，于是就产生了译文 3，这样整个句子一气呵成，不必断成两句，在风格上也更忠实于原文。

另外，在英美媒体上，"气"被表达为 Chi，而不是 Qi。

蜗阳苔干，名优特产，驰名中外，声震古今，翠绿、鲜嫩、清脆、可口，有"天然海蜇"之称；清乾隆年间奉献皇宫，故又名"贡菜"。

〖译文 1〗Taigan (a kind of dry stemmed vegetable) is a famous special local product of Woyang, Anhui Province. It is well known all over the world. It can be regarded as "jellyfish on land" It's green, tender, crisp and pleasant to taste.

It was once an article of tribute in Qing Dynasty. [15]

〖译文 2〗 Taigan (a kind of dry stemmed vegetable), a special local product of Woyang, Anhui Province, famous as "jellyfish on land", and offered as royal tribute in Qing Dynasty, is well known all over the world for it's greenish tinge, and tender, crisp and pleasant taste.

〖译文 3〗 As a special local product of Woyang, Anhui Province, famous as "jellyfish on land", and offered as royal tribute in Qing Dynasty, Taigan (a kind of dry stemmed vegetable) is well known all over the world for it's greenish tinge, and tender, crisp and pleasant taste.

某大学汉英翻译教程对译文 1 的评论是："较完整地传达了原文的意义，句子也合乎英语语法规则。但通篇不见任何句际衔接手段，结果语篇不连贯，逻辑性不强。此外，译文句式简单呆板，缺乏变化，因而表现力也不佳。"

可惜的是，作者没有给出修改建议。我们用散点—透视转换的要求来对照一下，就很清楚了，原文是一个句子，在某种程度上反是透视式。译文却是五个句子，反成了散点式。这五个句子的主语是同一事物，如果将主要信息译作主句，次要信息用从句，或介词短语，或分词短语，或形容词短语，或同位语之类译出，亦即将四个句子合并成一个句子，情况就会好得多。我们用译文 2、译文 3 作为译文 1 的修改建议。译文 2、译文 3 的句子成分，90% 以上都是用鼠标在译文 1 上复制粘贴而成。

与上面的几个例句不同，本句一定要用透视式译出，非此不足克服"语篇不连贯，逻辑性不强。句式简单呆板，缺乏变化，表现力也不佳"种种弊端。

八达岭这一段是 1957 年修复的，是长城的典型建筑，平均高 7.8 米，底部宽 6.6 米，顶部宽 5.8 米。

〖译文 1〗 The section at Badaling was restored in 1957, and it is typical in its structure. It is 7.8 metres high on an average, 6.6 metres wide at the bottom, and 5.8 metres wide on the top. [40]

〖译文 2〗 The section at Badaling, which was restored in 1957, is typical in its structure, with the average height of 7.8 metres, the bottom width of 6.6 metres, and the top width of 5.8 metres.

〖译文 3〗 The section at Badaling, restored in 1957, is typical in its structure, having the average height of 7.8 metres, the bottom width of 6.6 metres, and the top width of 5.8 metres.

译文 1 三个句子的主语 The section at Badaling, it, It 系指同一事物，比较容易合并，仍需采用各种语法手段。

他的译文使用的是维多利亚英语，与当代英语有一定的距离，而且译得不那么严谨，所以他的这个译本历来得到的评价并不太高，无法跟他的译诗相比。

〖译文1〗His translation of *Zhuangzi* is done with Victorian English，somewhat different from contemporary English. Moreover，this translation is not universally acclaimed as it is not so accurately done，not up to par with his translation of the Chinese Poems.[8]

〖译文2〗His translation of *Zhuangzi* is done with Victorian English，somewhat different from contemporary English. Moreover，this translation is not universally acclaimed as it is not so accurately done as up to par with his translation of the Chinese Poems.

〖译文3〗His translation of *Zhuangzi* is not so universally acclaimed as up to par with his translation of the Chinese Poems，for he rendered *Zhuangzi* with Victorian English，which is somewhat different from contemporary English，and not so accurate.

译文1是按原文语序译出的，其中第二句的后半部分可以改由is not so…as…句型译出，使句子紧凑，流畅。也可以将is not so…as…句型作为主句提到前面，其他成分作为原因状语从句放在后面。

第五节　汉语多主题转换为英语单主语

当然，有时汉语句子的散点各有各的主语，并非指同一事物，这就为我们翻译带来困难。但是我们还是要将句子转换为英语单主语。一山实在容不得二虎。一个英语句子一般只容得一个主语。

Of the intrinsic differences that separate American from English the chief have their roots in the obvious disparity between the environment and traditions of the American people since the seventeenth century and those of the English.

〖译文1〗将美语同英语分开来的本质区别的主要方面根植于美国人自17世纪以来的环境和传统与英国人的环境和传统之间明显的差异。

〖译文2〗许多本质上的不同造成了美语从英语中分出来。而主要的不同是两种语言根植于两个完全不同的社会环境和文化传统。自17世纪以来，美国人和英国人在这两方面的差异十分明显。[75]

译文1按照英语的结构用汉语来表达，它的意思没错，在一位比较宽松的英语老师手下，也许不会被扣分。但是我们朗读这个句子时，最好先吸一口气，然后慢慢读，慢慢运气，以免中间停顿。如果你一边读，一边想在中间找个什么地方停顿一下的话，你还没有来得及找到，句子却结束了。这是一个典型的西式汉语句子，具有浓重的翻译腔，句子虽短，但是你几乎很难只读一遍就能完全领会它的意思。它的毛病出在这是一幅透视式的泼墨山水，在油画布上画中国画。

译文2晓畅自然，明白如话。其特点是将原文一个句子用汉语三个句子译出，形成三个主题，三个散点，符合汉语表达习惯，故也适合读者阅读习惯。

汉语采用多短句形式，正因为句子短，理解起来不费吹灰之力。但是短句之间的连接需要靠读者的悟性，好在它们有一种节奏感、韵律感，读者只要稍稍注意一下它们的联系，不难从整体上把握。

反观英语依靠它严谨的句法和词汇的句法功能，使我们在阅读时自然而然产生一种期望，当这种预期得到满足时，我们同时也得到了美感的享受。

At noon, we picnicked in a dense forest, through which ran a murmuring creek. The water was so clear that we could see reflections of bamboos and trees and soft lazy clouds drifting across the sky.

正午时分，我们野宴于密林深处，林中小溪潺潺流过，溪水清冽，岸边竹树，天上闲云，尽映水底。❶

这个例句原文英语是两个句子，一是事件记叙，以 we 为主语；一是环境描写，以 water 为主语。汉语译文没有如此泾渭分明的结构，而是采用多主题的散点句式，包括："我们野宴""小溪流过""溪水清冽""岸边竹树，天上闲云，尽映水底"。其中"岸边竹树"和"天上闲云"是比较松散的对仗。译文整个句子流畅谐美。

综上所述，英译汉是一个将英语"透视式"句法转换成汉语"散点式"句法的过程。反过来，汉译英就要将汉语"散点式"句法转换成英语"透视式"句法。

天刑之，安可解？(《庄子》德充符)

〖译文1〗When the heaven is punishing him, how can I free him?[8]

〖译文2〗How can he be free from Heaven's punishing?

庄子原文的意思是"上天要惩罚他，怎么可以解除呢？"而译文1的意思是"上天正在惩罚他，我怎么可以放他自由呢？"他需要解除的不是人身自由的限制，而是天谴神咒的施魇。译文1显然不符合原文句意。

问题出在哪儿呢？原来原文句中有两个主语："天"和"之"（他）。译文又

---

❶ http://www.for68.com。

加了一个主语“I”（我），使句子松散了，散点化了。

解决的办法是将句子透视化，形成一个主语。我们可以将原文倒过来理解为“安可解天刑之?”以 he（他）作主语，以 be free from 短语紧扣“解”，如译文 2。

他爸爸死了，死于车祸；妈妈又改嫁了，顾不了他，真可怜。

〖译文 1〗 His father died of an accident, and his mother, remarried, could not afford to attend to him. He was then a poor boy indeed.[45]

〖译文 2〗 He was then a poor boy indeed, for his father died of an accident, and his mother, remarried, could not attend to him.[93]

原文又是一个典型的汉语散点句，主体隐藏得很深，或者说根本就是无主语句。实际上句中有三个主语，代表三个人物：“他爸爸”“妈妈”“他”。其中“他爸爸”“妈妈”是主格，“他”是所有格和宾格，没有以主格身份出现，被深深埋在信息流中。全句是讲“他”的人生遭遇，“他”才是中心人物。译文 1 很好，作为记叙文，可以这么顺序表达。译文 2 则把原文中的“他”提取出来充当主语，按聚焦透视要求译出。

没有电，人们生活水平的提高将会受到阻碍。日常生活的欢乐和方便将大大减少，风景、音响和信息将靠肉眼和耳朵交流。

〖译文 1〗 Without electricity, the rise in man's standard of living would have been checked. Everyday life would be much less pleasant and convenient, and the communication of sights and sounds and messages would still rely on the naked eye and ear.[43,45]

〖译文 2〗 Without electricity, man would have been dogged by low standard of living with much less convenience and pleasure in his daily life, receiving video and audio messages on the spot with his naked eyes and ears.

汉语原文有三个句子，其三个主题分别是“人们生活水平的提高”“日常生活的欢乐和方便”“风景、音响和信息”。译文 1 将主语稍作调整后，全句完全按原文结构译出，所以不算很准确、流利的英语。由于断句，译成“散点式”英语，更造成阅读理解的障碍。其中第三句虽然与第二句连在一起，仍嫌头重脚轻。

要改变这些状况可以将译文 1 三个句子捏合在一起。按照“散点式”转换成“透视式”的原理，我们首先设法将三个主语合并成一个主语，需要在“人们生活水平的提高”“日常生活的欢乐和方便”“风景、音响和信息”之间找一个主语，或者在三者之外重新找一个主语。运用第二章介绍的主题主语转换的原理，我们在原文主语“提高”的前面找到了“生活水平”“人们”和“人”这三个主语。经过权衡，我们确定用“人”man 作主语，“生活水平的提高将会受到阻碍”作主句，“日常生活的欢乐和方便将大大减少”用介词短语译出，“风景、音响和信息将靠肉眼和耳朵交流”用分词短语译出。

总之，微波只能以直线的方式传播，没有一系列的转播塔，它们就不能越过漫长的距离，把消息传递到遥远的地方。

〖译文 1〗In short, microwaves can only travel in straight line. Without a series of relay towers, it is impossible for them to send messages over long distances to remote places.[40]

〖译文 2〗In short, it is impossible for microwaves to send messages over long distances to remote places without a series of relay towers, for they can only travel in straight line.

〖译文 3〗In short, it is impossible for microwaves, which can only travel in straight line, to send messages over long distances to remote places without a series of relay towers.

译文 1 将原文断句翻译，分成两句，形成两个话题，前一个讲微波的性质，后一个讲微波的应用，所以是准确无误的译文。译文 2、译文 3 只是为了说明句式转换的可能性，提供两种参考方案。

1955 年国务院决定把交通大学迁移至西安，1956 年 5 月学校开始迁移，至 1957 年 9 月交通大学有两个部分，一个在西安，另一个在上海。

〖译文 1〗In 1955, the State Council decided to move Jiaotong University to Xi'an. In May of 1956, it began to move. In September of 1957, Jiaotong University has two parts, one was in Xi'an. The other was in Shanghai. ❶

〖译文 2〗In May of 1956, Jiaotong University began to move to Xi'an according to a decision of the State Council in 1955, so in September of 1957, it had two parts, one in Xi'an, the other in Shanghai.

〖译文 3〗In September of 1957, Jiaotong University began to have two parts, one in Xi'an, the other in Shanghai, after it moved to Xi'an in September of 1957 according to a decision of the State Council in 1955.

原文有三个句子，包含三个主语：“国务院”“学校”和“交通大学”，呈散点式。译文 1 分别用 the State Council，it 和 Jiaotong University 译出，也分成三个句子，故也呈散点式。译文 2 只用 Jiaotong University 一个主语，句子顿时显得流

---

❶ http://www.xjtu.edu.cn。

畅起来。我们也可以按照逆序翻译的要求，先表1957年，然后1956年，最后1955年。如译文3。

我们不仅因为今天科学技术落后，需要努力向外国学习。即使我们的科学技术赶上了世界先进水平，也还要学习人家的长处。

〖译文1〗It is not just today, when we are scientifically backward, that we need to learn from other countries. After we catch up with the world's advanced levels in science and technology, we shall still have to learn from the strong points of others.[43]

〖译文2〗We need to learn from other countries not only when we are scientifically backward just today, but also we shall still have to learn from the strong points of others after we catch up with the world's advanced levels in science and technology.

〖译文3〗We shall still have to learn from the strong points of others after we catch up with the world's advanced levels in science and technology, needless to say, we need to learn from other countries when we are scientifically backward just today.

〖译文4〗We shall still have to learn the strong points from other countries when we catch up with the world's advanced levels in the future, let alone when we are scientifically backward just today.

原文的两句话实际上是一句话。这是一个用“不仅……而且……”连接起来的递进句，只不过连接词“而且”省略了而已。前半部分又包含一个因果句，用“因为……所以……”连接，“所以”也省略了。后半部分则包含一个让步句，用“即使……也要……”连接，都没有省略。那么我们如何组织英语句子呢？一个办法是用not only…but also…搭配译出“不仅……而且……”，如译文2。

如果再作“主次—主从”转换分析，我们可以看到，原文的重点落在后半部分：我们现在落后了，需要学习，自不待言。作者告诫我们的是，将来我们先进了，不能忘了也还要学习。为了突出重点，可以把这一部分句子成分放到前面去。见译文3。

如果我们进一步作“意合—形合”转换分析，就可以看到，这个译文中含有大量的原文形合零信息，亦即有大量的词语可以归并。瘦身后的译文显得精炼了，而且与原文更贴近了。见译文4。

为了挽救这座精美的古塔建筑，1979年国家拨款修复，在此过程中，曾在塔内发现了木塔柱，佛像和佛舍利等珍贵文物，这些文物和塔本身对了解研究我国古代建筑和雕刻艺术以及中外文化交流史都具有重要参考价值，所以为全国重点文物保护单位。

〖译文 1〗For the remedy of the exquisite pagoda, the government appropriated funds in 1979 for repair. During the repairs people found some valuble cultural relics such as wooden pagoda pillars, Buddhist figures and relics. The pagoda and those things found are of great value for the knowledge and study of the ancient construction, the art of carving and the history of cultural exchange between China and other countries. Therefore, it is now the major state-class historic reservation.[29]

〖译文 2〗The repairs funded by the government in 1979 for the remedy of this exquisite pagoda found some valuable cultural relics such as wooden pillars, Buddhist figures and relics, which together with the whole pagoda are of great value for the study of the ancient arts of architecture and sculpture, and the history of cultural exchange between China and other countries. Therefore, the pagoda is now among the major state-class historic reservations.

本句原文体现了汉语形散神不散的风格，看起来一逗到底，句子直到结束才有一个句号，但是全句包含了许多分句，从不同的角度描述、说明这座古塔，从而使读者从整体上理解其历史文化价值。译成英语可以设法从原文中提取一个主语，例如译文 2 以“修复”repair 作主语。原文中间的“建筑和雕刻”建议译作 architecture and sculpture，两词押尾韵。

目前，国有纺织企业占用着上亿元的资产，却连年巨额亏损，其重要原因是资源重复配置，企业过度竞争，而败者又难以被淘汰，资源难以实现优化配置。

〖译文 1〗Currently, state-owned textile enterprises have assets worth over 100 million yuan, and yet they have suffered huge losses for successive years. An important reason is duplication in resources allocation. In the excessive competition among enterprises, the losers can hardly be eliminated, and the allocation of the resources can hardly be optimized.[94]

〖译文 2〗Currently, the huge losses suffered for successive years by the state-owned textile enterprises, whose assets amount to 100 million yuan or more, is due to the duplication of investments, the excessive competition, the encumbrance of the inferior, and the ejection of the resource allocation from optimization.

译文 1 将原文译作三句，呈散点式。译文 2 尝试将三句归并为一句。

汉语句子成分的顺序，往往是“弱—次弱—次强—强”，英语则相反，表现为“强—次强—次弱—弱”。按此原理，也可将汉语的散点式转换成透视式。

第六节 句式结构的降格

我们在第三节谈到独立分句用副词译出，使句子透视化。散点—透视转换的一个有效的手段就是句子结构的降格。亦即能够用简单句表达的句意，就不一定用复合句；能够用复合句的，就不断句，不采用独立的散点句子。语法层次越少越好，句法结构越简单越好。

冯正中词虽不失五代风格，而堂庑特大，开北宋一代风气。（王国维《人间词话》）

〖译文1〗Although Feng Yen-ssu retained the air and form (feng-ko) of the Five Dynasties in his tz'u, the side effects of his writings were considerable. He initiated the style (feng-ch'i) which was to become characteristic of the Northern Sung period…[10]

〖译文2〗Although Feng Yen-ssu adopted some manner of the Five Dynasties in his works of lyrics, he was the pioneer of style in the Northern Sung period with his profundity.

提示："冯正中"系指宋代文学家冯延巳。"堂庑"，厅堂和廊屋，句中系指文思深邃的堂奥。译文中的 tz'u 系指原文的"词"，相当于欧美现代的 lyrics。很明显"词"和 lyrics 两者是大致对应的。在中国古代，李煜、柳永、苏轼、秦观等词作家（lyricist）的作品也曾经被谱曲，流行于秦楼楚馆、舞榭歌台，千年之后，时至今日，仍然久盛不衰。

译文1用两个句子，译文2用一个句子，这是一种降格。

唐、五代、北宋之词，可谓生香真色。（王国维《人间词话》）

〖译文1〗It may be said that the tz'u of Tang, Five Dynasties, and Northern Sung have a living fragrance and true colour.[10]

〖译文2〗The lyrics of Tang, Five Dynasties, and Northern Sung may be said to be really fragrant and colorful.

我们看到汉语"可谓"，容易联想到英语的 It may be said that，这就产生了译文1，单单"可谓"一词用主句译出，其余用从句译出，增添了层次。仔细分析，发现可以用"可谓"作谓语动词，"可谓"前面是主语，后面是宾语，全句是简单句，见译文2。这是又一种降格。

而且译文1的 a living fragrance and true colour 太抽象，难以把握。建议去掉 a，将 living 换成 fresh，将 true 换成 vivid。

世界虽大，但艺术行业步人后尘亦步亦趋者必无立锥之地。

〖译文1〗Although the world is big, in the field of arts you will find no footing to hold if you blindly imitate your predecessors. （上海交通大学英语专业2004年研究生入学试题参考答案）[2,6]

〖译文2〗Even in this boundless art world there is no way for slavish imitation.

译文1的一头一尾各有一个状语从句，中间还有一个介词短语作状语，句子不流畅。如果将这些状语降格，归并起来，使全句更紧凑。

嘉庆甲子年，痛遭先君之变，行将弃家远遁，友人夏揖山挽留其家。（［清］沈复《浮生六记》）

〖译文1〗The tragedy of my father's death occurred in the spring of the 8th year of the the reign of the Emperor Chia Ching; I was about to leave home and become a recluse when my friend Hsia Yi-shan insisted that I stay a while at his home.[9]

〖译文2〗Because of the tragedy of my father's death in the spring of 1804, I was about to leave home and become a recluse when my friend Hsia Yi-shan invited me to stay a while at his home.

〖译文3〗Hsia Yi-shan, a friend of mine, kept me at his home when I was about to abandon my family after the tragedy of my father's death in the spring of 1804.

译文1将"嘉庆甲子年，痛遭先君之变"译为单独一句，可以降格为介词短语；"挽留其家"的宾语从句可以降格为动词不定式。两处句子成分的降格顿时便使全句语气贯通了。见译文2。

从原文来看，这是一段文章的开头，全段落记叙友人夏揖山邀请作者造访崇明县的见闻。因此，译文可以用"友人夏揖山"作主语，采用倒叙，形成右重。见译文3。

足球运动员必须能不停地奔跑，有时得用头顶球，撞别人或被别人撞，忍受双脚和肌肉的疼痛，所以说，足球是一项难度很大的运动。

〖译文1〗Soccer is a difficult sport. A player must be able to run steadily without rest. Sometimes a player must hit the ball with his or her head. Players must be willing to bang into and be banged into by others. They must put up with aching feet and sore muscles.[45]

〖译文2〗What a soccer player must be able to do is running steadily without rest, sometimes hitting the ball with his or her head, being willing to bang or to be banged into by others, and putting up with aching feet or sore muscles. So, soccer is a difficult sport.

译文1语法到位，词句精当。我们却从整体上提出修改意见：文中有 A player, a player, Players, They 四个主语，分别组成四个句子，实际上说的是一个对象——“足球运动员”。如果将四句归并起来，四个谓语动词改为动名词，这样，就只需要一个 player 作主语，组成了一个句子。译文1将“足球是一项难度很大的运动”放在开头译出，完全符合英语结论在前、论证在后的行文习惯。我们把它放在最后只是想说明，在长句子之后，用短句收尾，也能增添文章的力度。

清末立宪以来，中国宪政走过了百余年的历程，产生了十多部宪法与宪法性文件，反映了中国走向宪政与法治的艰辛与曲折。

〖译文1〗Since China's constitutionalism in late Qing, China has been in purser of constitutionalism for more than a hundred years with tens of constitutions and constitutional statutes as its result. It reflects that China's enterprise constitutionalism and rule of law is full of difficulties and frustrations.[95]

〖译文2〗For a hundred plus years since late Qing dynasty, China has given birth to a dozen of constitution versions in her long and arduous course of constitutionalism.

如果把译文1许多重复的信息散点加以合并，就可能成为透视式。

在散点透视转换过程中，汉语词组或短句可以用英语单词（大多是抽象名词）翻译。汉语的主谓、动宾、偏正结构英语用抽象名词表示。

他的秘书是一位思想成熟、精明能干、为人诚实的小伙子。

〖译文1〗His secretary is a young man who has mature thinking, great capacity and honesty.

〖译文2〗His secretary is a mature, dynamic, and honest young man.

〖译文3〗His secretary is young man of matureness, capacity and honesty.

在译文2，主谓结构“思想成熟”、并列结构“精明能干”、偏正结构“为人诚实”均译作形容词。译文3译作抽象名词。

颜渊问仁。子曰：“克己复礼为仁。一日克己复礼，天下归仁焉。”

〖译文1〗Yan Yuan asked about humanity, Confucius said, "Humanity means to restrain oneself and observe the rites. Once one does this, the whole world will be embraced in one's humane mind."[96]

〖译文 2〗Restraining yourself and restoring the rites.[97]

〖译文 3〗Yan Yuan asked about humanity, Confucius said, "Humanity means self-restraint and ritual-abiding. Once these prevail, the world will embrace humanity."

"克己复礼"译文 1 用动词不定式译出，译文 2 用动名词，译文 3 用名词，各有各的考虑，供读者参考。

武汉大学培育了"自强、弘毅、求是、拓新"的优良校风。

〖译文 1〗During the past 100-old years after its founding, Wuhan University gradually developed a fine school spirit and study style of its own, i. e., "improve oneself, promote perseverance, seek truth and make innovation". ❶

〖译文 2〗Improve Oneself, Carry Forward Stamina, Seek Truth and Develop Innovations.[98]

〖译文 3〗Improve Yourself, Carry Forward Stamina, Seek Truth and Develop Innovations. ❷

〖译文 4〗self-improvement, perseverance, truthfulness and originality

我们进入一些企事业单位，常常能看到诸如此类的标语："团结、拼搏、开拓、创新"。它既可以是皮鞋制造厂或建筑工程队的企业精神，也可以是师范学院或医科大学的校训。

武大的这个校训，四组词语中三组是动宾结构，故译者将它们全部化作英语的动宾结构，以求流畅。殊不知英语的动宾结构用在这儿成了祈使句，那么，我们听了您的话，该怎么去 improve 呢？oneself 又落实到谁呢？perseverance 又如何 promote 呢？stamina 怎么个 carry forward 法呢？其实，汉语的许多动宾结构都可以用英语名词表达。本句用名词译出，不仅贴切，而且庄重隽永。如译文 4。

今君实所以见教者，以为侵官、生事、征利、拒谏，以致天下怨谤也。（［宋］王安石《答司马谏议书》）

〖译文 1〗Your admonitory charge against me can be itemized separately as infringement on other people's authority, stirring troubles, extorting and amassing wealth, rebuffing remonstrances, thus causing disaffection in the country.[14]

〖译文 2〗You admonitorily charge me with infringement, incitement, ex-

---

❶ http://www.whu.edu.cn。

❷ http://www.exam8.com。

cessive collection, arbitrariness, thus causing disaffection in the country.

〖译文 3〗Your admonitory charges against me can be itemized separately as infringement, instigation, expropriation, opinionatedness, thus causing disaffection in the country.

原文句意为：您之所以来信赐教，是您认为我侵官、生事、征利、拒谏，以致民怨鼎沸。译文 1 将“侵官、生事、征利、拒谏”分别译作“侵犯别人的权威、制造麻烦、勒索和积聚财富、拒绝谏诤”，没有突破原文动宾结构模式，使行文显得冗长。

“侵官”可以译为名词 infringement（侵权）；“生事”可以译为名词 instigation（鼓动），provocation（挑起事端）或 incitement（煽动）；“征利”可以译为 excessive collection（过度征收），expropriation（剥夺财产土地等）；“拒谏”可以译为 obstinateness（顽固、倔强），arbitrariness（专断、武断），dictatorship（专制），stubbornness（执拗、固执），opinionatedness（自以为是）等。

在教学中他（孔子）讲究教育方法，注重启发、诱导，注意有的放矢，因材施教。

〖译文 1〗He was particular about teaching methods, and preached that teachers should teach with enlightenment and guidance, with a purpose, and should vary his methods to suit the students. ❶

〖译文 2〗He was particular about teaching methods, namely being heuristic, attractive, object-oriented, and competency-based.

原文的“讲究”“注重”“注意”是一个意思，不必全部译出；而“启发”“诱导”“有的放矢”“因材施教”是“教育方法”的具体内容，是对“教育方法”的阐发，被包含在“教育方法”之中。因此英译可以一气呵成，不必另起炉灶。

孟子突出的民本思想和平等倾向在晚清受到一定程度的重视和发扬。

〖译文 1〗Mencius's conspicuous thought that the people are the most important thing and equality tendency received some kind of notice and development in the later period of the Qing dynasty. [99]

〖译文 2〗Mencius' unique populism and equality tendency was accepted with a certain revaluation and elaboration in the late Qing dynasty.

译文 1 非常怪诞，以致我们不对照原文就根本无法破译它的含义。它的症结

---

❶ http://ahonggi.blog.sohu.com。

在于“民本思想”的翻译有点问题。其实这儿可以借用表示美国历史上“平民党”和俄国历史上“民粹派”的 populism 一词。将主张礼乐征伐自天子出的儒家，同“平民党”“民粹派”挂起钩来，恐怕有风马牛之嫌。然而，孟子曰“民为贵，社稷次之，君为轻。”意谓人民是可贵的，政权是次要的，君权更应轻视。孟子的这种思想，与强调民众的需要、权利、愿望的 populism（平民主义）相比，可谓有过之而无不及。只不过孟子的思想诞生于公元前四百多年，而 populism 出现于十八、十九世纪，且孟子的表述比他们更简捷、更透彻一点罢了。当然，两者都与 democracy（民主主义）不是一回事。用 populism 译出“民本主义”或“民本思想”也可算铢两悉称，当然，populism 和“民本思想”之间的内涵和外延究竟有多少重叠和交叉之处，这在学术上仍是可以商榷的。无论如何，这总比译者无以名之，随意发挥为好。

对现代生活的渴望太理想化了：丰厚的收入、宽大的住房、理想的职业、美满的婚姻……这还不够，动不动薪水少点就跳槽，带孩子责任太大就“丁克”，为了自由就做“周末夫妻”。家里闹了意见就离婚，单位有了矛盾就“炒老板鱿鱼”……反正是看哪儿都烦，看谁也不顺，心情糟透了。

〖译文 1〗People want to have everything that the urban life might mean—a good income, a spacious apartment, a decent job, a happy marriage, and that's not all. Urban people are always ready to change jobs if the salary is not satisfactory. They don't want to have any kids as that is too much responsibility. Marriage has taken the form of the so-called "weekend couple", which allows them total freedom. If they have to face arguments at home, they will choose divorce as the quick solution. If anything gets tangled at work, they will fire the boss. In such an urban culture, many people feel really bad, getting upset by just about everything and everybody.[100]

〖译文 2〗Modern people expect too much of the urban life, namely good income, spacious apartments, decent jobs, happy marriage, and furthermore, job hopping for higher salary, DINK family—Double Income and No Kid with less responsibility in truth, illicit love affairs, reckless divorce, getting boss the sack to avert the tangles, all of which in turn cause depression, upset, and anxiety.

汉语句子虽短，但是许多散点连缀起来，却可以表达相当复杂的意思。英语句子虽长，但是结构却比较清晰。汉语原文有许多散点，比如“家里闹了意见就离婚”，如果也对应地译成 If they have to face arguments at home, they will choose divorce as the quick solution，那就无法组织英语句子。可以用英语词组 reckless divorce（草率离婚）译出。这样做不但篇幅缩减，而且表达更清晰。

这就足以证明三中全会以来路线、方针、政策的正确性……

〖译文1〗This fact suffices to prove the correctness of the line, principles and policies adopted since the Third Plenary Session of the 11th CPC Central Committee.

〖译文2〗This suffices to prove the correctness of the line, principles and policies adopted since the Third Plenary Session of the 11th CPC Central Committee.

〖译文3〗This is adequate evidence to show that since the Third plenary Session of the 11th CPC Central Committee, our lines, principles and policies have been correct in nature.[101]

〖译文4〗This can adequately justifies the political line, principles and policies adopted by the Third Plenary Session of the 11th CPC Central Committee.

译文3认为:“汉语是一种动态表达法较多或倾向于动态表达的语言,而英语则是一种静态表达法较多或倾向于静态表达的语言。此句的三个译文中译文3的译者注意到了这一点,将‘足以证明’翻译成adequate evidence to show更加符合英语习惯,而译文1和译文2将其翻译成suffices to,相对而言就要稍逊一筹了。”

我们这里提供另一种方案:原文中的“证明……正确性”可以用justify一词表达。justify相当于show sth. correct by giving good reasons。例如:

The belief that women may give up a job to have children is repeatedly used to justify giving a job to a man and not to a woman.

人们相信女人可以放弃工作生孩子,这样一种观念被反复用来证明把一份工作给予男人,而不给予女人是正确的。

译文4进一步降低了语句的层次。

我们的东邻日本,市场上就有一种专门收集消费者意见、揣摩消费者心理的跑街先生。

〖译文1〗In the market of Japan, China's eastern neighbour, there are Paojie xiansheng or "street-running gentlemen", that is, people who do a kind of roving market research. These people specialize in collecting the opinions of consumers and in trying to figure out what goes on in their heads.[65]

〖译文2〗In Japan (to the east of China), there are so-called "Mr. Street Rover"s in marketplaces, who specialize in investigating what consumers want and think.

读译文1我们首先看到rove research动宾搭配不当。读完后又发现全文取散点式,将原文简洁的句子译成了两句。

第五章
意合与形合：语言中的语言

第一节　以物喻人，以人喻物

汉英翻译中的“意合”“形合”问题，已经被译界探讨、论述得相当多了。有一种观点把这个问题归因于中西文化的历史渊源、宗教渊源、风俗习惯形成、社会体制沿革、艺术审美变迁的差异，归因于中英文修辞的题旨情景不同，从而选择的语言手段不同，选择的表达方式不同。

我们首先看到，“意合”“形合”是存在的。然后我们也看到，中西文化及其语言的差异和不同也是存在的。接着，我们的问题来了：既然“意合”“形合”是中西文化的差异造成的，那么何以汉语一定是“意合”，英语一定是“形合”呢？“意合”“形合”的内涵和外延又是如何厘清和界定的呢？

有的专家指出：所谓“形合”，指借助语言形式手段（包括词汇手段和形态手段）显示句法关系，实现词语或句子的连接；所谓“意合”，指不借助语言形式手段而借助词语或句子的意义或逻辑联系实现它们之间的连接。前者注重语句形式上的接应，后者顾及行文意义上的连贯。

但是，细心的读者稍做观察便不难发现，事情远没有表面上看起来那么简单。汉语固然重语义轻形式，但是也有它的规范和法则，也有它的形式手段和句法关系。英语固然重结构轻感悟，但是也不乏高度意合的表达方式，亦即完全依靠约定俗成、固定搭配传递信息。

汉语语境不仅改变了主语，遮蔽了主体，也使其他句子成分，甚至整个句子非人格化了。与此相反，英语不仅在主语中突出了主体，在整个句子中也时时不忘照应主体。

科学是讲求实际的。

〚译文 1〛 Science deals with things in a practical way.[102]

〚译文 2〛 Science means to be pragmatic.

原文出自时任中国科学院院长郭沫若的讲话《科学的春天》，是一个高度汉化的句子，句中没有“我”，甚至没有“人”。实际上表达的是“我”的要求，“人”的责任。译文 1 也是拟人句，可谓明白晓畅。译文 2 用不定式译出“讲求实际”，充当表语，曲曲折折，隐隐约约地回归了主体。

当然，这并不等于说中国人讲话写文章时只见树木，不见森林，完全否定了主体的存在或取消了主体的作用。恰恰相反，中国人赋予万物以人格和灵性。日月星辰、山川河流、飞鸟走兽，万事万物皆有三头两绪，七情六欲，客体只是主体的外化。万物皆备于我，主体只是客体的内化。这种主客一体的有情宇宙观，我们仍能从天人合一中找到根源。

不少专家指出，汉语的拟人化程度非常高，大量非人物性词汇、词组、短句可以充当行为的施行者或接受者。科学可以讲求实际，技术可以勇攀高峰，在中国人看来顺理成章，天经地义。但是如果直译成英语恐怕外国人会觉得不可理喻，所以在英语中，这被视为修辞或逻辑上的一种语病。

实际上，以物喻人、以人喻物是一个普遍的语言现象，汉语英语，概莫能外，只是各自的本体喻体各不相同而已。“意合”“形合”的相互转换是英汉互译十分重要的方面。

汉语是意合式语言，英语是形合式语言，这是各种教科书众口一词的说法。但是对于“意合”“形合”的定义和内涵，却各有各的说法。通过学习，我们体会大约汉语句子成分之间的联系比较松散，有时甚至字面上根本没有联系。它们的语义关系、意思点到为止，明人不必细说，全靠读者语感的契合，故谓之“意合”。但是英语句子成分之间的联系，必须用句式和词汇等形式表示出来才合度，故谓之“形合”。

低速度就等于停步，甚至等于后退。要抓住机会，现在就是好机会。(《邓小平文选》)

〚译文 1〛 Low speed equals stagnation and even retreat. Opportunity must be grasped. The present offers excellent chance.[12]

〚译文 2〛 Slow growth equals stagnation and even retrogression. We must grasp opportunities; the present offers an excellent one.[12]

〚译文 3〛 We must grasp the present excellent opportunities for high speed development, because slow growth equals stagnation and even retrogression.

如果我们没有理解错误的话，上面即是“意合”“形合”的例证。

汉语句子有“低速度就等于停步，甚至等于后退”和“要抓住机会，现在就是好机会”两个部分。这两个部分各自可以独立成句，但是放在一起却表达了一个新的，更复杂、更完备的意思。虽然两者没有过渡和连接，然而我们还是能够准确无误地把握和理解全句。

原文在中国人听来绝无理解障碍，译成英语怎么就成了天书？原来译文1和译文2都是打一枪换一个地方，将原文两句话译成三句话三套主谓宾，句际无启承关系，令读者摸不着头脑。

译文3则将原文两部分意在言外的因果关系，用严谨的形式规整于一个句子中。

“意合”“形合”的原理，也适用于英汉翻译。

The crisis has arisen as a result of recent uncontrolled inflation having outweighed the benefits of devaluation.

〖译文1〗近来不加控制的通货膨胀在后果上超过了货币贬值所带来的裨益。[103]

〖译文2〗近来通货膨胀的失控已经造成危机，货币贬值弊大于利。

此例的英语原文是典型的形合句，特点鲜明，朗朗上口。译文1也译作形合句。译文2改为意合，前后两部分字面上没有什么联系，但是读者理解却没有多大的障碍。

第二节 意合形合的范围和分类

也有另一部分专家把意合形合理解为中英语修辞的题旨情景不同，从而选择语言手段不同，选择表达方式不同。他们认为，语言是一个民族文化心理、思维方式和表现风格最深刻的体现。所谓“意合”（Parataxis），指由于社会文化的影响和语言习惯的积淀，文句的表达可以脱离词汇的字面意义，突破句法的结构规定，常常表现为主体移情或客体拟人的主客换位。所谓“形合”（hypotaxis），指完全借助语言形式手段，包括词汇意义和句法关系，实现其语义功能。

本书赞同并采纳这种比较宽泛的界定。从翻译技巧的角度看，研究这种泛义的“意合”“形合”转换才有实质性意义。

《周易·系辞上》云：“书不尽言，言不尽意。”用现代汉语说就是“语句在文字之外，意义在语句之外。”书写和言语要留有三分余地，要相信受众的理解能力。也许这是关于汉语意合最早的论述。

英语是一种由拼音文字发展而来的表音文字，有的专家称为音位文字。它的单词语法功能较弱，全靠连接词、介词、副词、物主代词等扶持才能起作用，就像一部机器，一台马达，没有螺丝和轴承的连接就是死物，与一堆废铁无异。

反过来看，汉语句法活跃，但是文字结构相对固定。“大”字加一点，不是“更大”或者“最大”，而是“太”或者“犬”，无论读音、释义、词类都发生了根本变化。

同样，英语的一个特点或优点就是词形变化活跃。单词通过词形变化以后，就可以影响和参与整个句子的语义表达。

所以，在翻译中我们要把原文意合的内涵，用明明白白、简简单单的英语表达出来，我们称之为“意合—形合”转换。

“意合—形合”转换的具体内容可谓千头万绪，但是大致可以归纳为以下几类：

（1）文化背景差异；

（2）历史典故、文学典故、宗教典故；

（3）成语，包括谚语、俚语、俗语、歇后语等；

（4）修辞，包括对仗、排比、比喻、比兴、拟人、借代、双关、互文、通感等。

我们把英语汉语中上述的语言文字特点，把它们的固定搭配、习惯用法、谚语、成语等，把语言修辞的辞格等，都纳入本章意合形合研究讨论范围。

向来主张多一事不如少一事的赵举人也在茶馆里发表议论。（叶圣陶《倪焕之》）

〖译文1〗Even the county graduate Mr Zhao, who had always urged people to avoid trouble rather than make it unnecessarily, now propounded arguments in the teahouse that were quite at variance with this principle of his.[51]

〖译文2〗Even Mr Zhao, the county graduate, who was a firm believer in letting sleeping dogs lie, now stood out to air his views in the tea-house.

“多一事不如少一事”的翻译可以用上一个英语典故：Let sleeping dogs lie。这个词语分别出现于乔叟的《特罗勒斯与克里希德》（Geoffrey Chaucer：*Troilus and Chriseyde*）：

A sleeping dog is better left alone.
一条酣睡的狗最好别去招惹它。

和狄更斯的《大卫·科布菲尔》（Charles Dickens：*David Copperfield*）：

Let sleeping dogs lie—who wants to rouse ‘em?
让睡着的狗躺着，谁会去搅醒它们？

这两句话的意思都是“多一事不如少一事”“不要自找麻烦”，简化成 Let sleeping dogs lie。用了这个典故，译文就和原文很接近了。

唯女子与小人为难养也，近之则不逊，远之则怨。（《论语》）

〖译文1〗Of all people, girls and servants are the most difficult to behave to. If you are familiar with them, they lose their humility. If you maintain a reserve towards them, they are discontented. ❶

〖译文2〗We cannot live with or without women and lower class. To be close to them invites their discourtesy, and to be estranged from them does their discontentment.

翻译孔子的这句话，可以借鉴与孔子同时代的古希腊剧作家阿里斯托芬（Aristophones）的话：

These impossible women! How they do get around us! The poet was right: can't live with them, or without them!

这些不可理喻的女人！在我们身边搞什么鬼？诗人说得对：不能和她们在一起，又不能没有她们。

众所周知，所谓人类文明是伴随着私有制和家庭的产生而产生的。作为人类文化的代言人，孔子和阿氏竭力维护这种以等级和男权为基础的制度本不足为奇。在西方，阿氏受到了后世文人的推崇和效仿。例如古罗马诗人奥维德（Ovid）说：

So I can't live either without you or with you.

所以我不能没有你，又不能和你在一起。

另一位古罗马诗人马希尔（Martial）说：

Difficult or easy, pleasant or bitter, you are the same you: I cannot live with you—nor without you.

不论你倔强还是和顺，快乐还是忧伤，你总是同样的你；我不能和你在一起，又不能没有你。

在中国，孔子却成了统治者歧视和摧残女性的替罪羊，体现了中西文化环境的巨大差异。

大凡女人都是水性杨花。（［清］曹雪芹《红楼梦》）

〖译文1〗have a disposition as changeable as water[1]

〖译文2〗a woman of loose morals[1]

〖译文3〗a woman as unstable as water[1]

〖译文4〗easy to seduce[1]

---

❶ http://www.ldbj.com。

〖译文 5〗 ever unstable as water[1]

〖译文 6〗 of easy virtue[1,64]

〖译文 7〗 ranging fancy[1,51,64]

〖译文 8〗 water disposition and aspen flowers-fickle and lascivious[1]

〖译文 9〗 light-o-love like[64]

〖译文 10〗 fickle as an easy woman's disposition[64]

〖译文 11〗 skittishly[64]

〖译文 12〗 of variable character[64]

〖译文 13〗 an inconstant woman[64]

以上译文摘自辞典的"水性杨花"词条，都或多或少反映了原文的意象。显然，"水性杨花"是汉语的一种形象说法，那么在西方语言中是否有这种比喻呢？有。古希腊戏剧家索福克勒斯（Sophocles）说过：

A woman's vows I write upon the wave.

我把女人的誓言写在水波之上。

意谓女人的山盟海誓口不应心，虚情假意，靠不住得很。这是"水性杨花"最早的西方版本。古罗马诗人卡图卢斯（Catullus）：

But what a woman says to her lusting lover it is best to write in wind and swift-flowing water.

一个女人对她热恋中的情人所说的话，最好记录在清风流水之上。

有"水"有"风"，与"水性杨花"最为贴近。莎士比亚（W. Shakespeare）：

Men's evil manners live in brass; their virtues we write in water.

男人的丑行镌刻在金石之上，凿凿有据；他们的德行记录在流水之上，化为泡影。

女人水性杨花，男人杨花水性，有过之而无不及。英国哲学家培根（Francis Bacon）说：

Who then to frail mortality shall trust, But limns the water, or but writes in dust.

谁会相信脆弱的德性，它只不过写在水波上或尘土里。

世风浇薄，人心不古，非关性别。英国作家梅瑞狄斯（George Meredith）的小说中有个自私自利的家伙，曾经气急败坏地说：

Women are women; they swim in infidelity, from wave to wave!
女人毕竟是女人，她们趟不贞节的浑水，水性杨花！

这已经纯属典故活用，了无新意了。综合参考以上典故，我们推出以下建议：

〖译文 14〗Most women write their vows on the wave.
女人大都把山盟海誓写在水波之上。

一句看似简单的“水性杨花”，竟然先后惊动了古代、中世纪、人文主义时期、近代和现代的五位西方作家。

英语典故应该成为我们的参考和尺度。

那地方是块肥肉，谁都想吃。
〖译文 1〗That place is an attractive piece of meat coveted by all.[104]
〖译文 2〗That place is the sweet fat coveted by all.

在英语中 fat 一词解释“脂肪”，也引申为“事物中最好的一部分”。美国诗人惠特曼（Walt Whitman）说：

I found no sweeter fat than sticks to my own bones.
长在自己骨头上的肥肉是精华。

英国作家罗伯特·伯顿（Robert Burton）说：

They lard their lean books with the fat of others' works.
他们用别人作品中的精华来润饰自己浅薄的书。

Longman Modern English Dictionary（《朗文现代英语词典》）对 fat 的释义，其中一条是：the best part of something（某物最好的部分）。该词典举例：living on the fat of the land（住在最肥沃的地方）。所以 a feast of fat things 是“山珍海味的筵席”，而不是“大块吃肉的筵席”。

我们认为英语汉语都存在一个意合形合问题，而且都存在一个相互转换的问题。

英译汉的意合形合转换有三种情况：

（1）意合向形合的转换：

town and gown
市民们与学术界

在字面上，town，城镇，与商铺和街道有关；gown，长袍，与款式和面料有关。但是两者放在一起，与这些都无关，意义发生了根本的改变。

（2）形合向意合的转换：

All good things come to an end.

天下没有不散的筵席。

英语句意是“所有的好事都要收场结束”。汉语则取天人合一的意念。在所有的汉语词典上，“筵席”都没有“好事”（good thing）的释义，读者只可意会，不可死抠字眼。

（3）意合向意合的转换：

No rose without a thorn.

〖译文1〗世上没有不带刺的玫瑰。

〖译文2〗世上没有十全十美的快乐。

一般的翻译家大多高估我们读者的领悟力，大多不把这个句子译作译文2，我们也没有辜负翻译家的期望。因为“玫瑰”是美丽的花朵，象征着爱情和幸福，大家都有这个共识；“刺”则令人讨厌，碰上“刺儿头”人人头痛，大家也有这个默契。“玫瑰”和“刺”合在一起会是什么效果，大家都心领神会，于是就意合了。另外，英语的rose放在句子前面，汉语的“玫瑰”放在后面，泾渭分明。

汉译英的意合形合转换也有三种情况：

（1）意合向形合的转换：

狮子林

〖译文1〗The Lion Forest Garden[9,105]

〖译文2〗The Lion-shaped Rock Garden

苏州园林“狮子林”中既没有狮子又没有森林，其命名是汉语一种意合表现手法。英译必须还原这个名称的真实含义。译文1摘自某翻译教程和某中国古典文学英译，由于没有转换，将使读者误以为狮子是庄园主人的宠物。笔者久闻狮子林盛名，还是读了下文，才知道它的意义：

狮子林因园中有许多太湖石头，看上去像狮子林立，所以称为狮子林。

Shizilin is a garden where numerous Taihu Lake stones shaped like lions have been positioned. That's why it bears the name Lion Grove.[27]

（2）形合向意合的转换：

偷得浮生半日闲

take time to smell the roses

在汉语中，“偷得浮生半日闲”寓意“忙中偷闲，享受生活”。在英语中，take time to smell the roses 字面意思是“抽时间闻闻玫瑰花”，实际意思是 take time out and enjoy life。两者的本体旨趣相同，表现方式各异。

While he described Jenny as a “phenomenal woman”, he also calls her a “workaholic”. “She just doesn't take time to smell the roses,” he said.

他把珍妮说成是“杰出女性”，他又把她称为“工作狂”。他说：“偷得浮生半日闲的事，她是没有的。”

（3）意合向意合的转换：

猪都笑了

Enough to make a cat laugh

说的是某事物完全荒唐可笑，said of smth. utterly ridiculous。

The idea of a chop like that composing a music: it's enough to make a cat laugh.

一个像他那样的伙计要谱写一首乐曲，想一想简直让猪都笑了。

意合形合的对立统一和相互转换为英汉这两种语言增添了无穷的艺术魅力，可以说是语言学习者和研究者思维的盛宴。世界上没有一种语言仅仅只有单纯的一面。一位美国语言学专家把 rhetoric，修辞，称为 language-within-a-language，其实，我们把意合形合看作“语言中的语言”，也是恰如其分的。

第三节　汉语意合转换成英语形合

汉语的意合，在作者是“意表”，读者是“意会”，译者则是表达上“迎合”之。

然而，翻译京剧此类很纯粹的中国艺术，是一项艰巨的工作。

〖译文 1〗To translate and interpret this typically Chinese cultural form as Peking Opera, however, is by no means an easy task.[69]

〖译文 2〗To translate and interpret so typical Chinese artistic form as Peking Opera, however, is by no means an easy task.

〖译文 3〗However, it is by no means an easy task to translate and interpret so typical Chinese artistic form as Peking Opera.

按照英语形合的要求，译文 1 可做如下修改：首先 typically 应该改为 typical，形成 typical，Chinese，cultural 共同修饰 form。然后 this 一定要改为 so，形成 so

…as…的搭配，英语的这种形合倾向非常明显。另外 cultural form（文化形态）可以改为 artistic form（艺术形式）。

庙内多秦槐汉柏，大皆三四抱。（沈复《浮生六记》）

〖译文 1〗Inside the temple grounds were many Chin Dynasty locust trees and Han dynasty cypress trees, most as big around as the span of three or four men's arms.[9]

〖译文 2〗In the courtyard were many locusts and cypresses of Qin or Han dynasty, most as big around as the span of three or four men's arms.

〖译文 3〗On the temple grounds grow many locusts and cypresses from ancient times, their trunks taking several people to encompass.

〖译文 4〗In the courtyard were many antique locusts and cypresses, whose trunks are as big around as the span of three or four men's arms.

原文记叙作者游历"华阴庙"。文中"秦槐汉柏"是汉语一种特殊的表达方式，修辞学称为"互文"。根据这种辞格，"秦槐汉柏"不能理解成"秦代的槐树，汉代的柏树"，而应该是"秦汉时代的槐树和柏树"。见译文 2。

秦汉是中国历史上两个早期的大一统王朝，因此汉语中往往将"秦汉"比作"古代的"或"年代久远的"。例如"秦砖汉瓦""秦楼楚馆""秦时明月汉时关"，不一定实指秦汉时代。鉴此，"秦槐汉柏"也可以理解成"古代的槐树柏树"，或"年代久远的槐树柏树"。见译文 3 和译文 4。

在庞然大物中，左找，右找，找不到商品究在何处。

〖译文 1〗Search left and right, and you still cannot locate the commodity in the huge box.[66]

〖译文 2〗Fumbling here and there in the huge box, you still cannot find where the main body is.

原文批评商品的过度包装，有时包装很大，商品却很小，买椟还珠，舍本逐末。本句汉语的"商品"是个意合概念，我们中国人很好理解，就是那个主件。但是在英语中，包装、说明书、附件也是商品，句中"商品"一词直译作 commodity，可能引起误解。建议译作 main body（或 main item，main part）。

二人同心，其利断金。

〖译文 1〗If the two people are of the same mind, their sharpness can cut through metal. ❶

---

❶ http：//www. fane. cn。

〖译文 2〗Two heads are better than one.

〖译文 3〗Two persons with the same mind have the strength greater than metal.

原文当然是高度意合的句子。译文 1 介于形合意合之间。首先，第一个定冠词应该取消。其次，sharpness 意为“敏捷”“机灵”，与后面的谓语搭配不当。译文 2 用意合译出。译文 3 用形合译出。

三十而立。

〖译文 1〗At thirty, I had planted my feet firm upon the ground. [24]

〖译文 2〗At thirty, I stood firm. ❶

〖译文 3〗At thirty, I was a success in my career.

〖译文 4〗At thirty, I stood on my own legs.

这儿如何理解原文的“立”，是准确翻译的关键。译文 1 和译文 2 理解成“站立”，形合意不合。译文 3 理解成“事业上的成功”，只求意合，不汲汲于字面上的形合。译文 4 采用英语成语 stand on one’s own legs，它表示“独立”“自立”。例如：He is old enough to stand on his own legs.（他长大了，可以自立了。）

调查有两种方法，一种是走马观花，一种是下马观花。

〖译文 1〗There are two ways of making investigations, one is to look at flowers on horseback and the other is to get off your horse and look at them. [13]

〖译文 2〗There are two kinds of investigations, one is the superficial and the other is elaborate.

译文 1 的句意是：做调查研究有两个途径，一个是骑在马背上看花，另一个是跳下马看花。

对“走马观花”的理解需要绕一个圈子。唐代孟郊《登科后》诗：“春风得意马蹄疾，一日看尽长安花。”表示愉快的心情，后世用“走马观花”比喻粗枝大叶地观察一下。“下马观花”是仿词，比喻仔细观察研究。翻译成英语只解释喻体，不点明本体是不行的，例如译文 1，西方读者会感到莫名其妙。反过来，丢下喻体不管，只译出本体倒是可以的。译文 2 的句意是：调查研究有两种类型，一种是马虎肤浅的，一种是认真详尽的。

同仁堂人的目标是：加强品牌意识，推行品牌策略，研制更好、更多品种的药品，为世界人民服务。

---

❶ http://www.ldbj.com。

〖译文1〗Tongrentang people aim to strengthen the sense of quality, carry out the brand policy and manufacture better medicines in wider variety to serve the people of the world.[43]

〖译文2〗Tongrentang people aim to sharpen the sense of quality, carry out the brand policy and, and offer better products in more extensive line for the health of the people of the world.

〖译文3〗Tongrentang people aim to promote the public health of the world by high sense of the quality and the brand, and offering better products in more extensive line.

“为人民服务”中也含有意合，译文1译作 serve the people 是不错的，但是没有考虑到该企业的产品是药品，所以应该补足 health 一词。

春到田间耕作忙。

〖译文1〗With spring looking on, everyone has been busy plowing and planting.[50]

〖译文2〗Spring comes along urging plowing and planting.

译文1虽然将“春”作拟人化翻译，但是整句仍然是形合，故译文补足 everyone 一词，反而更忠实于原文。译文2彻底地拟人化，属于意合。

读万卷书，行万里路。

〖译文1〗To read ten thousand books, and to go ten thousand li.[7]

〖译文2〗Read extensively and practice earnestly.

古人的“读万卷书，行万里路”用来鼓励学生多读书多接触社会实际。译文1译成“读一万本书，走一万里路”没有译出原文字面背后的真实涵义。

知己知彼，百战不殆；不知彼而知己，一胜一负；不知彼不知己，每战必殆。

〖译文1〗You can fight a hundred battles without defeat if you know the enemy as well as yourself. You will win one battle and lose one battle if you know yourself but leave yourself in the dark about the enemy. You will lose every battle if you leave both the enemy and yourself in the dark.[106]

〖译文2〗You will be invincible if you are acquainted with the enemy as well as yourself. Your average will be half and half if you are only acquainted with yourself but not the enemy. You will lose every battle if you are acquainted with neither yourself nor the enemy.

"百战不殆"并不是说您打第101仗必败无疑，而是说您"战无不胜"，"百战"不能真的译作 a hundred battles。同理，"一胜一负"也不是说您赢一次，输一次，而是说您的概率"一半对一半"。至于"不知彼不知己"更不是让自己和敌人都蒙在鼓里，而是说您自己蒙在鼓里。

文化搭台，经济唱戏。

〖译文1〗Cultural events set the stage, trade activities play the title role.

〖译文2〗Cultural programs provide arenas for trade activities.

〖译文3〗Cultural events set the stage for business to play the title role. [107]

〖译文4〗Business promotion in the name of cultural events.

〖译文5〗Theatrical performance for business purpose.

title role 是戏剧、电影等中被用作剧名或片名的剧名角色或片名角色，比如《哈姆雷特》中的哈姆雷特，《白蛇传》中的白娘子。所以译文1、译文2的意义不明确。

我们说，你没有挑过水，所以没有摘桃子的权利。

〖译文1〗We say, "You never carried any water, so you have no right to pick the peaches." [31]

〖译文2〗We say, "Since you never watered the tree, you have no right to pick the fruit."

"挑水"和"摘桃子"是比喻说法，表示"付出劳动"和"获得成果"。但是直译成 carry water 和 pick the peach 就不符合原意了。carry water（搬运水）固然是"付出劳动"，但是与 pick the peach（摘桃子）没有逻辑联系。"桃子"在汉语中指代"即将到手的成果"，比如"跳一跳，摘桃子"，意思是再努力一把，将胜利成果拿到手。在英语中 peach 却指代"美女"，pick the peach 与"摘桃子"字面上不差毫厘，引起的联想却失之千里。

我们不妨把"挑水"换成"给树浇水"，把"桃子"换成"果实"，这样，两者就很自然地联系起来了，而且 water the tree 和 pick the fruit 形成语句的排偶，体现了语言的形式美，这个问题我们在第六章将详谈。

不诚信的人，不可能做好人，也难处世。与没有诚信的人交往，是十分危险可怕的。

〖译文1〗A dishonest man cannot be a good man or easy to get along with. And it is dangerous to befriend dishonest men. [6]

〖译文 2〗 A dishonest man cannot be well-behaved or easy to be got along with, and will turn out to be a harmful company.

原文“不可能做好人”可以有两种解读：(1)不可能做,好人;(2)不可能做好,人。

译文 1 可能按前一种理解翻译。译文 2 则换成后一种理解。最后一句“与没有诚信的人交往，是十分危险可怕的”也可以换一种说法，按“没有诚信的人是损友”译出，以便文章更连贯。

市场经济下的公平竞争是促进经济繁荣的重要因素，但竞争过了头，其负面影响就不容忽视。

〖译文 1〗 In the market economy, the crucial factor for prosperity is fair competition. But if the competition spins out of control, the negative effects must not be overlooked. [6]

〖译文 2〗 Although fair competition is the catalyst for a big boom in market economy, overheated competition should not be neglected for its negative consequences.

〖译文 3〗 Although fair competition fuels a big boom in market economy, overheated competition should not be neglected for its negative consequences.

〖译文 4〗 Although fair competition acts as engine of a big boom in market economy, overheated competition should not be neglected for its negative consequences.

译文 1 是考研真题的参考答案。很明显，这个答案是译者将“促进”“繁荣”“重要”“因素”等逐一查阅汉英词典后组装起来的。

像原文这样的经济学话题，西方媒体却不乏采用科技词汇来表达。译文 2 将“公平竞争是促进经济繁荣的重要因素”用“催化剂”（catalyst）来表示。译文 3 用“燃料”（fuel）表示。译文 4 用“发动机”（engine）表示。

人只要真正找到了自己，就找到了品牌，就找到了恰当的包装。

〖译文 1〗 As long as one finds himself indeed, he finds a brand and finds his proper package. [57]

〖译文 2〗 Only when people discover true oneself, he finds the brand, and the appropriate package as well. [57]

〖译文 3〗 He, who can see oneself, can find the brand and the proper package. [57]

〖译文 4〗 It is not difficult for people to find the right brand and the right package when he can find himself. [57]

〖译文 5〗 As long as one finds where one stands, one knows how to package oneself, just as a commodity establishes its brands by the right package. [57]

〖译文 6〗 As long as one finds where one stands, one knows how to package oneself, just as a commodity establishes its value by being true to its character and enhances its brand by virtue of the right packaging. [57]

〖译文 7〗 As long as one knows himself, he finds his own brand of manner and appearance.

译文 1 至译文 6 摘自某汉英翻译教程，该书对于原文及译文 1 至译文 4 评论道：此句字面意义很明了，但是内涵却异常丰富。这种“矛盾”在很大程度上体现了汉语的特点。若译者未能得其赅意，而急于思考“直译”还是“意译”，岂不误事？……译者很可能未能读懂原句。以上 4 译“依样画葫芦”，均为拙译。

该书对译文 5 的评论是：译者对原文的理解不存问题，但是，其英译在 native speaker 看来，仍不能接受。Bill Hofmann 教授对原译修改如译文 6。教授还就此修改特作如下说明：

I have made a few changes in brackets. With the exception of the very last line, I have changed only a word or phrase. I have suggested a revision in the last line that seems more logical to me.

我在括弧中做了一些改变。除最后一行之外，我仅作了一词或一语之改。对最后一行的修改意见在我看来似乎更合乎逻辑。（本书译）

我们对原文和诸英译的评论如下：

原文含义不难理解：人只要找到了自己，也就找到了自己特立独行的精神风貌和处世方式。作者由于长期浸润于市场经济和商品文化之中，借用了一些广告用语设喻，本无新意。说几位译者未能读懂这几行文字，似无可能。其实未能完全读懂的恐怕是 Hofmann 教授。

译文 1 是及格的。虽然它没有挑明人的商品之譬，但是读者仍能朦胧地把握它的意思。

译文 2 有语病。句中的 people 一词最好改为 one，以便与后文的 oneself 和 he 连贯。连带地将谓语动词 discover 加 s。

译文 3 听起来似乎一个人在照镜子，看到自己时，找到了什么东西，比如化妆品的品牌和包装。句中 oneself 须改为 himself 才算通顺。

译文 4 说的是两回事：“他”发现他自己之时，于是广大人民大众也不难找到正确的品牌和包装。

译文 5 是准确的。但是译文后面的 one，one，oneself 一定要用代词。

译文 6 的译者大约出于礼貌，全盘接受译文 5 的思路和框架，结果非但没有找到自己，反而迷失在“商品”之中，离原文渐行渐远。

译文 7 是本书自译，意在还原原文本来的意思。译文采用的 brand 一词有两重意义：一是“品牌”，“商标”。二是“独特的一种”，“自成一格的一类”。

结论：汉语的“意合”有时也能以英语意合之。

最后顺便指出：该翻译教程有表达错误，其中“内涵”是“涵义”之误，前者是逻辑学术语，后者才有“含义”的意思。“拙译”是“绌译”之误，前者是“我的译文”的谦辞，后者才是“有瑕疵的译文”。

我们的毛病还很多。我们不怕说出自己的毛病，我们一定要改正自己的毛病。

〖译文 1〗 We still have many failings. We are not afraid to admit them and are determined to get rid of them. [31]

〖译文 2〗 We still have many faults. We do not deny them and are determined to correct them.

〖译文 3〗 We still have many shortcomings. We are not blind to them and are determined to overcome them.

“毛病”用 failing（失败）译出是一种误译，可以用 fault（过失）或 shortcoming（缺点）译出。

“不怕说出”不能逐字译作 not afraid to admit。其中 admit 意为“供认”，或者“承认……合理”。虽然英语中有 I admit that I was wrong.（我承认我错了。）admit failure（认输）等说法，但是 admit 隐含“不得不”“不情愿”（unwilling）的意味。本句可以用 not deny（不否认），或者 not overlook（不忽略），或者 be not blind to（不视而不见）取代 be afraid to admit。

“改正”用 get rid of 译出不妥，与 failure 搭配更不恰当。可译作 correct，fix，rectify，repair，compensate for，eliminate，make up for，overcome，remedy 等。

夫至德之世，同与禽兽居，族与万物并，恶乎知君子小人哉。同乎无知，其德不离；同乎无欲，是谓朴素；朴素而民性得矣。(《庄子》第 9 章)

〖译文 1〗 In ancient times when perfect virtue prevailed, people lived together with birds and animals and mixed with everything in the world. How did they know the distinction between superior men and inferior men? All ignorant, they did not lose their virtue; all desireless, they were in state of natural simplicity as uncarved timber, which kept intact their inborn nature. [8]

〖译文 2〗 In ideal times of perfect virtue, there was no discrimination between superior men and inferior men among people who were competing with other creatures and circumstances. All innocent, they retained their virtue; all free from covetousness, they live simple life, which in turn kept intact their inborn nature.

为了方便理解，首先将原文译为现代汉语：

在那盛德的时代，人们与禽兽杂处，与万物共存，哪里知道君子小人的区别呢？同样都无知，就不会离弃道德；同样都无欲，这就叫本真质朴；只要本真质朴，人民的本性就保持了。

原文含有大量意合词语。

“至德之世”系指史前原始社会，那个社会是什么样子的，由于没有文字记录，所以大家有发挥自己想象的余地。庄子认为那是一个道德完美的理想社会。

“同与禽兽居，族与万物并”的意思恐怕不仅仅是“与飞鸟走兽居住在一起，与世界万物混杂在一块”，人类至少不会像在伊甸园那样养尊处优。

“其德不离”可以译作 retain virtue（保持美德）或 do not stray from virtue（不偏离美德），不宜译作 lose virtue（失去贞操，堕落）。“无欲”不宜译作 desireless，其中的“欲”不是 desire（愿望）而是 lust（贪欲），covet（贪求），craving（渴求）。

“朴素”一词重复一次。古人的文字需要刻在竹简或金石上，故惜墨如金。作者重复“朴素”，是为了强调“朴素”的作用与反作用。

重庆大学的毕业生因综合素质高，工作能力强非常受用人单位的欢迎。

〖译文 1〗Graduates from Chongqing University are very much welcomed by employers for their high overall quality and strong capability. ❶

〖译文 2〗Graduates from Chongqing University find favor with their employers for their comprehensive quality and potential capability.

原文的“欢迎”含有意合语意，表示受到用人单位的赞赏、偏爱。不能用词典上的 welcome 译出。

科学家对新事物要非常敏感，敢想敢干。

〖译文 1〗Scientists should be very sensitive to new things, and should dare to think and dare to do.

〖译文 2〗Scientists should be sensitive, initiative and courageous.

〖译文 3〗Scientists should be of sensibleness, courageousness and broad-mind.

---

❶ http://international. cqu. edu. cn。

“敢想敢干”是意合词组，它包含的意义可以理解成“敢于突破传统的思维和行为的禁区”，因此可译作 dare to break through the shackles of the old conventions。译文 1 的 dare to think and do，成了“胆敢想，胆敢做”，背离了原文的精神。为了忠实于原文言简意赅的风格，我们可以把“敢想”译作 initiative（有首创精神、进取心的）、innovative（有创新精神的）、broad-minded（思路开阔的）。“敢干”的意思就是 courageous（有勇气的）。另外 sensitive 本身就含有 showing the feeling to new things or changes（对新事物或变化有感觉）的意思，因此译文 1 中 to new things 是冗词。

道家哲学可粗略分作三个阶段，初始阶段、发展阶段及世俗道教阶段，第三阶段有时也称衰退阶段。

〖译文 1〗 Taoism as a philosophy may be divided roughly into three stages, the original stage, the stage of development, and the stage of Popular Taoism, sometimes called the stage of degeneration. [22]

〖译文 2〗 Taoism evolved as a philosophy roughly in three stages, the stages of origin, development, and popularization, the last of which sometimes is called the stage of degeneration.

“道家哲学”在其演化过程被“分作三个阶段”。

第四节 汉语形合转换为英语意合

他赚钱多，但是花销更多。

〖译文 1〗 He earns much, but spends more.

〖译文 2〗 He is a big earner, but a bigger spender.

译文 1 是正规的，又是我们最常见的译文。译文 2 是我们中国人不习惯，却是外文资讯常见的表达。汉语倾向于多用动词，英语多用名词，这种表达习惯的不同，值得注意，也颇值得我们在翻译实践中效仿。

计算机比人检查更仔细，更勤快。

〖译文 1〗 The computer inspects more carefully and industriously than human does.

〖译文 2〗 The computer is a more careful and industrious inspector than human.

计算机也可以被说成 inspector（检查者），而且可以与“人”比较。

这把钥匙怎么也打不开房门。

〖译文1〗This key couldn't open the door anyhow.

〖译文2〗This key refused to open the door.

英语中许多用来描述人的动作的词汇，例如 accept，invite，put，help，refuse，speak，tell，betray，allow 等等，都可以用于物，使文句的叙事生动、形象鲜明。拟人和拟物在英汉互译中是一个互为转换的过程，如何分解和区别，仍然是意象和境界转换的重要方面。

在公文、公函、科技论文、政府文件、历史文献等特殊的书面语中，作者为了尽量客观冷静的描述、评论某事物，往往尽可能避免使用与人或人称有关的词语。科技论文中的话题，如果与主体关系不大，英语常常使用带有动作意义的抽象名词充当主语或其他句子成分。汉语常常用主谓结构或动宾结构的短语充当主语或其他句子成分。

在某些更特殊的场合，人们甚至小心翼翼地避开 I，we，my，our 等人称代词。

A current search of the files indicates that the letter is no longer in this Bureau's possession. It is noted that the letter was received two months ago, and after study, returned to your office.

〖译文1〗我们最近查看了卷宗，发现本局并无此信。可以肯定的是，我们于两个月前收到此信，经研究后，已寄还贵处。[13]

〖译文2〗倾阅卷宗，本局查无此信。此信两月前即已收悉，经研究后，已寄还贵处，特此奉告。

我们知道，办公室政治有一条不成文游戏规则，就是尽可能规避责任。英语原文这封公函没有违背这条规则。作者既不失礼貌，又摆脱干系，全文增一词则太多，减一词则太少，显得异常冷静，有条不紊。文中根本不用 I，we，my，our 等人称代词，主句用名词和 it 做主语，从句用 letter 做主语。说到“本局”，不说 our Bureau（我局）而说 this Bureau（该局），也不让做主语，只做介词宾语。全文唯一一个人称代词指向对方：your，又放在倒数第二的位置，作者在不否认基本事实的前提下，干净利落地把皮球踢还给对方。另一个代词 it 不作人称代词，而作形式主语。

译文1用了两个原文没有的“我们”，而且将 note（通知）一词误译作犹犹豫豫，勉勉强强“可以”的“肯定”。另外，译者按原文词序译出，note 在原文的句子开头，是一个主要信息的位置，“可以肯定”在汉译句子的开头却是一个次要信息位置，这样就大大削弱了原文的语势。在风格上，原文是一种庄重的公文体书面语，译文1则倾向于口语化。

译文 2 采用半文半白的汉语，语气接近原文。

A nobler want of man is served by nature, namely, the love of Beauty.

〖译文 1〗人的一个更高尚的需求被大自然满足了，那就是爱美之心。

〖译文 2〗大自然除了提供人类衣食所需之外，还满足了人类一种更高的追求——那就是爱美之心。[78,108]

原文出自美国作家爱默生（Ralph Waldo Emerson）的随笔《论美》（Beauty)，这是开宗明义的第一句话。译文 1 无论从哪方面看都是不错的。但是译文 2 也有它的道理。

对西方人来说，大自然提供人类衣食之需，人类为了提高生活质量还应该不断向大自然索取。但是在中国文化“天人合一”的观念中，人与大自然不是予取予求的关系。在爱默生看来，大自然满足我们爱美之心之前，还有一种满足是不言而喻的，而中国人却不明白：这个不言而喻的满足是什么呢？您老人家“不言”，我怎么“而喻”呢？译文 2 刚好解答了我们的疑问。因此我们把这也称为英语意合向汉语形合的转换。

一个人开始去爱谁的时候，他可以有所选择，但当他要结束爱情的时候，可就没有选择了。

〖译文 1〗When a man begins to love, he has many choices. When he ends it he has none.

〖译文 2〗A man has choice to begin love, but not to end it.[33]

英语借助 connectives 组成复句，而汉语更多地依靠语序直接组合复句。这儿的 connectives 是指连词或副词之类。

本译例的情况刚好相反。原文“的时候”“但”“当……的时候”都起了一个连词或副词的作用，而译文 2 只用了一个 but，表示前后意思的转折关系。原文“开始去爱谁的时候”，译文 2 只用 to love 表示。“开始”“去”“谁”“的时候”都省略了。后面，“当他要结束爱情的时候”也是如此，而“可就没有选择了”只用 not 表示。

也许人们会说这只是一个例外。但是当这种“例外”太多，“例外”“例内”的比例达到三七开或四六开，甚至倒四六或倒三七时，“规则”本身就站不住了。意合形合是英汉互译中双向转换的问题。

同事们都很欣赏他的观点。

〖译文 1〗His colleagues appreciate his opinion very much.

〖译文 2〗His colleagues think highly of his opinion.

“欣赏”可以用 appreciate，admire 等“大词”，也可以用 think highly 译出。同样，“朋友们对她的为人评价很高”，其中“评价”一词可以译作 evaluate，assess，estimate，也可以将“评价很高”译作 speak highly，即 Her friends speak highly of her behavior.

尽管对电的确切性质人们还不清楚，但对电能做些什么已了解得很多了。

〖译文 1〗While the exact nature of electricity is unknown，a great deal is known about what it can do. [13]

〖译文 2〗We know more about what the electricity can do than what it is.

〖译文 3〗What the electricity can do is better known than what it is.

原文借助语言形式手段，包括词汇和形态，通过连词显示句法关系，实现词语或句子的连接。句中“确切”“性质”“尽管”“但”“对”等词汇都起了这样的作用。译文 1 将这些词汇一一对应地译出，信则信矣，却不通达。

译文 2 首先运用了第一章介绍的技巧，将“对电能做些什么已了解得很多”作为主要信息，放在前面；将“对电的确切性质人们还不清楚”作为次要信息，放在后面。然后运用第二章介绍的技巧，提取“人们”作主语，以回归主体。接着运用第三章的知识，将 We know 放在句首。运用第四章内容，化散点为透视，将原文两个分句用英语一个完整的句子译出。最后在第五章技巧的运用上，将“确切”“性质”“尽管”“但”“对”等，不做字面对译，都用意合表达。

译文 3 则取译文 1 之长，以“电能做些什么”作主语，以“电的确切性质”作宾语。

据我粗略的统计，有的商品在大包装中仅占空间十分之一，二十分之一，甚至五十分之一。

〖译文 1〗According to my rough statistics，some commodities take up only one tenth，one twentieth or even one fiftieth of the space in the huge package. [66]

〖译文 2〗I put some commodities at only one tenth，twentieth or even fiftieth of the space in the huge package.

“据……粗略的统计”可以用英语短语 put something at 译出。这个短语意为 estimate that it is a certain amount，number etc without trying to be very exact。例如：I' d put her age at around 40.

他还问了我们分手后我的情况。

〖译文 1〗He also asked my circumstances since we separated.

〖译文 2〗 He also asked what had happened to me since we separated.

译文 2 用 what had happened 代替 circumstances 译出“情况”，似乎更准确。

对于这些条件，他们大伙有的同意，有的不同意。

〖译文 1〗 Some of them agreed on the terms, but some disagreed.

〖译文 2〗 All of them did not agree on these terms.

本句的肯定形式是：

对于这些条件，他们大伙一致同意。

All of them agree on the terms.

对于肯定句式英汉比较一致，无形合意合之别。但是一旦成为否定形式，本句应该用意合翻译，英语句意是：并非他们全都同意这些个条件。

世有贤妻良母，也有泼妇浪女。

〖译文 1〗 There are not only good wife and loving mother but also shrewlike ladies and immoral girls.

〖译文 2〗 There are women and women.

人和人不一样，女人也如此。有的女人勤劳节俭，有的好吃懒做，有的相夫教子，有的连邻居也敢欺负，所以才有原文这种说法。译成英语不必逐字对译，可以采用意合。译文 2 的 There are × and × 常被使用，已成句型。比如，There are snakes and snakes. 蛇有多种，有的有毒，有的无毒。

公司因我发展，我因公司生存。

〖译文 1〗 I coexist with the company. ❶

〖译文 2〗 I am conductive to company development on which my own existence depend. ❶

〖译文 3〗 Each for company, company for each.

一位网友说：请问“公司因我发展，我因公司生存”怎么译呢？I coexist with the company，可不可以呢？

第二位网友说：coexist 有摒弃歧见，互相忍让而共存的意思，容易引起误会，有点不太恰当。可以直译：I am conductive to company development on which my own existence depends.

---

❶ http://www.translator.com.cn。

第三位网友说：Does that mean that without you the company would have no development?（是不是说没有你公司就不发展了？——本书译）

我们认为，“我”不一定要用 I 或 you 译出，可以用 each 译出。贵公司以“公司因我发展，我因公司生存”做宣传标语是不错的。因为 company 一词源自拉丁语，本义“某人和另一人一起吃面包”，所以它与 each 是很对应的。译文 3 丢掉了“我”“发展”“生存”字样，保留了“公司”company，增添了 each，就是采用意合手法。我们推荐译文 3 还因为它保留了原文的对仗，贵公司如果把原文译文一起贴在墙壁上，视觉效果也不错。

溪口千层饼采用传统工艺，制作精细、质地松脆、清香可口。

〖译文 1〗Xikou Thousand-sheeted cake is homemade, using natural foods and traditional procedures. The cake tastes good, smells good and is crisp. [13]

〖译文 2〗Xikou Qianceng cake, with numerous clear sheets in it, is finely made in a traditional way. It is tasty and crisp. [13]

〖译文 3〗Xikou sheeted cake is fragrant, crisp and tasty owing to its fine traditional processing.

汉语表达习惯采用数字，以增添文采。但是这些数字如果直译成英语，有时非但不能增添文采，反而显得沉闷。譬如“万里长城”不能译作 Ten Thousand Miles Wall，而必须采用意合手法，译作 Great Wall。“凭我三寸不烂之舌”不一定译作 I will trust to this tireless three-inch tongue of mine 或 use my three inches of never-failing tongue，可以通过意合译作 on the strength of my eloquence 或 with my eloquence。译文 1 将“千层饼”译作 Thousand-sheeted cake 是误译。译文 2 采用音译手法，译作 Qianceng cake，这只有当老外操着生硬的汉语对商店营业员说他要买“钱衬瓶”时，才有意义。从信息传递功能的角度看问题，“千层饼”只要简单地译作 sheeted cake 或 multi-layer cake 即可。

我们许多同志缺乏分析的头脑，对于复杂事物，不愿做反复深入的分析研究，而爱做绝对肯定或绝对否定的简单结论。

〖译文 1〗Lacking an analytical approach, many of our comrades do not want to go deeply into complex matters, to analyze and study them over and over again, but like to draw simple conclusions which are either absolutely affirmative or absolutely negative. [31]

〖译文 2〗Lacking an analytical approach, many of our comrades do not want to go deeply into complex matters, to analyze and study them over and over again, but are prone to be torn between absolutely affirmative or absolutely negative conclusions.

〖译文3〗Lacking an analytical approach, many of our comrades do not want to go deeply into complex matters, to analyze and study them over and over again, but to draw simple conclusions between two extremities.

首先，原文的“爱”作“老是”“常常”解，比如：“他这个人就是爱犯这种低级错误。”其中“爱”不能理解成 love 或 like。“简单结论”是“绝对肯定或绝对否定”的包裹层，也就是说“简单结论”不必译出，全句可以译作：我们许多同志在绝对肯定和绝对否定之间首鼠两端。如译文2。

“绝对肯定或绝对否定”译作 absolutely affirmative or absolutely negative，重复了 absolutely 一词，如果换成“在两种极端之间”，between two extremities，则可避免之，这就是报纸上常说的“从一个极端走向另一个极端”。如译文3。

中国千年来的科举制度滋生出八股文这个独特的文化奇观。这种文字既不能经世济用，又无涉个人情感，更不是什么语言艺术。士人皓首穷经，思想僵化，对于时务一窍不通，只指向一个唯一的目标——做官。顾炎武《日知录·拟题》指出：“八股之害等于焚书，而败坏人才，有甚于咸阳之郊所坑者但四百六十余人也。”毛泽东将媒体和公文中的党腔党调贬之曰“党八股”。其实，商八股、官八股、学八股（包括学术八股和学生八股）远未绝迹，这就是我们称之为汉语形合的一种，而且是谬种。孰料现代的大学教授对此类空话、套话甚为偏爱，纷纷收入汉英翻译教材。他们不了解此类文本仍有许多陷阱。

本公司期待着与国内外的新老朋友开展更多的合作机会。

〖译文1〗We look forward to more cooperation opportunities with new and old friends at home and abroad.

〖译文2〗We look forward to your partnership.

译文1深受原文影响，而原文则是受了中国千年八股文风的影响，实属现代“商八股”。其实“国内外”“新老朋友”云云，可以用一个“你”字 you 代替。“开展”“更多”“机会”等字样统统都可删除。上海有一家印刷机械公司在自己的网页上写道：“在新老客户的关注和支持下，本公司将不懈地为新老客户提供更多、更好、更新的服务。”该句被依样画葫芦地译作：

With the support and concern from our old and new customers, we would provide even more services for both of our old and new customers.

该公司最好把这个令人望而生畏的广告词改得简洁、醒目一点，比如改作

We will offer more services for you.

或许宣传效果会更好一些。

处在世纪之交的×××铁路车辆（集团）有限责任公司，正在奋力实现“再现国家队雄风、再造新世纪辉煌、再为社会主义增光”的宏伟意愿，朝着“发展规模集团化、产品品种系列化、市场经营国际化、企业规模现代化”的目标迈进。公司将一如既往地坚持“信誉第一、用户至上”的宗旨，不仅以更多的高质量、高品位、高档次的新产品满足市场，而且以良好的作风，为广大用户提供一流的全过程的服务。

〖译文 1〗 At the turn of the century， ××× Railway Rolling Stock （Group） Co.,Ltd. is now striving hard in confidence and well on the way towards a global-market-oriented enterprise group to be well developed in management, marketing and product series. Focusing on our clients, we will continue with our credit to provide our customers with high quality and advanced products as well as our cover-all services. [45]

〖译文 2〗 We will continue to offer our cover-all services as well as our quality products for you.

本广告如果套用一句套话，可谓集官八股商八股于一体，熔老生常谈陈词滥调于一炉。作者收集领导动员讲话，职工表决心鼓干劲和市场常见广告、宣传标语的勤奋和耐心给人留下深刻印象，可惜广告本身不会产生什么影响。读者还未及完整地读一遍，大抵都会抱头鼠窜着离开。微软公司松下公司如果这样讲话，恐怕生意都会滑坡。贵公司最好结合自己的行业和产品的特点设计广告语，并且在实际运销中打响广告，擦亮品牌。我们可以在这儿赠送贵公司一条广告语：

See the world in a ×××(贵公司品牌).

这个句子的意思是，坐上我们的铁路车辆可以看外面精彩的世界，同时，通过我们的产品可以看到世界先进水平。我们免费赠送，分文不取，是为了不再看到原来那个非常可怕的广告。须知语言文字应该是很美很可爱的。

我们真诚希望大使先生阁下能介绍一批有识之士来中国考察，共谋发展大业。我们的目标是依靠我们点点滴滴、锲而不舍的卓越追求，实现两地经济的共同繁荣。

〖译文 1〗 We sincerely hope Mr. Ambassador can introduce a group of insightful men into China for reviewing and seeking/designing the development cause. Our goal is to implement common prosperity both two economies, through relying on hairlike and persistent pursuit of excellence. ❶

---

❶ http：//www. translator. com. cn。

〖译文 2〗 We sincerely hope that the Honorable Mr/Ms/Mrs XYZ will send us groups of learned people to investigate opportunities for business cooperations. Our goal is that by bits and drabs, and persistence in the pursuit of excellence mutual economical prosperity between the two countries can be achieved. ❶

〖译文 3〗 We shall appreciate Your Excellency if you should introduce groups of learned people to investigate opportunities for business cooperation. Our goal is to benefit our mutual economical growth by the constant and persistent efforts of our part.

汉语原文是中国大陆地方官员的口吻。他可能是在经贸交流，或招商引资的宴会上说这番话的。他的态度可能是真诚的。正是为了表示真诚，他的话未免落入“官八股”窠臼。译文 1 和译文 2 偏偏一头钻入形合词语“点点滴滴”“锲而不舍”“卓越追求”的牛角尖，结果弄得译文语句点点滴滴很不连贯，殊不知这些词语可以用英语意合表达。而且译文 1 和译文 2 显得小家子气，与中国官员前呼后拥、颐指气使的派头不相吻合。

健康茶在我国有着相当久远的历史，随着科学的发展，国内外科学家对茶叶及中草药的研究也日益深入。茶叶的药用价值也随着研究的深入而不断有新的认识和提高。此外还发现茶叶与某些天然植物药材配伍，其疗效可以发挥得淋漓尽致。

〖译文 1〗 Health Tea has quite a long history in China. With the development of science, the tea leaves and traditional medicinal herbs are increasingly brought to further research by the scientists in the world. Also, the medical value of tea leaves has been risen to some new concept gradually with further studies. Moreover, finding that tea leaves mixed with some natural rare plants ingredients gives literally efficacious therapeutic effects. [43]

〖译文 2〗 Health Tea has quite a long history in China. Modern scientific research has found much more medical value in tea leaves, which mixed with some natural rare herbal ingredients can give obvious efficacious therapeutic effects.

〖译文 3〗 Health Tea has quite a long history in China. Modern scientific research has found much more medical value in tea leaves, which mixed with some rare herbal ingredients can give apparent therapeutic efficacy.

译文 1 语法、句法、词汇都正确。但是我们希望对原文提出一些改进。让我们先分析原文：

---

❶ http://www.translator.com.cn。

“随着科学的……日益深入”有28个字，似乎内容比较空洞，不妨并入后面的“随着研究的深入”。

“茶叶的药用价值也……不断有新的认识和提高”实际上就是“发现茶叶新的药用价值”的花哨说法。

“此外……”句没有提供新的信息，只是对“药用价值”的解释和发挥，所以“此外还发现”是冗词。

经过分析，原文便可整理如下：

健康茶在我国有着相当久远的历史，现代科学研究发现茶叶又有不少新的药用价值，茶叶与某些天然植物药材配伍，可以发挥显著的疗效。见译文2。

整理后的原文也还是有不必要的形合成分，比如“天然植物”。一般来说人工植物是摆设，供观赏，不入药，所以“天然”不必对应地译作 natural。再如 efficacious…effects 是同源词重复，可用 efficacy 一词代替。译文经过再次整理后大概更容易理解一些了。见译文3。译文3囊括了原文的全部信息，但是篇幅不足译文1的一半。

任何人要获得新知识，途径只是一条，那便是“学”，向具有这门知识的人学，向记有这门知识的书本学。

〖译文1〗There is only one way for anyone to acquire new knowledge, and that is “learning,” from those who are versed in it, and from books that record it.[21]

〖译文2〗Knowledge can only be acquired by learning, from those who are versed in it, and from books that record it.

译文1准确无误，唯一需要修改的是把“learning,”的逗号放在引号外面。如果我们换一种思路，就可以看到本句原文有一些形合词语“任何人”“要”“新”“途径”“一条”可以不必译出。句中“只是一条”和“那便是”可以择一而取，也不必全译，见译文2。

穷亲戚和富亲戚来往，就是只能沾光，不会受害的事情。（柳青《创业史》）

〖译文1〗Contact between poor relatives and rich relatives could only bring profit to the poor. Nothing bad could come of it.[51]

〖译文2〗It could have everything to gain and nothing to lose for the poor relatives to contact rich ones.

原文“只能沾光，不会受害”，说得有点儿势利和直率。如果将“只能沾光”译作 bring profit，“不会受害”译作 Nothing bad could come of it，那就说得更直率更势利，超过了原文的分量，而且对谁“不会受害”也不清楚。因此，原文“只能沾光”和“不会受害”是同一事物的两面，不宜分说。

第五节　句子成分的简省和增益

在英译对汉中，减省和增益句子成分是我们常用的技巧之一。译文之所以对原文增删，是为了适应意合形合的转换。

劝君莫作守财虏，死去何曾带一文。(《增广贤文》)

〖译文 1〗It is better not to be a miser, even a penny after one's death is impossible to cling to.[51]

〖译文 2〗Never be a miser during our lifetime, as money is meaningless after we deceases.

〖译文 3〗During your lifetime, don't worship money, which is meaningless to you when you pass away.

〖译文 4〗Never spend your life worshiping money and end your days as a worthless miser.

原文是对人生和金钱的思考，虽然字面上只有“死”，但是我们不难对“生”的意义心领神会。而英译最好在字面上补足“生”。

这个工程项目正在按计划有条不紊地进行。

〖译文 1〗This project is processing as planned in good order.

〖译文 2〗This project is processing as planned.

译文 1 的 processing as planned 就是“按计划有条不紊地进行”，不必再增加 in good order。

并非在太空遨游的一切星球都可以称为行星。

〖译文 1〗Not all of the stars wandering in space can be called planets.

〖译文 2〗All wandering stars can not be called planets.

译文 1 中 in space 是冗词。换句话说，“在太空”我们根本就可以考虑不译出。

一些中国品牌以有竞争力的价位为后盾，已经挤进了国际市场，但同时也采用了其他战略。

〖译文 1〗Some Chinese brands have nudged into the international market on the back of competitive pricing, but have also utilized other strategies. [43]

〖译文 2〗Some Chinese companies have done more than nudging into the international market with their brands on the back of competitive pricing.

译文 1 可能在上半句遗漏了 not only 字样，故造成句意不通顺。从全句来看，"战略"应该比"竞争力""价位""挤进"等层次更高，它可以译作 strategy，但也能以意合之。

上海 20 世纪三四十年代电影佳作迭出，群星灿烂，具有与世界先进文化同步发展的深刻的现代性。

〖译文 1〗The Shanghai cinema in 1930s and 1940s has a large quantity of excellent films and well-known stars. Thus it displays a deep modernity of keeping a simultaneous development with the world's advanced culture. [41]

〖译文 2〗The Shanghai cinema in 1930s and 1940s boasts a large number of excellent talents and films, displaying the spirit of modernity and universality.

在汉语中，一个概念可以用自身的定义来解释，以突出作者的观点。"与世界先进文化同步发展"是"现代性"题中应有之义，如果按照原文直译，比较困难，如译文 1。可以考虑译作 modernity and universality（现代性和普世性），形成词语排偶（详见第六章介绍）。

同理，star（明星）不必用 well-known 修饰。modernity 不必用 deep 修饰。

译文 1 选择"电影"作句子主语，可以考虑采用 boast，be endowed with 之类作谓语。a quantity of 不能用来修饰人，只能修饰物，quantity（数量）是与 quality（质量）相对而言的。本句可以采用 a number of，它既能用来修饰人，又能修饰物。

你或许已是一位老师，或许将要成为一名老师。你可知道一名合格教师必须具备什么样的条件吗？

〖译文 1〗You may have already been a teacher, or you may become a teacher. But do you know what prerequisites are required of a qualified teacher? [6]

〖译文 2〗Perhaps you are or will be a teacher, but do you know what are the prerequisites of a qualified teacher?

〖译文 3〗Perhaps you are or will be a teacher, but do you know what is the most important part of a qualified teacher?

〖译文 4〗Perhaps you are or will be a teacher, but do you know what is the chief part of a teacher?

译文 1 的头一句有两个 teacher，以对应于原文的两个"老师"，根据减译原则,可以去掉一个。"已是一位老师，将要成为一名老师"可以合并起来,见译文2。

显而易见，译文1是译者通过查阅汉英词典"合格""条件"等词条后组织起来的。句中 prerequisite 一词源自拉丁语，意为"前提""先决条件"。该词由 pre（预先）+ requisite（要求）构成。其中 requisite 由 re（再）+ quisite（寻求）构成。一般来说 prerequisite 不能做 require 的宾语，require prerequisite 就相当于说"要求一个已经预先要求了的东西"。

而且，prerequisites 是一个大词，常用于比较正规、庄重的文体中。本句则可以用英语意合表达。见译文3。

最后，译文1、译文2和译文3中的 qualified 一词都可以去掉，译成译文4。

知识产权保护的环境营造有待于社会整体知识产权保护意识的提高。

〖译文1〗The construction of IPR protection environment builds upon the effective improvement of IPR protection awareness in the whole society. [63]

〖译文2〗The IPR protection environment should builds upon the effective improvement of IPR protection awareness in the whole society.

〖译文3〗Only by the awareness of the whole society can the IPR protection environment be effectively improved.

原文"环境营造"是一种比喻说法，从字面上对译是没有必要的。从逻辑学角度看,"知识产权保护意识"是"知识产权保护"的必要条件，但不是充要条件。亦即没有这种"意识"，绝对不行，有了"意识"，还要加上其他条件才行。译文1逐字直译，意思似乎有点过头了。

他虽然在飞机坠毁时幸免于难，结果却死在沙漠里。

〖译文1〗Although he survived the crash of the plane, he died in the desert in the end.

〖译文2〗He survived the crash only to die in the desert.

译文1译出了原文"虽然""结果"等形合连接词。译文2的 only 暗含这些意思。

词人者，不失其赤子之心者也。(王国维《人间词话》)

〖译文1〗Tz'u writers can be considered among those who have not lost their childlike heart. [10]

〖译文2〗A real lyricist could not have lost his childlike heart.

原文的两个"者"，就像数学方程式两边的公约数，可以约去。这样，我们就可以用单数的 lyricist 译出全句，同时，在前面加上 real。

第六节 打破常规，词义活用

词性转换是英汉互译中最常见的方法之一。词性转换体现了在忠实原文的基础上，突破原文的词性束缚，达成句式的转换。汉语倾向于动态，行文多用动词，英语静态，行文多用名词。我们这儿所谓词性的转换主要是指将汉语的动词转换成英语的名词。

The latest exhibitions, films, or plays are only a short bus ride away.

参观新展出的展览会，欣赏新上映的电影或新献演的戏剧，只要坐短途公共汽车就到了。

这个英语译例取自《新概念英语》，全句仅有一个动词 are，主语和表语都采用名词。译成汉语则采用大量的动词，包括“参观”“展出”“欣赏”“上映”“献演”“坐”。英译汉要补足这些动词，语句才能通顺。同样的道理，如果把这个汉语句子译回英语，这些动词就不必见诸字面了。

每按一次键将取消一个数字。

〖译文 1〗Every time you press a key will cancel a digit.

〖译文 2〗Each key press will cancel one digit.

原文有“按”“取消”两个动词，译文 1 是正确的，但是译者把两个动词全部译出，不得不补出“you”作主语，句式采用主从复合句。如果将“按”press 理解成名词，句式就成为简单句了。

不耻下问才能有学问。

〖译文 1〗Asking questions makes you learned.

〖译文 2〗A man becomes learned by asking questions.

〖译文 3〗Asking questions invites knowledge.

译文 1 无疑是正确的。译文 2 的意思是：“不耻下问就能有学问”。实际上一个人有学问除了不耻下问，还需要攻读和历练。译文 3 采用拟人手法，“有学问”用名词译出，这样，在译文中就不必添加 you 或 A man 等词，句式简单化了。

芙蓉镇街面不大。十几家铺子、几十户住家紧紧夹着一条青石板街。(古华《芙蓉镇》)

The main street of Hibiscus was not big. Paved with flagstones it was wedged between a dozen shops and a few scores of houses. (杨宪益译)

原文分两句。“街”在第一句中是主语，在第二句中是宾语，遥相呼应。译文也分两句。第一句 street 作主语，第二句用 it 指代，还是作主语，被动语态，使文句显得紧凑，流畅。

最值得称道的是，译文所下的 wedge 一词，译出“紧紧夹着”，译得出神入化，以一当十。所谓修辞就是在最恰当的地方使用最恰当的词汇，恐怕英美作家也不过如此。文章本天成，妙手偶得之，此之谓也。

译文中 wedge，“楔子”，名词，这儿活用作动词，意为“楔进，挤入”。名词用作动词是英语的一大特色。

意合打破常规，词义活用。形合用词准确，表达严谨。

词语在长期的应用中，词义会有所引申和偏移，经过变化后，与本义差别很大。有的可以词性活用，甚至临时发挥。

每个插座都有标记，说明应该插哪一根电线。

〚译文 1〛 Each socket is marked indicating it should be inserted by which cable.

〚译文 2〛 Each socket is marked for the appropriate cable.

医疗器械在一位病人用过之后必须消毒才能给另一位病人用。

〚译文 1〛 After medical instruments has been used by one patient, it must be sterilized before it can be used by another patient.

〚译文 2〛 Medical instruments must be sterilized between patients.

语言的意合有言简意赅的特点，有时达到四两拨千斤的程度。但是英语的形合，有时也可以表达得很简洁。译文 2 一个 between 取代了译文 1 的 after，has been used by one，before it can be used by another 和一个 patient，就是一个生动的实例。

译文 2 的单词数量是译文 1 的三分之一，篇幅缩水三分之二，但是原文的内容无任何脱落。

但一窝蜂的国际化造城运动将给城市建设带来致命伤。

〚译文 1〛 However, if they rush swarm to carry out an “internationalized” cities campaign, it will fatally damage the construction of cities. [65]

〚译文 2〛 However, if they hurriedly swarm to carry out an “internationalized” Cities campaign, it will fatally damage the construction of cities. [65]

〚译文 3〛 However, the “internationalization” boom among Chinese cities would fatally damage the construction of cities.

“一窝蜂的运动”英语可以用 boom 表示。这个词是拟声词，听起来好像“嘭”的一声响，非常形象地描绘人的活动一窝蜂，使事物迅速达到高潮，例如价格暴涨、营业激增、经济繁荣等等。甚至一窝蜂地生孩子都可以是 baby boom。上海“洋泾浜”英语说某事物受人追捧，势头蓬勃，就说它“起蓬头”了。这个说法可能起源于此吧。

当前国际产业分工格局呈现出服务贸易与商品贸易并重、产业内和产品内垂直分工快速发展和发达国家主导的特点。

〖译文 1〗The current international division of labor shows these characteristics: service trade is balanced with commodity trade; intra-industry specialization and intra-product specialization grow fast; and the advanced countries are pivotal and predominated.[109]

〖译文 2〗The spectrum of the current global industries is characterized by the parallelism of service trade with commodity trade, the fast increasing specializations of intra-industry and intra-products, and the predominance of the advanced countries.

译文 1 的 division of labor，分工，系指大家协商，根据各自的专业特长，各尽所能，分头负责，也可指“劳务部门”。原文的“产业分工”可译作 distribution of industries，“产业的分布”，或 category of industries，“产业的门类”，或 spectrum of industries，“产业的谱系”。

市场经济下的公平竞争是促进经济繁荣的重要因素，但竞争过了头，其负面影响就不容忽视。

〖译文 1〗In the market economy, the crucial factor for prosperity is fair competition. But if the competition spins out of control, the negative effects must not be overlooked.（上海交通大学英语专业 2004 年研究生入学试题参考答案）[2,6]

〖译文 2〗Although fair competition is the catalyst for a big boom in market economy, overheated competition should not be neglected for its negative consequences.

〖译文 3〗Although fair competition fuels a big boom in market economy, overheated competition should not be neglected for its negative consequences.

〖译文 4〗Although fair competition acts as engine of a big boom in market economy, overheated competition should not be neglected for its negative consequences.

译文 2 中，促进经济繁荣的“重要因素”可以用 catalyst（催化剂）一词译出，它表示“催熟了经济繁荣”。也可以用 fuel（燃料）一词作谓语动词，表示“为经济繁荣提供燃料”。或者说成 acts as engine of（起发动机作用）。总之，英语在经济学文本中使用科技术语司空见惯，不足为奇。

下坡顺滑，速度加快，需要全神贯注。（曲波《林海雪原》）

〖译文1〗Traveling downhill, their pace was rapid and required complete mental concentration.[51]

〖译文2〗Traveling downhill with more rapid pace required their all eyes.

表示“需要某人全神贯注”英语可以用 to require one's all eyes 表达。

世界上第三代博物馆是充满全新理念的博物馆。在这里，观众可以自己动手操作，自己细心观察。

〖译文1〗The third-generation museums in the world are those designed with new concepts. In such museums, visitors can operate with their own hands and observe with their own eyes.（2000年全国高校英语专业八级考试汉译英试题参考译文）[27,61,62]

〖译文2〗The third-generation museums are devised with new concepts. Instead of "hands-off", such museums encourage visitors to be hands-on as well as eyes-on.

世界上任何博物馆最常见的公共标识语大约是“请勿动手”和“hands-off”。因为人手上的汗渍和污秽对展品有腐蚀作用。但是一些青少年体验型博物馆，即如例句所说的第三代博物馆则有所不同，它将真品束之高阁，代之以高仿真的复制品，鼓励观众亲手操作。于是“欢迎动手”取代了“请勿动手”。“hands-on”仿“hands-off”应运而生。译文2的 eyes-on 则仿 hands-on，其意义一目了然。

第六章 逻辑类比排偶，美学修辞排偶

第一节 对仗、排偶与 parallelism

人是美的杰作，美的精华。人体具有匀称、和谐、庄严的美。除了人，大多数动物和植物都具有与人体一样的对称美。这种美对人类审美认识和审美趣味的影响就是对称艺术美。无论在东方在西方，人类的许多建筑、家具、服饰、器皿都取对称形态。语言艺术作为美的反映形态也不例外。汉语的对仗和英语的排偶就是这种艺术美的体现。

汉语的对仗和英语的排偶，用英语说都是 parallelism。该词派生于 parallel。Parallel = alongside one another，意为“相互沿着边”，即“平行”，源自希腊语。

汉语的 parallelism 和英语的 parallelism 可以类比，但是要分为几种情况。一是汉语完全严格对称的，多见于古代汉语的对仗骈俪诗文。英语的排偶不完全，不严格，只是大致对应。

一粥一饭，当思来处不易。半丝半缕，恒念物力维艰。

〖译文 1〗The growing of rice and of grain / Think on whenever you dine; Remember how silk is obtained / Which keeps you warm and looks fine. ❶

〖译文 2〗Remember that every bowl of rice and porridge has not been got easily. Be ever mindful that each cotton or silk garment has taken much material and labor to make. [17]

〖译文 3〗Every grain of rice or corn should be considered as the result of

---

❶ http：//www. exam8. com。

toil. Each string of cotton or silk should be regarded as precious resource.

无论译文1、译文2，还是译文3，只是力图在内容忠实的基础上，做到形式上、风格上的对应。

二是现代汉语句子成分部分对称，英语也部分对称。

这家公司铺天盖地的广告只开花，不结果。

〖译文1〗This company's overspread advertisement blossoms but does not bear fruits.

〖译文2〗This company's overspread advertisement blossoms but never bears.

译文1中，bear可以是及物动词，譬如bear apples（结出苹果），也可以是非及物动词，作“结出果实”解，后面不跟宾语。所以译文1后面的fruits是冗词。

译文1不是语法问题，是修辞问题。译文2删除了fruits后，使blossoms和bears对称，两词押头韵，取得结构严谨，音韵和谐的效果。与此相似，汉语原文“只开花，不结果”也是一种平行对称的结构。

它既是排偶句，也是比喻句，而且是隐喻。它将公司比做一棵树，广告投入的人力物力好比施肥浇水，广告的炒作和造势好比开花，公司的销售业绩好比结果。这些都不难理解，所以在英汉互译中都没有必要将喻体还原本体。

西方文化的机械自然观认为整体可以拆分为独立的部分，将人类的观察与世界分隔开来，譬如亚里士多德提出的形式逻辑同一律、矛盾律和排中律，以及三段论式的推理方法，其影响表现在西方人观察问题非此即彼的思维方式和有限的相对的局部的对称审美认识上。英语也追求对称的整饬美，然而这种对称往往是“单边主义”的。我们很难在英语典籍中，找到排偶句的主谓宾完全不相同，甚至没有一词重复的例句。因此，第三种情况是：汉语绝大多数是二项式，英语可以是多项式。

Courage in excess becomes foolhardiness, affection weakness, thrift avarice. (Francis Bacon)

勇敢过度，即成蛮勇；感情过度，即成溺爱；俭约过度，即成贪婪。(钱歌川译)

上面句子形式对仗，无一词重复，但是这又可以看作是一个省略句，省略了相同部分in excess becomes。译成汉语就必须按现代汉语习惯补足、重复省略部分“即成”，以求形成整个译文词语的排比，节奏的明快。

parallelism，或者对仗、排偶，是修辞中一个很大的课题。这个课题既关涉语言表达能力的培养，又是对语言形式美的追求，所以我们强调它既是重点，又是难点，以至于不得不专门辟出一章篇幅加以详解。在汉译英中，我们要将原文优美的对仗转换成译文晓畅的排偶，则是重点中的重点，难点中的难点。

除此之外，我们还观察到英语汉语都有在对称中词语重复的现象，例如下面二例：

Better to know everything of something than something of everything. (Francis Bacon)

知识泛而陋，不如少而精。

上例是 everything of something 与 something of everything 的完全对称，在重复中显示文人对文字纯熟的把玩。

子与我衣，我活也，我与子衣，子活也。(《吕氏春秋》)

〖译文 1〗If you give me your clothes, I will survive. If I give you my clothes, you will survive.

〖译文 2〗If you give me your clothes, I will survive, and vice versa.

本句汉语原文前半部分与后半部分完全对称，英译可以用省略对应，见译文 2，其中 vice versa 相当于汉语的“反之亦然”。

第二节 汉语对仗的英译

有的汉语的对仗不一定能够英译成排偶。

话说古时候有一位妇女触犯了刑律，主审官员在案牍上写道：“情有可原，法无可逭。”这时恰有一位绍兴师爷动了恻隐之心，便在报呈上司的文件中把这个结论的两句话掉一个头，改为“法无可逭，情有可原”。经他这么轻轻一改，疑犯得到了从轻处罚。

这句话大概可以译作：

法无可逭，情有可原

〖译文 1〗commiserable though unpardonable

〖译文 2〗Though she is guilty in sight of the law, her conduct should not be condemned on moral grounds.

译文 1 的句意是：虽不可原宥，却值得怜悯。译文 2 的句意是：尽管她在法律上是有罪的，但她的行为不应该在道德上受到谴责。

这两句译文丧失了原文的词序对上司量刑的心理暗示作用。汉语对仗的词序作用由此可见一斑。

曹操名为汉相，实为汉贼！

〖译文1〗 Although Cao Cao acts in the name of Prime Minister of the Han court, he is in fact a traitor of the Han Dynasty. [14]

〖译文2〗 Cao Cao is a traitor rather than a Prime Minister of the Han court.

〖译文3〗 Cao Cao is really the traitor in the name of Prime Minister of the Han court.

原话是影视剧中的周瑜说的，而影视剧则根据《三国演义》《三国志》《资治通鉴》改编。"名为汉相"，揭露曹的伪装，"实为汉贼"，指出他的真相，所以本句可以不译作主从复合句，而译作简单句，可以不译作排偶句，而在英语句子内部建立起对称关系。

早知今日，何必当初。

〖译文1〗 If it has to be like this now, it's a pity it was ever like it in the beginning. [1,64]

〖译文2〗 If I had only known beforehand what will happen today I would have repented (of…) before this. [1]

〖译文3〗 If I'd known then what was going to happen, I wouldn't have acted as I did. [1]

〖译文4〗 If you had known this day must come you would have repented long since of your evildoing. [1]

〖译文5〗 If I had known it would come to this, I would have act differently. [57]

〖译文6〗 Had I known to have this day, I would not have done it before. [64]

〖译文7〗 If I'd known what was going to happen, I wouldn't have done as I did. [64]

原文是地地道道的中国话，句子没有主语，主语随语境而定，不言自明。英译必须补足 I，we，you 之类的主语。

我们建议做如下修改：

〖译文8〗 If only I had known what happens today!

〖译文9〗 If only I had known!

英语短语 if only 带有丰富的感情色彩，表示"但愿……""要是……就好了”“还不如从来就这样”“早就应该如此”。只要深刻理解它的含义，这个句子就可以译得非常简洁。

下面援引一段原文：

After the armies of Imperial Germany invaded Belgium in August 1914, launching one of the most destructive and futile conflicts in history, Prince von Bulow asked German chancellor why all the diplomatic steps taken to avoid the war had failed. “At last I (Bulow) said to him: ‘Well, tell me, at least, how it all happened.’ He raised his long, thin arms to heaven and answered in a dull exhausted voice: ‘Oh—If I only knew.’”

德意志帝国军队于1914年入侵比利时，发动了一场人类史上最残酷、最无聊的冲突。事后，比洛王公询问德国总理，为何避免战争的外交努力全部都告失败。“最后，我（比洛）问他：‘好吧，你总得告诉我，这一切是怎么发生的。’他向上苍举起细长的双臂，声嘶力竭地回答：‘啊，我早知道就好了。’”

好事不出门，恶事传千里。

〖译文1〗Good deeds are never heard of outside the door, but bad deeds are proclaimed for three hundred miles.

〖译文2〗Good deeds always stay indoors, while scandals travel a thousand li.

〖译文3〗Good works most frequently remain hidden, while evil deeds become known at a distance of a thousand li.

〖译文4〗Honor goes on crutches while discredit flies apace.

〖译文5〗Misdeeds always receive the maximum publicity, while good deeds are relegated to obscurity.

〖译文6〗News of good works seldom go beyond the threshold of the house, but reports of evil deeds are quickly circulated for a thousand miles around. [71]

原文十个字，两句话，其含义犹如小葱拌豆腐，一清二白。道出了人言啧啧，众口铄金的炎凉世态，而且大多数国人或许都有过这种人生体验。从语言艺术的角度看，其中似乎并没有多少值得分析的地方。也许正因为如此，众多的英译显得有些轻率，其中大多数都没有分析和提取主要信息，尽管采用了主从复合句，但是重点不突出，带有浓重的翻译腔。

上列译文的句意分别为：

译文1：好的行为从不被门外人听到，但是坏的行为却被宣布到了三百英里之外。

译文2：好的行为老是待在室内，而丑闻却旅行了一千里。

译文3：好的作品最为频繁地被隐藏起来，而坏的行为却在一千里的距离外为人所知。

译文4：荣誉拄着拐杖蹒跚而行，而丢脸的事漫天飞舞。

译文5：不端行为往往最为引人注目，而良好行为则归于默默无闻。

译文6：良好行为的消息很少跨过门槛，但是罪恶行径的报道很快传播到一千英里的方圆之内。

请看例句：

A lie can be halfway round the world before the truth has got its boots on.

真理未及穿上靴子，谎言却跑遍了半个世界。

这是一个用连接词before连接的主从句，主次分明，“谎言跑遍了半个世界”作为主要信息放在主句位置，“真理未及穿上靴子”作为次要信息放在从句位置。如果套用这个句型，“好事不出门，恶事传千里”可以译得简洁清晰：

〖译文7〗A scandal can be halfway round the world before a good deed has got known to someone else.

好的行为未及为人所知，丑闻却跑遍了半个世界。

如果用次主—主次转换原理来分析一下，我们便可以发现：在句法结构上，“好事不出门”是次要信息，是陪衬；“恶事传千里”是主要信息，是重点。在语意内含上，“好事不出门”，好事不为外人所知，其后果顶多是做好事者没有得到应有的赞扬和鼓励；“恶事传千里”，恶事流传开来的后果却不堪设想，当事人颜面丢尽，名誉扫地，弄得不好夫妻会闹离婚，官员会遭查办，总统会被弹劾。经过这么一番分析之后，我们可以重新翻译如下：

〖译文8〗A scandal can travel far away before a good deed has got known to other people.

在良好行为被人知晓之前，丑闻可以旅行得很远。

让我们再看一句中国通俗小说很常见的对仗句。

天有不测风云，人有旦夕祸福。

〖译文1〗In nature there are unexpected storms and in life unpredictable vicissitudes.[1]

〖译文2〗Unforeseen, into storm can nature burst; overnight, a man may have his fortune reversed.[1]

〖译文3〗Storms gather without warning in nature, and bad luck befalls men overnight.[1]

〖译文4〗Sudden storms spring up in nature and men's fortune may change overnight.[1]

〖译文5〗Human fortunes are unpredictable as the weather.[1]

〖译文6〗The unexpected always happens.[1]

〖译文7〗The weather and human life are both unpredictable.[100]

上列译文的句意分别为：

译文1：大自然有不可预期的暴风雨，人生有不可预料的变迁。

译文2：大自然会不可预测地突发暴风雨，人的命运会在一夜之间突遭逆转。

译文3：大自然没有征兆暴风雨集结了，一个晚上厄运降临到人们头上。

译文4：暴风雨突然降临于大自然，人们的命运也会一夜之间改变。

译文5：人的命运犹如天气变化莫测。

译文6：料想不到的事总是发生。

译文7：天气和人生都是不可预测的。

原文采用汉语谚语和诗歌中常见的比兴手法，以天象喻人事。译文1、译文2很好地表达了这样一种比喻。译文3写一种情景，而不是人生感悟。译文4乍看之下，好像是一部惊悚小说的开头。译文5突破原文的形式，没有逐字直译，但是仍然忠实于原文。唯有一个小瑕疵是：原文小说家关心的并不是全人类的前途，而是个人的命运，所以译文开头的Human最好改为Man's。译文6稍稍背叛了原文，比如某人的钱包失而复得，我们可以说“料想不到的事总是发生”，但不是“旦夕祸福”。译文7大大背叛了原文，可能译者不知道天气和人生都是可以预测的，从字面上看译文7有强调天气不可预测的暗示。

上有天堂，下有苏杭。

〖译文1〗There is Paradise above and Suzhou and Hangzhou below.[1]

〖译文2〗There is Paradise in heaven whereas on earth are Suzhou and Hangzhou. The beauty of Hangzhou is concentrated in the beauty of the West Lake.(上有天堂，下有苏杭。杭州之美在西湖。)[7]

〖译文3〗In heaven there is paradise, On earth Hangzhou and Suzhou.[110]

〖译文4〗In the sky, the best is heaven, on the earth, the best are Suzhou and Hangzhou.[13]

〖译文5〗Above is paradise, below is Suzhou and Hangzhou.[13]

〖译文6〗Suzhou and Hangzhou are Paradise on earth.

“上有天堂，下有苏杭”是传诵千古的名句。也许我们每个中国人从人生识字起，就熟悉这个句子了，它几乎积淀成了一代代中国人先入为主的思维范式，要摆脱是不容易的。但问题是，在不具备这种思维范式的西方人看来，上有“天堂”，下有的应是“地狱”。英语把地狱也称作 the place below。

我们无法证实个别西方人有没有这样的理解偏差。译文 1 逐词直译，很可能造成误解。译文 2 听起来好像一位有神论者对我们说：“我们头顶上有一座天堂，您瞧，我们人间不也有苏州杭州吗?”译文 3 的情况同译文 1，而且英语单词大小写有误。译文 4 既保留了对仗形式，又不造成误解。译文 5 同译文 1。

由此可见，汉语的对仗有时可以不译成英语的排偶，于是我们试着撰写了译文 6。

劳心者治人，劳力者治于人。

〖译文 1〗 Those who work with their minds rule others; those who work with their strength are ruled by others. [111]

〖译文 2〗 Those who work with brains rule and those who work with their brawn are ruled.

译文 1 上半句的 Those who work with their minds 可以理解为“劳动脑力者”，也可以理解为“努力用心工作的人”；下半句的 strength 可以理解为“力量”，也可以理解为“长处”“强项”，或因人数优势而形成的权力。

译文 2 简洁无歧义，其中 brain 和 brawn 是亮点。

炮炙虽繁必不敢省人工，品味虽贵必不敢减物力。

〖译文 1〗 making the best medicines, irrespective of the cost of materials and time consumed. [55]

〖译文 2〗 No processing too laborious, no material too expensive.

原文系北京同仁堂公司的宣传标语，是其制药宗旨。译文 1 有三个问题：一是以“形合”译“形合”，结果貌合神离；二是原文对仗工整的艺术效果丧失殆尽；三是广告用语采用 best 可能会引起争议，而且不留余地，给人言过其实之感。译文 2 采用意合，用 no + too 译出可收以少胜多，简约醒目之效。

皮掌之厚无以复加，利润之薄无以复减。

〖译文 1〗 The leather shoes made here are thick enough; the profit that's attained is slight enough. [21,112]

〖译文 2〗 No leather too thick, no profit too small.

这是上海某皮鞋商店的广告词。这副对联的横批是“天下第一厚皮”，颇具幽默感。译文 1 保留了原文的对仗，但是逐字直译，反而词不达意。shoes 用 thick 来修饰，搭配不当。在语义忠实于原文的基础上，译文应该尽可能在形式上对称，使原文译文的整饬美相得益彰。

外国也包装，也走人情，也行贿，但以包装作欺蒙则我们传统中早有提示：金玉其外，败絮其中。

〖译文 1〗People in foreign countries are also particular about packaging, and also bribe with gifts, but we have a longer tradition of hoodwinking customers by means of packaging, as witness the ancient Chinese saying, "gold and jade without, rubbish within."[113]

〖译文 2〗There are also worldly wisdom, hypocrisy, or even bribery among people outside China, but we have a longer tradition of hoodwinking customers by means of packaging, as witness the ancient Chinese saying, "roselike without, rubbish within."

本句的"金玉"当然可以译作 gold and jade，译文 2 根据内含意义译作 roselike。

人要脸，树要皮。

〖译文 1〗"Face" is as important to man as the bark is to the tree.[1]

〖译文 2〗"Face" to man is what bark is to the tree.

从表面看，原文是一个对仗工整的并列句，实际上是一个含偏正关系的比喻句，"人要脸"是本体，"树要皮"是喻体。这也不能刻板的英译成排偶句。

有时候，如果在句式上不译作英语排偶句，应该尽可能在译文句子内部建立对称关系。

第三节 逻辑类比对称

有一种说法，似乎汉语逻辑混乱，英语逻辑严密。这不符合事实。我们还没有找到哪个正确的规范的汉语句子不讲逻辑。但是汉语的逻辑具有朦胧性、模糊性、随意性、暗示性，却是不争的事实。我们这儿所讲的逻辑类比对称，系指词语所包含的概念，必须在逻辑上对应。英译必须比汉语在逻辑上更清晰，更精确。

休闲体育的兴起及其社会意义

〖译文 1〗rising of leisure sports in China and its significance[114]

〖译文 2〗the rise and significance of leisure sports in China

〖译文 3〗the rise and its significance of leisure sports in China

原文是个局部对称的短语，亦即“兴起”和“意义”对称，共同被“休闲体育”统领。英译可以按原文的结构，将 rising 和 significance 对称，共同被 leisure sports 统领。译文 1 却将对称的双方放在一头一尾，所以不合逻辑。而且它的物主代词 its，究竟指代它前面的 rising，sports，还是 China？不明确。

越南有着摄人心魄的景色，连绵的群山和美丽的海滩。

〖译文 1〗Vietnam is a place of breathtaking scenery, wild mountains and idyllic beaches.[115]

〖译文 2〗Vietnam is a place of breathtaking scenery, with wild mountains and idyllic beaches.

“景色”在逻辑上包孕了“群山”和“海滩”，亦即“景色”是由“群山”和“海滩”等组成，因此三者不是并列关系，不能用 and 或 or 连接。“景色”倒是可以与原文后面提到的“建筑”和“美食”并列。

国家财政的重点，应放在推动农村经济和西部开发，以及东北老工业基地改造上。

〖译文 1〗State financing will focus on stimulating the rural economy, China's western region and the old industrial base in the northeast.[116]

〖译文 2〗State financing will focus on stimulating the economies of the rural area, western region, and the northeast old industrial base.

译文 1 试图组成英语排偶句，可惜排偶的句子成分无法对举。句子宾语是 the rural economy, China's western region and the old industrial base in the northeast（农村经济，中国的西部地区和东北老工业基地），三者逻辑关系混乱。经整理后我们可以得到译文 2。

天塔城环境优雅，交通便利。

〖译文 1〗Environment around Sky Tower City is elegant and the traffic is convinent.[117]

〖译文 2〗Sky Tower City is surrounded by favorable environment and traffic network.

原文用“环境优雅”和“交通便利”两个主谓结构对称，是常见的汉语对仗结构。译文 1 大概受汉语“对对子”的影响，译成全对称，是误译。

另外，译文不能照搬词典将“优雅”译作 elegant。因为 elegant，graceful 等只能修饰人或与人有关的事物，例如 elegant in taste（speech，dress，manner）（优雅的趣味、谈吐、服饰、举止）。本句原文“优雅”系“幽雅”之误，译文

1 中 convinent 系 convenient 之误。“环境幽雅”可以译作 have（或 be surrounded by）favorable（有利的），beautiful（美丽的），quiet（宁静的），cordial（亲切的）environment。为了让这个形容词与“交通”共享，就选择 favorable 吧。

……传递出的上述三个信号，既有高等教育本身的问题，也有教育管理决策部门的问题，还有大学生自身存在问题。

〖译文 1〗The above signals sent by the survey concern the problem of higher education, educational management and the students themselves.[13,118]

〖译文 2〗The survey casts light on problems of the higher education system and management and the students themselves.

〖译文 3〗The survey throws light upon problems of both the system and management of higher education, and the students themselves.

译文 1 的 higher education（高等教育），只能与 elementary education（初等教育）、specialized（专业教育）等对应。educational management（教育管理部门），只能与 educational establishment（教育机构设置）、educational policy（教育方针政策）等对应。因此它们本身不能构成英语句子中的排偶关系。可以在 higher education（高等教育）中增添 system（体制）一词，使之与 management（管理）对应。至于 students（大学生），属于受教育者，是可以与 system（体制）、management（管理）这些教育者对应的，但是要用定冠词 the 将两者分开。

……在全国范围内开展了大规模的污染防治和生态环境保护。

〖译文 1〗It will be carried out across the country with large-scale measures for pollution prevention and control as well as ecological environmental protection.[110]

〖译文 2〗Large-scale measures will be carried out across the country to control and prevent pollution, and to protect ecological environment.

It 作形式主语可以代替句子中的不定式、动名词或名词分句等。译文 1 在句子中除了几个介词短语外，找不到任何不定式、动名词或名词分句，所以句子不能成立。解决办法是设立一个主语。我们知道，用 as well as 可以连接英语排偶的句子成分，但是在 A as well as B 句型中，A 得到了强调和突出，而本句原文“污染防治”和“生态保护”同样重要，如果存在倚轻倚重关系的话，也应该是后者更重要。所以两者只能用 and 连接。

为保护海洋环境，促进海洋经济发展，必须提高对海洋环境监测的认识，增加投入，加强“热点”海域的监测，减少海洋的损失，加强海洋生物监测，避免潜伏的海洋灾害发生。

〖译文 1〗In order to promote the development of sustainable marine economy and conserve marine environment, we should pay great attention to reinforcing awareness of marine environmental monitoring, increasing investment and strengthening the monitoring in "hot spots" as well as biological monitoring to avoid marine calamity.[119]

〖译文 2〗In order to conserve marine environment and develop marine economy, we should pay great attention to marine environmental monitoring, increase investment and strengthen the "hot spots" monitoring as well as biological monitoring to avoid marine calamity.

译文 1 对原文有所调整和发挥，译文 2 在译文 1 句式的基础上再作调整，试图再现原文的对称结构。

荀子……战国后期赵国人，生卒年月无考。

〖译文 1〗A native of the state of Zhao in the later years of the Warring States period, his dates are still subjects for debate.[77]

〖译文 2〗His birthplace was the state of Zhao of the later Warring States period, but his exact dates of birth and death remained to be verified.

译文 1 前半部分是一个独立结构，指的是"人"，a native。后半部分的主语是"日期"，dates。两者不是一回事，没有逻辑联系，句子不能成立。解决办法是将两回事分开来说，中间用连接词连接起来。

老聃的思想在春秋末年已形成，成书和传播可能在战国前期。

〖译文 1〗The thought of Laozi took shape possibly in the later years of the Spring and Autumn Period, but the book was written down and circulated in the early years of the Warring States Period.[56]

〖译文 2〗Laozi probably fermented his thought in the later Spring and Autumn Period, and wrote his book and had it circulated in the early Warring States Period.

严格地说，原文有语病。在此种情况下"老聃思想的形成"英译最好以"老聃"作主语，或许可以弥补，至少可以采用一个主语将译文捏成一个句子。"形成"在汉英词典中固然作 take shape 或 form 解，但是它们不宜和 thought（思想）搭配。而且本句前后两部分并不形成转折关系，所以不能用 but 连接，可以用 and 连接。

本文首先讨论了人文学科为什么必须有批评研究，其次指出翻译批评与翻译批评学的区别。

〖译文1〗This paper first discusses the necessity of criticism for the disciplines in humanities, then it points out the differences between practical translation criticism and theory of translation criticism.[120]

〖译文2〗This paper firstly looks into the necessity of criticism for the disciplines in humanities, then points out the difference between the practice and theory of translation criticism.

译文2将谓语动词look into和point out对称，将宾语practice和theory对称，of translation criticism作共同修饰语。

我国目前正在修订专利法和商标法，拟议要修订的许多内容都要进一步向国际标准和国际化靠拢；有的即使准备分两步甚至三步走，那也是为了做好协调工作，稳妥前进，避免欲速则不达。

〖译文1〗China is at present revising its Patent Law and Trademark Law, and many of the contents recommended for version are coming closer to international standards and internationalization; in respect of some other contents, although preparation are being made to revise them in two or even three steps, it is only for the sake of accomplishing the task of harmonization properly, ensuring steady progress and avoiding the hazard of "more haste, less speed".[33]

〖译文2〗China is at present revising its Patent Law and Trademark Law, and many of the contents recommended for version are coming closer to international standards and practices; in respect of some other contents, preparation are being made to revise them in two or even three steps to make them more harmonious, ensuring steady progress and avoiding casual negligence.

本句的"国际标准"和"国际化"不属逻辑并列关系，而是包孕关系。译文1按字面直译，使连接词and两边的句子成分不对等。"国际标准和国际化"可以译作：internationalization including international standards（包括国际标准在内的国际化）。但是这与译文1一样，同时出现international和internationalization，也不妥。可将"国际化"译作international practices（国际惯例），使standards（标准）和practices（惯例）并立，这样同时从理论和实践两方面概括了"国际化"。

原文"即使"属于句子连接符号，删除后句子意义不改，所以是个冗词。

一国法律之制订，当然要考虑社会关系和社会影响的协调，但是本文的"做好协调工作"主要是指法律条文本身的协调。因此译文2译作：to make them more harmonious，使之与to revise them in two or even three steps排偶。

"欲速则不达"在汉英词典上确实注为 more haste, less speed。但是本句可以按照作者的真实思想，译作"出现不应有的疏忽或疏漏之处"。如译文 2 将"避免欲速则不达"译作 avoiding casual negligence，这样可以与前面的"稳妥前进" ensuring steady progress 形成排偶。

随着中国经济最近几年的迅猛发展，中国的外贸在外贸政策、开放政策和外贸体制几个方面，开始实行许多符合实际的、灵活的新措施。

〖译文 1〗With the rapid growth of China's economy in recent years, China's foreign trade has begun a number of new pragmatic and flexible practices in foreign trade policy, open door policy and foreign trade system.[40]

〖译文 2〗With the rapid growth of economy in recent years, China has introduced a number of more pragmatic, flexible and open practices in her foreign trade policy and system.

这是一个用"外贸"将主体"中国"包裹起来的句式。"中国的外贸……开始实行……"译成英语要换成"中国……开始实行……"，所以译文 1 中第一个 foreign trade 和它前面的's 是冗词。China 成了全句的主语后，也理所当然地成了介词短语的逻辑主语，所以第一个 China's 也是冗词。"开放政策"如果系指我国的改革开放，那么它统领"外贸政策"。如果"开放政策"系指外贸政策的开放，那么它从属于"外贸政策"。所以它与"外贸政策"不属于并列关系，"开放"必须放开，换到别的位置上。

今后，我们要继续坚持以人为本的管理思想，强化企业文化建设，塑造与弘扬有利于社会主义商品经济发展的企业精神、价值观念、经营哲学和行为规范。

〖译文 1〗In the future, we should stick to the human-oriented management, strengthen the cultivation of enterprise culture and foster as well as advocate the enterprise spirit, values, management philosophy and code of conduct, which would be helpful to the development of socialist market economy.（上海对外贸易学院英语专业 2002 年研究生入学试题参考答案）[6,121]

〖译文 2〗From now on, we should maintain the human-oriented management, cultivate the enterprise culture, including spiritual values, company identifications, and behavior patterns in conformation to the socialist market economy.

原文所谈的"管理思想""企业文化""企业精神""价值观念""经营哲学""行为规范"之类，有的属于逻辑并列，有的属于包孕，或重叠关系，不能一股脑并列。因此修改后的译文 2 将"精神价值""企业形象""行为模式"按由内向外的顺序从属于"企业文化"。

在当今激烈竞争的世界上，只有以质取胜和改善售前售后服务才能行得通。

〖译文 1〗 Now in the highly competitive world the concepts of "fine quality or else no export" and "good service before and after sales" should be used to increase the added value on export commodities. ❶

〖译文 2〗 Now, in the highly competitive world the concepts of "fine quality or else no export" and "good service before and after sales" should be the order of the day.

〖译文 3〗 In this worldwide keen competition, only prime quality and perfect service will be infallible.

〖译文 4〗 In this worldwide keen competition, only will prime quality and perfect service get you to anywhere.

本句可以用"以质取胜"和"改善售前售后服务"对称。

作为最早生产空调器厂家，所有的关键设备及先进的生产工艺均从美国飞歌公司引进。

〖译文 1〗 As the earliest manufacturer of air conditioners, all the key equipment and advanced manufacturing techniques are introduced from Philco International Company of the U. S. A. [68]

〖译文 2〗 As one of the earliest manufacturers of air conditioners, this company is the first to introduce the key equipment and techniques from Philco International Company of the U. S. A.

原文在句首省略了主语"我厂"字样，译文 1 照此办理，结果主句主语与前面介词短语的逻辑主语不一致，故造成语病，亦即介词短语说的是"生产厂家"，主句说的却是"设备工艺"。为了照顾"最早"和"先进"的逻辑联系，主句中可增添 the first 一词，以便与前面的 the earliest 对称。

学校（上海外国语大学）积极开展学术交流与合作，与 30 多个国家和地区的 110 多所著名大学建立了合作关系。

〖译文 1〗 SISU maintains close academic and exchange relations with universities overseas. So far, it has established collaborative relationship with more than 110 universities in over 30 countries and regions. ❷

---

❶ http：//www. mofcom. gov. cn。

❷ http：//www. shisu. edu. cn。

〖译文 2〗So far SISU has collaborated with more than 110 universities from some 30 countries or regions maintaining close academic exchange relations with them.

逻辑对称涉及连接词的使用。在译文 1 中，形容词 academic 和 exchange 不能用 and 连接起来。用 and，or 或 as well as 等连接是有条件的，必须两个形容词属逻辑并列关系。比如：

a pretty young girl（一个年轻漂亮的女孩）不能说成：

a pretty and young girl

我们可以说：

a tall and slim girl（一个高挑、苗条的女孩）

因为 tall、slim 逻辑并列。也可以说：

close academic and economic relations（密切的学术和经济关系）

其中 academic，economic 逻辑并列。

中国古代散文是优秀的中国古代文学和文化的一个重要组成部分。

〖译文 1〗Ancient Chinese prose constitutes an important component part of the the splendid ancient Chinese literature and culture.[14]

〖译文 2〗Ancient Chinese prose is an important component of the the splendid ancient Chinese literature.

译文 1 的 component 是机器、结构或系统中的“组成部分”。part 是机器或结构的“零部件”。component = part，相互不能构成修饰关系。

Constitute，“构成”，它的前面应该是构成的零部件，后面是完整的构成产物。例如：

Ancient Chinese prose，poet，novel，drama constitute the the ancient Chinese Literature.

中国古代散文、诗歌、小说、戏剧构成了中国古代文学。

但是不能说“某物”constitute“另一物的组成部分”。

另外，literature and culture 的并列关系不存在，两者是包孕关系。所以 literature 后面的 and culture 应该删除。不谈文化，文化也脱不了关系。

大学的研究所才是初步研究学问的所在，在这里做学问也只能算是粗涉藩篱，注重的是研究学问的方法与实习。

〖译文 1〗Research done in the university is only the most preliminary stage of study and the first attempt at conducting research and the emphasis is on the methodology and practice of research.（南开大学英语专业 2004 年研究生入学试题参考答案）[6,122]

〖译文 2〗 The research institute of a university, however, is the place for preliminary scholarship. But even there you get only the first taste of learning and the emphasis is on the methodology and practice of research.[59]

〖译文 3〗 Even in the research institute of a university, students begin to cross the threshold of research work there with the emphasis on the methodology and practice.

首先，原文有语病。“粗涉”为“初涉”之误。“藩篱”可以比做“限制条件”或“屏障”，不能作“登堂入室”之喻，因此“粗涉藩篱”可以改为“初登堂奥”。

其次，译文 1 没有将原文的信息加以整理，而是按原文语序逐字直译，故显得随意、凌乱。译文 2 是准确的。译文 3 吸取译文 2 的优点，再加整理。

第四节 美学修辞对称

所谓美学修辞对称系指在符合逻辑的前提下，追求译文形、义、音的整饬美。这比单纯的逻辑对称要求更高，做好了，我们不但能够更好地传达原文的美感，我们的表达也更精确，更容易为读者接受。

上海有些小市民精明而不聪明。

〖译文 1〗 Some urban petty bourgeois in Shanghai are shrewd but not intelligent.

〖译文 2〗 Some of small potatoes in Shanghai are penny wise and pound foolish.

本句翻译可以采用英语成语 penny wise and pound foolish，“便士”聪明，“英镑”愚蠢，亦即小事精明大事糊涂。这是一种对仗工整的英语排偶修辞手法。

我们抵挡不住变化，就像树叶到秋天挡不住要变黄、变枯，球茎在春天挡不住要钻出土壤，萌出新芽一样。

〖译文 1〗 We couldn't stop the change, as leaves turn yellow and fall off the trees in autumn and tubes can't wait breaking through the soil to sprout new buds.（上海理工大学英语专业 2004 年研究生入学试题参考答案）[6,123]

〖译文 2〗 We couldn't stop changing, nor the leaves stop turning yellow and falling off the trees in autumn, the tubes breaking through the soil to sprout new buds in spring.

原文大约是女生的作文，文辞优美，译文1打了一点折扣。比如译文的连接词用 as，可以理解成"就像"，也可以理解成"当……的时候"，容易被误读。

首先我们把译文1的 the change 改为 changing。原文的前面说我们的主观世界和客观世界都在变，无时无刻不在变，据此，我们可以把"变化"用动名词，不用名词译出，这也为后面的对称做好了准备。后面，nor the leaves turning yellow = nor could the leaves stop turning yellow，其中 could stop 承上省略。同理，the tubes breaking = nor could the tubes stop breaking，其中 nor could stop 承上省略。

最后，句末还得搁上 in spring，一为忠实于原文，二为求得与前面的 in autumn 对称。

这种作风，拿来律己，则害了自己；拿了教人，则害了别人；拿了指导革命，则害了革命。

〖译文1〗To govern one's own conduct by this style is to harm oneself, to teach it to others is to harm others, and to use it to direct the revolution is to harm the revolution. [11]

〖译文2〗This style, if followed to govern one's own conduct, will do harm to oneself; to instruct others, will mislead others; and to direct the revolution, will damage the revolution.

原文是典型的排比辞格，有一个主语"这种作风"，谓语包含三组假设句，从"自己""别人"到"革命"，层层剥笋，步步深入。译文1试图译成马致远或培根式的全对称，毕竟语境不同，效果并不好。在译文1的对称结构中 to govern one's own conduct，to teach it to others 和 to use it to direct the revolution，三个句式三个样，很不好看，而且还出现了三个 harm，更不好看。

再从语义关系来看，本句的翻译应该以"这种作风"为主语。作者批评了某些领导干部想当然，瞎指挥的工作作风，指出了海归留学生缺乏创新精神的毛病。紧接着本句的上文是："有哗众取宠之意，无实事求是之心，……自以为是，老子天下第一，钦差大臣满天飞。这就是我们队伍中若干同志的作风。"然后是本句"这种作风，……害己……害人……害革命"。下文是："总之，这种反科学的反马克思列宁主义的主观主义的方法，……是党性不纯的一种表现。"很明显，文章写到本句，作者已经完全对事不对人了。译文1与相邻句子不连贯，不协调，因而不忠实于原文。另外原文的三个"害"，根据其深层含义，可以分别译作 harm（伤害）、mislead（带坏、误导）、damage（损害）或 ruin（葬送）。"教"不是 teach，而是 instruct。

《现代汉语词典》出版后，承读者关心和爱护，不少读者来信指出不足，这里，谨表衷心感谢，并希望对修订本继续提出宝贵意见，以便不断修订。

〖译文 1〗 Since its first publication, *the Contemporary Chinese Dictionary* has drawn considerable attention from our readers. Some have written to us with valuable criticism. We would like to thank all our readers and hope you will continue to contribute your comments and suggestions and help us with future revisions of the dictionary.

〖译文 2〗 We would like to thank the readers who pay attention to *the Contemporary Chinese Dictionary* after its first publication, who write to us with valuable criticism, and who will continue to contribute their comments and suggestions and help us with future revisions of the dictionary.

我们分别在第一章和第三章详细讨论过英语表态在前，叙事在后的特点。我们也可以采用这个方法将译文 1 的三个句子捏合成一句，然后，我们还要注意这个长句子谓语宾语的排偶关系。译文 1 的三个句子分别包含三种读者对象：关心和爱护的读者，来信指出不足的读者，提出宝贵意见的读者，这就有条件将三者组织成排偶关系。

政府责任法制化，是责任政府、法治政府、服务政府题中应有之意。

〖译文 1〗 The systematized legislation for the governmental responsibilities should be included in responsible government, the government ruled by law as well as service government. [124]

〖译文 2〗 A responsible, law-ruled, and service-providing government should institutionalize its responsibilities.

由于逐字对译，译文 1 将原文很简单的句子译得叠床架屋，佶屈聱牙。如果吃透原文精神，译文也可以很简单。这个所谓“题中应有之意”系指一个责任政府、法治政府、服务政府应该将其政府责任法制化。原文“意”疑为“义”之误。

〖译文 1〗 明中叶后，科举功名成为决定士子前途和政治资源分配的决定性因素。

After the middle age of the Ming Dynasty, imperial examinations has become the decisive factors in determining the future of students and in the distribution of political resources. [95]

〖译文 2〗 Since the mid-Ming dynasty, imperial examinations has become the decisive factors for determining the students’ future and distributing the political power among them.

本句可以用 determining the students’ future（决定士子前途）和 distributing the political power（政治资源分配）这两个动名词+宾语结构取得对称。

它（体育旅游）增加了体育文化的内涵，促进了比赛举办地的经济、文化发展。

〖译文1〗It increases the culture meaning of sports, and promotes economic and cultural development in the host city. [125]

〖译文2〗It marries sports to culture, and promotes economic and cultural development in the host city.

"内涵"是一个逻辑用语，表示概念中所反映的对象的特有属性。这是一个被媒体和学界用得最滥，又100%误用的词。它往往被用来表示"内容""内含""含量"等意思。本句原文未能免俗，也是这种用法。英译不但可以将"体育"与"文化"并列，而且可以说成将两者"联姻"。

我说中印两国友好的时间有2000多年，可以说占99.9%，两国的冲突的时间很短，不到0.1%。即使这个冲突，也已化干戈为玉帛。

〖译文1〗I told him that the duration of time when China and India enjoy friendly relations stretched 2,000 years, or 99.9 percent of our total interactions. In terms of conflict, the conflict between our countries only lasted two years, or less than 0.1 percent of the total. We could always turn swords into plows. [13]

〖译文2〗I told him that the last 2,000 years saw China and India enjoy friendly relations of 99.9 percent of our total interactions and only 0.1 percent of the conflict which lasted mere two years. We could always turn swords into plows.

本句可以用"中国"和"印度"，"友好"和"冲突"，"99.9%"和"0.1%"排偶，这样做还有一个好处，就是将原文散点句规整成透视句式了。

山西省五台山是闻名中外的佛教圣地境内迄今保存着北魏、唐、宋、元、明、清及民国历朝历代的寺庙建筑47座。

〖译文1〗On Wutai Mountain, located in Shanxi Province, there are 47 temples built during the seven dynasties, from the Northern Wei in the 4th and 5th century to the Republic of China in the first half of the 20th century. [105]

〖译文2〗On Wutai Mountain, Shanxi Province, there are 47 temples built in the seven dynasties, from the Northern Wei in the 4th and 5th century to the Republic of China in the first half of the 20th century.

〖译文3〗Wutai Mountain, Shanxi Province, is a holy place of Buddhism, where preserved are 47 temples built on and off from the Northern Wei dynasty (386—534 A.D.) to the Republic of China (1911—1949).

译文1没有注意对称。译者心里明白寺庙在山西境内五台山上。但是读者却有一种雾里看花之感，亦即要停下考虑寺庙、山西、五台山三者的关系。如果忍痛割爱，删除 located 一词，形成 On Wutai Mountain, in Shanxi Province 对称，理解障碍就会小得多。如果再把 in 删除，意思也不变，见译文2。

但是译文2给人印象似乎这47座寺庙造了七个王朝，这也不符合事实。所以还不如顺着原文的语序翻译，同时注意句子成分的对称。见译文3。

余冬日往视，但见衰柳寒烟，一水茫茫而已。

I went there, however, on a winter day and saw only a stretch of cold water against some sparse willow trees and a frosty sky.

本句摘自清代作家沈复的《浮生六记》，林语堂译。

有位专家认为，此译堪称扬英语之长。一个介词 against，“扼”了全句，令人寻味。a stretch of cold water against some sparse willow trees and a frosty sky 虽然译出了水平，但是，它和原句“衰柳寒烟，一水茫茫”相比，只是重在“写实”(write realistically)，而汉语句子在“写实”之外尚有韵律之美，意境之美。[57]

我们认为，原文看似漫不经心的白描写实，短短数语却节奏明快，境界全出，显现中国文人十年寒窗打造的文字功力。译文出自大名家之大手笔，比之原文确实铢两悉称，旗鼓相当。

我们在这儿想提一个小小的建议：将 willow trees 改为 willows，这样使 some sparse willows 和 a frosty sky 排偶，而且两者对仗工整，庶几与专家“韵律之美，意境之美”的要求稍稍靠拢。

另外说一点题外话。在现代汉语中，属类名词或专用名词一般都带有一个表示属类的后缀。例如“柳树”“黄浦江”，其中“树”和“江”即表示“柳”和“黄浦”的属类。英语则有所不同，“柳树”可以是 willow tree，也可以是 willow。“密西西比河”可以是 Mississippi River，也可以是 the River of Mississippi，更多的用法是 the Mississippi。这种标识符号缺位的语言现象为我们中国人学习英语带来一定的困难。但是，反过来，我们做汉译英工作，也应该了解并利用这一点。

中国2010年上海世博会是展示中国实力和形象的良机，它的举办对上海和整个国家的发展都具有深远的政治、经济和社会意义。

〖译文1〗 China's 2010 Shanghai World EXPO displays the strength and form of golden business opportunities in China, and hold the World EXPO for the development of Shanghai and the entire country has profound political, economic and social significance.[126]

〖译文2〗 Hosting Expo 2010 Shanghai will offer China a golden opportunity to display and enhance her prestige, and the Expo itself will be of political, economical and social significance to the development of Shanghai and other parts of China.

原文不怎么通顺，但仍然可读。译文 1 不但保留了原文的缺点，而且加上自己的自由发挥，放大了这种缺点。上海世博会正式的英文名称是 Expo 2010 Shanghai China，译者似乎不甚明白，这也太不应该。

解决问题的方法仍然是采用排偶。在译文 2 中，我们看到：display 和 enhance 对称；political、economical、social 排偶；Shanghai 和 other parts of China 对称，句子对称排偶整齐了，也就通顺了。

与其他发展中国家贸易摩擦迅速增多已经成为中国近年来对外经济贸易遇到的一个突出问题。

〖译文 1〗In recent years, China's trade frictions with other developing countries are increasing rapidly.[49]

〖译文 2〗In recent years, the trade frictions between China and other developing countries are on the rapid increase.

〖译文 3〗In recent years, China is confronted with the increasing knotty problems of trade frictions with other developing countries.

译文 1 选择“贸易摩擦”作主语是不错的，但是不能用“中国”来修饰，而应该用“中国和其他国家”修饰，使译文形成 China and other developing countries 对称。

另外，are increasing 如果改为 are on the increase，就显得更客观，更公正，而且后者含有“问题”“困难”等负面因素“增多”的意思。译文 3 仍用“中国”作主语。

灭火器和灭火剂应定期检查，以保持随时可用状态。

〖译文 1〗Fire extinguishers and fire extinguishing media should be kept ready and should be inspected at stipulated intervals.[20]

〖译文 2〗Fire extinguisher and extinguishant should be inspected at stipulated intervals and kept ready for use.

译文 1 是准确的。译文 2 将“灭火剂”译作 extinguishant，力图与“灭火器”extinguisher 对称。

第五节 词语排比与结构排比

现代汉语是多见词语排比，而英语则是一种结构排比的语言。词语排比要求引导词不更换，排比词更换，排比句式不变。结构排比则要求结构对称，但是词语最好不重复，该省略的就省略。现代汉语的排比非但不惮重复，而且词语的重复反增添了文句的力度和文采。而英语习惯使用省略句，一般都不重复。英语的特点是在省略中追求排比。

这些岩石，一半在水下，一半在水面上。

〖译文 1〗Half of the rock was under the water and half of the rock was above the water.

〖译文 2〗Half of the rock was under the water and half above.

译文 1 语法无误，但是读起来饶舌。

所愧少年失学，稍识之无，不过记其实情实事而已。（［清］沈复《浮生六记》）

〖译文 1〗Unfortunately I never completed my studies, so my writing is not very skillful. But here my purpose is merely to record true feelings and actual events. [9]

〖译文 2〗I merely record the true happenings and feelings of my own with my limited writing skill, which was due to my limited schooling in young age.

我们认为"实情实事"可以考虑译为 happenings and feelings。将"实情实事"调整为"实事实情"是基于"情"是对于"事"的反应，先有"事"后有"情"。体现了英语对逻辑的苛求。

其中 happening = event，前者表示非比寻常的"事"，后者表示意义重大的"事"。本句语境用 happenings 更准确。而且 happenings and feelings 具有排偶的形式美。这就是我们所谓的词语对称。

另外，"失学"和"稍识"也有对称关系，可以考虑译为 limited writing skill 和 limited schooling。对称了，读起来流畅又易于理解。

人知和靖《点绛唇》、圣俞《苏幕遮》、永叔《少年游》三阕为咏春草绝调。不知先有正中"细雨湿流光"五字，皆能摄春草之魂者也。（王国维《人间词话》）

〖译文 1〗Everyone knows that Lin Pu's Tz'u to the tune of "Tien chiang ch'un", Mei Yao-ch'en's Tz'u to the tune of "Su mu che", and Ouyang Hsiu's *Tz'u* to the tune of "Shao nien yu" were masterpieces on the subject of spring grasses, but what many did not understand was that prior to these were Feng Yen-ssu's five words, "Fine rain dampens the passage of time", which really captured the soul of spring grasses. [10]

〖译文2〗Well known is that Lin Pu's lyrics to the tune of "Dian jiang chun", Mei Yaochen's lyrics to the tune of "Su mu zhe", and Ouyang Xiu's lyrics to the tune of "Shao nian you" were masterpiece odes to the meadow scenery in spring, however, little known is that prior to them Feng Yansi's five words, "Drizzle maketh fleeting time dripping" was really a vivid touch in depicting spring grasses.

提示："和靖"，宋代文学家林圃。"圣俞"，宋代文学家梅尧臣。"永叔"，宋代文学家欧阳修。"正中"，宋代文学家冯延巳。

译文1的前半句 Everyone knows that，和后半句 but what many did not understand was that，在内容上、时态上、形式上都没有形成基本的排偶。

内容上，前半句是"人人都知道的是"，后半句是"许多人所不理解的东西是"，没有形成逻辑对照和结构对照关系，与原文"人知……不知……"结构不符。时态上，前半句是现在时，后半句是过去时，将"人知……不知……"的转折关系，误认为时间先后的对照关系。形式上的紊乱更是一目了然。

译文1中 Everyone knows 言过其实，不见得人人都知道。masterpieces on the subject of spring grasses 不是"咏春草绝调"，而是"论春草的雄文"。captured the soul of spring grasses 不是"摄春草之魂"，而是"捕获春草之魂"。

只需合上电闸，房屋便可照亮，轮子便可旋转，冰就可以制出，饭就可以做熟，远处的声音便可以听见，还有无数其他工作——平常的和不平常的——都能进行。

〖译文1〗By the mere closing of a switch, buildings are lighted, wheels are turned, ice is made, food is cooked, distant voices are heard, and countless other tasks—ordinary or extraordinary—are performed.[13]

〖译文2〗With a switch being turned on, buildings can be lighted, wheels revolved, ice made, food cooked, distant voices heard, and countless other tasks—ordinary or extraordinary—performed.

译文应省略连系动词，在省略中美化排偶句式。句中第二个 turned 改为 revolved 是为了避免与第一个 turned 撞车，也为了美化句式。

孟子说："天下之本在国，国之本在家，家之本在身。"

〖译文1〗He says, "The essence of the world is in the state, the essence of the state is in the home, the essence of the home is in the self."❶

---

❶ http://ahongqi.blog.sohu.com。

〖译文 2〗He says, "The essence of the world is in the state, the state in the family, the family in the individual self."

原文为排比句，词语的重复显示了作者高屋建瓴、顺势而下的雄辩力量。但是英译则不能照搬照抄，只能使用省略句法，省略句反而显得言简意赅，精辟警醒。

人之学也，或失则多，或失则寡，或失则易，或失则止。

〖译文 1〗The faults in learning include learning more than one can accept, learning within a narrow scope, learning inconstantly, and stopping at a smattering of knowledge.[127]

〖译文 2〗No learning is obtainable in speediness, insufficiency, inconstancy, or smattering.

〖译文 3〗No learning can be obtained with speediness, insufficiency, inconstancy, or smattering.

原文意谓："一个人的学问，或失之贪多求滥，或失之孤陋寡闻，或失之见异思迁，或失之浅尝辄止。"译文 1 含有四个 learning，显得不讲究修辞。其中"多"用 learning + 形容词短语译出，"寡"用 learning + 介词短语译出，"易"用 learning + 副词译出，"止"则用 stopping + 介词短语译出，而且两个介词短语的结构也不一样，使整句结构松散。如果稍稍变通一下，将原文说成"没有什么学问可以通过多、寡、易、止获得"，译文就晓畅、地道多了。

她完全失去了控制，她抬高了声调，笑声也变得更加奇异。

〖译文 1〗She was out of control completely, she raised her voice and her laughter became queerer.

〖译文 2〗Completely out of control, her voice had become louder and her laughter queerer.

译文 1 完全是合格的。但是行文至此，我们似乎已不能满足于此。我们先发现的是"她抬高了声调"和"笑声也变得更加奇异"，可以不用 she 和 her laughter 对举，而用 her voice 和 her laughter 对举，译作 her voice had become louder and her laughter had become queerer。其中后一个 had become 可以省略。

其次，"她完全失去了控制"可以从独立句子降格为介词短语，使全句透视化。

至于介词短语与主句是否造成逻辑问题，我们认为译文 2 中 out of control 的逻辑主语可以是 her voice 和 her laughter。如果是 she 或 her，在欧美作家那儿，这样的句式也有先例。

君子不可以不修身。思修身，不可以不事亲；思事亲，不可以不知人；思知人，不可以不知天。

〖译文1〗A man of virtue should not neglect self-cultivation. To conduct self-cultivation, he has got to care for his relatives. To care for his relatives, he has got to acquire knowledge of men. To acquire knowledge of men, he has got to know about the Way of Heaven. [127]

〖译文2〗A man of virtue should not neglect self-cultivation. However, he has to know about the Way of Heaven before he can know about men. To know about men before care for his parents. To care for his parents before cultivate himself.

提示：原文“亲”不作 relative（亲戚）解，而作 parents（父母）解。

原文开门见山地提出“君子不可以不修身”，这是一个独立的论断，强调“修身”的重要。以后依据由近至远的次序，依次提出“事亲”“知人”和“知天”的要求。英语的习惯刚好相反。英语译文最好将这个次序倒过来。“君子不可以不修身”是全句的立论，可以不改变位置，但是后面的“修身”“事亲”“知人”和“知天”则最好把次序颠倒过来。

译文1将“修身”和“知人”用一种动词+抽象名词译出：conduct cultivation 和 acquire knowledge，可改为直接用动词 cultivate 和 know 译出，这样它们可以与“事亲”和“知天”的动宾结构取齐、对称，使行文流畅。译文 has got to，常用于口语，可改译为 has to。

寻章摘句，世之腐儒也，何能兴邦立事？

〖译文1〗Those who are lost in selecting passages and choosing phrases are pedants. How can such men make their states strong and do great deeds? [27]

〖译文2〗How can those pedants, who are only good at citing and quoting, be leaders of a state or a cause?

很明显，本句“寻章”与“摘句”对应，“兴邦”与“立事”对应，问题是英语如何对应？下一节将进一步探讨。

第六节 隐藏的对称结构

有些汉语句子存在对称结构，但是不明显，所以我们说它是“隐藏的对称结构”，需要在英语译文中显现出来。有些则根本不存在对仗，但是翻译后为了译语的晓畅和美化，更为了便于读者理解，需要精心组织英语句子的排偶。

王小玉便启朱唇，发皓齿，唱了几句书儿。

〖译文 1〗 Now open her rosy lips and her ivory white teeth shine, her song begins. [27,32]

〖译文 2〗 Little Jade Wang then opened her vermilion lips, displaying her sparking white teeth, and sang several phases. [27,32]

〖译文 3〗 Little Jade then parted her lips and sang a few lines. [27,32]

〖译文 4〗 Now her rosy lips open and her white teeth shine, her song begins.

译文 1 开头是祈使句，如果将 open her rosy lips 改为 her rosy lips open，同时在后面的 ivory white 两者中的删除一个，全句形成排偶，我们可以得到译文 4。

从国内看，我们正处在经济结构调整的关键时期，改革处于攻坚阶段。

〖译文 1〗 At home, we are at a crucial juncture in economic restructuring, and reform is in a very difficult period. （南开大学英语专业 2006 年研究生入学试题参考答案）[6,42]

〖译文 2〗 At home, economical restructuring is at a crucial juncture, and reform in arduous phase.

原文隐藏着对称结构“经济结构处于调整的关键时期”和“改革处于攻坚阶段”。译文 1 用 we 和 reform 对称，不如用 restructuring 和 reform 对称。后者不仅押头韵，而且共用 economical 修饰，使译文句子更紧密。译文 2 在 reform in arduous phase 中省略 is。

这是一个汉语句子字面上存在的隐藏结构。下面的句子字面上不存在对称，需要在译文中发掘并表达出来。

因思《关雎》冠三百篇之首，故列夫妇于卷首；馀以次递及焉。（［清］沈复《浮生六记》）

〖译文 1〗 The very first of the three hundred chapters of the *Book of Odes* concerns husbands and wives, so I too will write of other matters in their turn. [9]

〖译文 2〗 Just as the first chapter of the Chinese classical poetry collection *Book of Odes* is a love song, so I will begin my story with my romance before the other events in their turns.

译文 1 没有将“故列夫妇于卷首”译出，所以 so 左右两边的内容根本无法形成逻辑关系。译文 1 句意为：《诗经》三百篇的第一篇是写夫妻的，所以我也将依次写到其他事情。哪里话？

其实原文隐藏着“《关雎》”和“夫妇”的对称关系，英译可以分别用 love 和 romance 译出，取对称结构。

帝子之尊，童稚之逸，尚能如此，况其庶士冀以自达者哉?（［南北朝］颜之推《颜氏家训》）

〚译文 1〛If a child prince who is entitled to a privileged and carefree life chooses to be a hard working student, shouldn't petty officials work harder to climb the social ladder?[19]

〚译文 2〛If a privileged and carefree young prince chooses to study diligently, shouldn't minor officials work hard to climb the social ladder?

本句原文讲某帝王少年好学，故有“帝子之尊”与“童稚之逸”的对仗，但是英译无法照搬，只能在文句中自洽，可以用 privileged 与 carefree 对称，用 study diligently 与 work hard 对称。

若必考订其文法，是责明于垢鉴矣。（［清］沈复《浮生六记》）

〚译文 1〛Criticism of my writing will be like the shining of a bright light into a dirty mirror.[9]

〚译文 2〛My writing has little to do with the rigid grammar rules, as a dusty mirror has little to do with luster.

原文是古人的自谦之词，而且是很高明的那种：如果我的写作有个别文法问题的话（我的文章还是有价值的），就像镜子有污垢（镜子还是好镜子）。

即使对照原文，也没有读懂译文 1，所以不便评议。

这个比喻句的本体和喻体是含有对称关系的。

林太乙先生从事文学创作多年，著作多以英文写就。

〚译文 1〛Ms Lin is a veteran in literature and a very productive author. Most of her works are in English.[22]

〚译文 2〛Ms Lin is a veteran and prolific writer in literature, and her most works are in English.

译文 1 中 productive 系指“工作效率很高的”。至于林先生是不是工作效率很高，一则我们无从知晓，二则读者不感兴趣，因此该词可以换为 prolific，表示“多产的”“著作颇丰的”，并与 veteran 并立对举。

词之雅郑，在神不在貌。（王国维《人间词话》）

〚译文 1〛The refinement or lack of refinement of tz'u lies in their spirit rather than in their outward appearance.[10]

〚译文 2〛The refinement degree of lyrics lies more in their inward spirit than in outward appearance.

译文 1 开头的 refinement 与 lack of refinement 不能排偶，应该取消。spirit 前面最好加上 inward，使 inward spirit 与 outward appearance 排偶。rather than 最好改为 more than，也是为了排偶。

原文属高度的意合表达，对英译可能有陷阱。“雅”，雅乐；“郑”，郑声，分别代表艺术的高端和低端，原文并非认为在这两个极端之间就不存在中间状态。“神”“貌”也不是非此即彼，势不两立，而是什么多一些，什么少一些的问题。

……觉西湖如镜，杭城如丸，钱塘江如带，极目可数百里，此生平第一大观也。（［清］沈复《浮生六记》）

〖译文 1〗 From there West Lake looked like a mirror, while the city of Hangzhou was as small as a ball and the Chientang River looked like a belt. We could see for hundreds of *li*, quite the most wonderful vista I have ever seen. [9]

〖译文 2〗 From there West Lake looks like a mirror, the city of Hangzhou a capsule and the River of Chientang a belt. We could look afar to hundreds of *li*, enjoying the most wonderful vista I have ever seen.

原文是排比句，可看作排偶的一种。英译也应该尽可能保持这种排偶。

我不敢说康桥给了我多少学问或是教会了我什么，我不敢说受了康桥的洗礼，一个人就会变气息，脱凡胎。我敢说的只是——就我个人说，我的眼是康桥教我睁的，我的求知欲是康桥给我拨动的，我的自我意识是康桥给我胚胎的。（徐志摩《吸烟与文化》）

〖译文 1〗 I dare not say how knowledgeable I have become through my education in Cambridge, I dare not say one can be regenerated and deified through the baptism of Cambridge. What I dare say is that it was Cambridge that opened my eyes, it was Cambridge that aroused my curiosity in knowledge, it was Cambridge that generated the awareness of “I” in me. ”❶

〖译文 2〗 I dare neither say how much knowledge I had acquired when I was educated in the campus of Cambridge, nor how much saintship I had attained when I was exposed in the culture of Cambridge. What I dare say is that it was Cambridge that broadened my horizons, it was Cambridge that aroused my desire for learning, and it was Cambridge that bled my self-consciousness.

上面的译例，原文出自大诗人的大手笔，有一些显性的排比语句，也有隐藏的对称结构。译文如何排偶，留待我们思索。本书正文以此作结。

---

❶ http://language.chinadaily.com.cn。

后　　记

显而易见，汉语英语的表达都存在一个意象和境界问题。翻译家在向读者传递信息的同时，更要注重审美空间的转换和移植，其中包括对汉语原文审美意象的把握和对英语译文审美境界的重构。

有些转换和移植比较浅显，一般译者也能对付，比如：

☞正语与反语转换：

这些民工们都归心如箭。

Those provincial workers couldn't get home fast enough.

☞人称转换：

我会找你算账。

You'll pay for this!

☞祈使句与疑问句转换：

请你说到点子上吧！

Will you please get to the point?

☞委婉说法与直率说法转换：

假如你以为他是好人，那你就大错特错了。

If you think he is a good man, think again.

☞主观感受与客观描述转换：

文学课程虽然艰涩，但是令人获益匪浅。

The literature course has been hard work, but very rewarding.

汉语英语作为思辨的语言，都有一些逻辑隽语，比如汉语成语“自相矛盾”和英语的 paradox，其翻译就颇费斟酌了：

“I always lie” is a paradox because if it is true it must be false.

“我老是说谎”是一种自相矛盾的说法，如果它是真的，那么它本身就是一句假话。

没有意象和境界的文字只是一串味同嚼蜡、令人费解的字符。只有语言的意象和境界得到体现，汉语英语所代表的异域文化特色才能得到反映。

一只碗不响，两只碗叮当。
It takes two to make a quarrel.

这一句的汉语原文很生动，另一种说法是“一个巴掌拍不响”，译成英语则不再出现这些形象。请看例句：

Sue：I think Mimi ought to apologize for arguing with me.
Mother：It takes two to make a quarrel，dear. Maybe you ought to apologize to her.
苏：我认为咪咪与我争吵就应该道歉。
母亲：一只碗不响，两只碗叮当。亲爱的，也许你应该向她道歉。

英语作为译入语，我们有时可以借助西方社会和西方文化的某些意象加以形象化表达：

爸爸已经从总工程师岗位退居二线，但他仍然每天按时上班。
〖译文1〗Dad has retired from the post of chief engineer，but he still goes to work in time everyday.
〖译文2〗Dad has taken a back seat from the post of chief engineer，but he still goes to work in time on weekdays.

“退居二线”不完全等同于“退休”（retire），故译文1不太准确。
译文2的 in the back seat 表示“坐在汽车后排位置”。一位负责人从领导岗位退居二线，犹如汽车驾驶员退居后排位置，仍然可以为如何驾车献计献策，发挥余热。
下面的例句以谚语译谚语：

得放手时须放手，得饶人处且饶人。（［元］关汉卿《窦娥冤》）
Live and let live.

元代杂剧中的这句话已成谚语，我们当然可以逐字直译，但是这样做很可能事倍功半，达不到原文警策醒目的艺术效果。英语有谚语曰 Live and let live，原意“自己活着也让别人活”，引申为“穷寇勿追，留有余地”“退一步海阔天空”“你好我好大家好”：

Father's attitude toward anybody who wasn't his kind used to puzzle me. It was so dictatorial. There was no live and let live about it.

从前我总不懂父亲为什么对那些脾气跟他不一样的人采取那么个态度，那么专制，一点儿“你好我好”也没有。（吕叔湘译）

汉语英语的意象和境界不拘一格，经纬万端，远远不止本书列出的这些译例。客观世界有多么复杂，语言就有多么复杂；人类的思维有多么微妙，其语言就有多么微妙。汉语和英语是世界上最为精确、精细、精美的语言。从《诗经》到《红楼梦》，从乔叟叙事诗到莎士比亚戏剧，无不体现了语言大师们的伟大和永恒。我们热爱汉语，如果我们能够以英语作为她的参照系，就会更深切地感受汉语的玄妙；我们欣赏英语，如果我们没有深厚的母语功底，就不可能真正地领略英语的美丽。

希望本书的解析没有牵强附会之处，如果读者对本书阐述的道理做出验证，甚至有助于自己的翻译、教学或研究工作，笔者无疑会感到欣慰。

本书就汉英翻译的各个方面举一隅而探赜索隐，如果读者以三隅返，钩深致远，提出新的独特的翻译方案，笔者一定竭诚欢迎。

对于语言意象的研究，西方的修辞学翻译学学者提出“形式意象和内容意象”（formal schema and content schema）和“具象意象和抽象意象”（concrete schema and abstract schema）的概念，似乎为我们开拓出可供深耕的学术研究园地。

也有人沿袭亚里士多德，提出语言艺术境界的“个性”（ethos），“逻辑”（logos）和“情感”（pathos）三要素。

所谓“个性”系指作者或译者的精气神，没有个性的作品，千人一面千部一腔，是不能获得生存权利的；“逻辑”是语言内在的理性力量，是人类共有的心理框架；“情感”是具体有形的诉诸感情的艺术形象。

对于这些方面的探索和研究无疑会推动翻译事业的前进，我们将期盼和关注着新的成果问世。

上海老克勒
曾凯民谨识

参考书目

[1] 吴光华. 汉英大词典[M]. 上海：上海交通大学出版社，1993.

[2] 上海交通大学英语专业 2004 年研究生入学试题参考答案.

[3] 李照国. 熵化 · 耗散 · 重构——汉英翻译理法探微[M]. 上海：上海科学技术出版社，2008.

[4] 梅德明. 新汉英口译实践——成功之路[M]. 北京：人民教育出版社，2005.

[5] 北京大学英语专业 2009 年研究生入学试题参考答案.

[6] 金圣才. 英语专业英汉互译考研真题与典型题详解[M]. 北京：中国石化出版社，2014.

[7] 王昊，徐齐平. 风景名胜[M]. 北京：人民文学出版社，2008.

[8] 大中华文库——庄子[M]. 长沙：湖南人民出版社，2012.

[9] 大中华文库——浮生六记[M]. 南京：译林出版社，2006.

[10] 大中华文库——人间词话[M]. 南京：译林出版社，2009.

[11] 毛泽东选集英文版[M]. 北京：外文出版社，1977.

[12] 王大伟，魏清光. 汉英翻译技巧教学与研究[M]. 北京：中国对外翻译出版公司，2005.

[13] 成昭伟. 新汉英翻译实务[M]. 北京：国防工业出版社，2007.

[14] 谢百魁. 中国历代散文一百篇[M]. 北京：中国对外翻译出版公司，1996.

[15] 陈宏薇，李亚丹. 新编汉英翻译教程[M]. 上海：上海外语教育出版社，2004.

[16] 冯树鉴. 古文今译与英译[M]. 北京：华语教学出版社，1990.

[17] 陈宏薇. 新实用汉译英教程[M]. 武汉：湖北教育出版社，2009.

[18] 王宏印. 中外文学经典翻译教程[M]. 北京：高等教育出版社，2007.

[19] 大中华文库——颜氏家训[M]. 长沙：湖南人民出版社，2004.

[20] 严俊仁. 汉英科技翻译新说[M]. 北京：国防工业出版社，2010.

[21] 黄振定. 英汉互译实践教程[M]. 长沙：湖南人民出版社，1999.

[22] 大中华文库——镜花缘[M]. 南京：译林出版社，2004.

[23] 厦门大学英语专业 2003 年研究生入学试题参考答案.

[24] 大中华文库——论语[M]. 长沙：湖南人民出版社，2009.

[25] 武汉大学英语专业 2003 年研究生入学试题参考答案.

[26] 厦门大学英语专业 2005 年研究生入学试题参考答案.

[27] 厦门大学外文学院英语系.《汉英翻译》课程介绍与教学重点.

[28] 亚历山大 L G. 新概念英语——课文中译本[M]. 黄次栋，等译. 上海：上海科学技术文献出版社，1987.

[29] 桑子长，徐彩霞，李飒. 中国名塔[M]. 重庆：重庆出版社，2001.

[30] 复旦学报. 2005(5).

[31] 庄绎传. 汉英翻译 500 例[M]. 北京：外语教学与研究出版社，1980.

[32] 戎林海. 新编实用翻译教程[M]. 上海：上海外语教育出版社，2010.

[33] 赵朋. 译海精要——英汉汉英翻译理论与实践[M]. 合肥：合肥工业大学出版社，2007.

[34] 卢敏. 英语笔译全真模拟试题及解析[M]. 北京：外文出版社，2010.

[35] 中国翻译. 2007(1).

[36] 郭富强．汉英翻译理论与实践[M]．北京：机械工业出版社，2009.
[37] 中国翻译．2007(5).
[38] 大中华文库——孙子兵法孙膑兵法[M]．长沙：湖南人民出版社，1999.
[39] 清华大学学报．2006(5).
[40] 陈宏薇．汉英翻译基础[M]．上海：上海外语教育出版社，2011.
[41] 上海大学学报．2007(4).
[42] 南开大学英语专业2006年研究生入学试题参考答案.
[43] 张蓓．汉英时文翻译实践[M]．北京：清华大学出版社，2001.
[44] 中国翻译．1988(6).
[45] 司显柱，曾剑平，等．汉译英教程[M]．上海：东华大学出版社，2006.
[46] 上海对外贸易学院英语专业2005年研究生入学试题参考答案.
[47] 孙海晨．汉译英实用技能训练[M]．北京：外文出版社，2008.
[48] 田传茂，杨先明．汉英翻译策略[M]．上海：华东师范大学出版社，1992.
[49] 上海大学学报．2007(11).
[50] 刘宓庆．新编汉英对比与翻译[M]．北京：中国对外翻译出版公司，2006.
[51] 尹邦彦．汉语熟语英译词典[M]．上海：上海外语教育出版社，2006.
[52] 上海大学学报．2007(7).
[53] 杨伯峻．论语今译[M]．济南：齐鲁书社，2009.
[54] 上海大学学报．2007(9).
[55] 曾诚．实用汉英翻译教程[M]．北京：外语教学与研究出版社，2002.
[56] 大中华文库——老子[M]．长沙：湖南人民出版社，2009.
[57] 毛荣贵．新世纪大学汉英翻译教程[M]．上海：上海交通大学出版社，2002.
[58] 上海交通大学学报．2005(3).
[59] 邵志洪．汉英对比翻译导论[M]．上海：华东理工大学出版社，2013.
[60] 范勇．新汉英翻译教程[M]．南京：南京大学出版社，2006.
[61] 2000年全国高校英语专业八级考试汉译英试题参考译文.
[62] 冯伟年．汉英笔译[M]．西安：西安交通大学出版社，2012.
[63] 上海画报．2006(9).
[64] 张常人．汉英古今常用语汇词典[M]．北京：外文出版社，2005.
[65] Simon Patton，高亮．译出地道的英文来：汉英翻译误区解析[M]．北京：外文出版社，2014.
[66] 英语世界．2009(1).
[67] 英语世界．2009(7).
[68] 丁树德，等．中英文广告实用手册[M]．天津：天津科技翻译出版公司，1995.
[69] 孙萍．中国京剧百部经典英译系列：霸王别姬典[M]．北京：中国人民大学出版社，2012.
[70] 中国翻译．2009(2).
[71] 薄冰．高级英语语法[M]．北京：世界知识出版社，2010.
[72] 韩素英青年翻译奖竞赛题参考译文.

[73] 西安外国语学院英语专业 2003 年研究生入学试题参考答案.
[74] 上海画报. 2010(9).
[75] 蔡基刚. 英汉汉英段落翻译与实践[M]. 上海：复旦大学出版社，2002.
[76] 今日中国. 1996(4).
[77] 大中华文库——荀子[M]. 成都：四川人民出版社，2013.
[78] 徐翰林. 最优美的散文[M]. 北京：中国对外翻译出版公司，2006.
[79] 浙江树人大学学报. 2006(11).
[80] 悠悠. 摩登上海：上海最炫室内设计[M]. 沈阳：辽宁科学技术出版社，2005.
[81] 英语世界. 2009(9).
[82] 全国高校英语专业八级考试试题参考答案.
[83] 上海翻译. 2007(4).
[84] 蓝田. 中国成语故事[M]. 北京：百花文艺出版社，2005.
[85] 马家驹. 中国历代微型小说一百篇[M]. 北京：中国对外翻译出版公司，1996.
[86] 刘会，张海让. 导游英语[M]. 天津：天津科技翻译出版公司，2006.
[87] 居祖纯. 新编汉英语篇翻译强化训练[M]. 北京：清华大学出版社，2002.
[88] 中国社会科学院语言研究所词典编辑室. 现代汉语词典（汉英双语）[M]. 北京：外语教学与研究出版社，2002.
[89] 武汉大学外语学院，今日武汉电视英语.
[90] 华东理工大学英语专业研究生入学试题参考答案.
[91] 英汉语比较与翻译[M]. 上海：上海外语教育出版社.
[92] 李照国. 译海心语[M]. 上海：上海中医药大学出版社，2006.
[93] 周志培. 汉英对比与翻译中的转换[M]. 上海：华东理工大学出版社，2003.
[94] 北京周报. 1998(22).
[95] 清华大学学报. 2006(6).
[96] 丁往道. 孔子语录一百则[M]. 北京：中国对外翻译出版公司，1999.
[97] 蔡希勤. 孔子的故事[M]. 北京：华语教学出版社，2001.
[98] 上海翻译. 2007(2).
[99] 北京大学学报. 2006(6).
[100] 陈秋劲，等. 英汉互译理论与实践[M]. 武汉：武汉大学出版社，2005.
[101] 杜争鸣，陈胜利. 英汉互译原理与实践教程[M]. 北京：中国经济出版社，2008.
[102] 李运兴. 汉英翻译教程[M]. 北京：新华出版社，2006.
[103] 章振邦. 新编英语语法[M]. 上海：上海外语教育出版社，1997.
[104] 郭著章，李庆生. 英汉互译实用教程[M]. 武汉：武汉大学出版社，2003.
[105] 张春柏，刘川. 英汉汉英翻译教程[M]. 北京：高等教育出版社，2003.
[106] 张燕清，席东. 英汉互译理论与实践[M]. 西安：西北工业大学出版社，2008.
[107] 魏志成. 汉英比较翻译教程[M]. 北京：清华大学出版社，2006.
[108] 任虹. 翻译引论[M]. 南京：东南大学出版社，2007.
[109] 国际经贸探索. 2015(1).
[110] 梅德明. 新英语口译资格考试分类词汇精编[M]. 北京：人民教育出版社，2010.

[111] 大中华文库——孟子[M]. 长沙：湖南人民出版社，1999.
[112] 谭卫国，蔡龙权. 新编英汉互译教程[M]. 上海：华东理工大学出版社，2005.
[113] 英语世界. 2009(3).
[114] 体育科学研究. 2006(3).
[115] I时代报. 2007(5).
[116] 杨新亮，段汉武. 中国媒体英语阅读[M]. 北京：国防工业出版社，2007.
[117] 丁树德. 英汉汉英翻译教学综合指导[M]. 天津：天津大学出版社，1996.
[118] China Daily. 2006(8).
[119] 冯志杰. 汉英科技翻译指要[M]. 北京：中国对外翻译出版公司，1998.
[120] 外国语. 2006(1).
[121] 上海对外贸易学院英语专业2002年研究生入学试题参考答案.
[122] 南开大学英语专业2004年研究生入学试题参考答案.
[123] 上海理工大学英语专业2004年研究生入学试题参考答案.
[124] 清华大学学报. 2006(2).
[125] 体育科学研究. 2007(3).
[126] 上海世博. 2004(2).
[127] 本社. 儒家名典箴言录[M]. 济南：齐鲁书社，2006.
[128] 蔡希勤. 孟子的故事[M]. 北京：华语教学出版社，2002.
[129] 常立. 实用汉英活译6000例[M]. 太原：山西教育出版社，2006.
[130] 陈文伯. 教你如何掌握汉译英技巧[M]. 北京：世界知识出版社，1999.
[131] 陈文伯. 译艺：英汉汉英双向笔译[M]. 北京：群言出版社，2004.
[132] 程镇球. 论汉译英的几个问题[M]. 北京：外语教学与研究出版社，1981.
[133] 范家材. 英语修辞赏析[M]. 上海：上海交通大学出版社，1992.
[134] 顾正阳. 古诗词曲英译美学研究[M]. 上海：上海大学出版社，2006.
[135] 胡文仲. 现代实用英语例解[M]. 上海：上海外语教育出版社，1987.
[136] 黄任. 英语修辞与写作[M]. 上海：上海外语教育出版社，2006.
[137] 居祖纯. 汉英语篇翻译[M]. 北京：清华大学出版社，1998.
[138] 居祖纯. 高级汉英语篇翻译[M]. 北京：清华大学出版社，2012.
[139] 居祖纯. 汉英翻译强化训练[M]. 上海：上海辞书出版社，2004.
[140] 李明. 英汉互动翻译教程[M]. 武汉：武汉大学出版社，2006.
[141] 李青. 新编英汉汉英翻译教程：翻译技巧与误译评析[M]. 北京：北京大学出版社，2005.
[142] 李云，李和庆. 新编大学翻译教程[M]. 北京：世界知识出版社，2007.
[143] 廖国强. 英汉互译理论、技巧与实践[M]. 北京：国防工业出版社，2006.
[144] 凌德祥. 走向世界的汉语[M]. 北京：文化艺术出版社，2006.
[145] 卢红梅. 华夏文化与汉英翻译[M]. 武汉：武汉大学出版社，2010.
[146] 陆谷孙. 英汉大词典[M]. 上海：上海译文出版社，2000.
[147] 陆乃圣. 新编大学翻译教程[M]. 北京：世界图书出版公司，2006.
[148] 马秉义. 汉英科技写作词典[M]. 北京：气象出版社，1996.

[149] 毛荣贵．英语幽默语言赏析[M]．上海：上海社会科学院出版社，1993.
[150] 钱歌川．翻译漫谈[M]．北京：中国对外翻译出版公司，1980.
[151] 石定乐，蔡蔚，王纯林．实用商务英汉互译[M]．北京：北京理工大学出版社，2007.
[152] 宋天锡．翻译新概念：英汉互译实用教程[M]．北京：国防工业出版社，2009.
[153] 王琼．英汉互译教程[M]．北京：知识产权出版社，2007.
[154] 王文华．翻译的概念[M]．北京：外文出版社，2007.
[155] 王正元．新编学生实用汉英翻译词典[M]．北京：中国大百科全书出版社，2003.
[156] 熊若磐，梁联发．汉英对照怀旧金曲[M]．上海：上海音乐出版社，2003.
[157] 徐应庚．西湖细语[M]．杭州：浙江大学出版社，2005.
[158] 曾祖选．实用汉英多种表达法词典[M]．成都：四川人民出版社，1989.
[159] 张培基，等．英汉翻译教程[M]．修订版．上海：上海外语教育出版社，2014.
[160] 朱明炬，等．英汉名篇名译[M]．南京：译林出版社，2010.
[161] 杨自俭，李瑞华．英汉对比研究论文集[M]．上海：上海外语教育出版社，1990.
[162] 邵志洪．英汉语研究与对比[M]．上海：华东理工大学出版社，1997.
[163] 冯至．世界散文精华[M]．南京：江苏文艺出版社，1994.
[164] 汉英词典[M]．北京：商务印书馆，2006.
[165] 汉英词典[M]．3 版．北京：外语教学与研究出版社，2010.
[166] 现代汉英词典[M]．新版．北京：外语教学与研究出版社，2001.
[167] 王振亚．实用英语语言文化[M]．保定：河北大学出版社，2004.
[168] 汪静．最易犯错的汉译英 268 例[M]．天津：天津科技翻译出版公司，2015.
[169] 张传彪，缪敏．汉英误译经典例析 1000[M]．上海：上海译文出版社，2013.
[170] 何琳．实用英汉互译快捷通[M]．天津：天津科技翻译出版公司，2009.
[171] 刘宓庆．翻译基础[M]．上海：华东师范大学出版社，2008.
[172] 顾雪梁，何建乐．汉英互译实用基础教程（上册）[M]．杭州：浙江大学出版社，2008.